Lecture Notes in Computer Science 8770

Commenced Publication in 1973
Founding and Former Series Editors:
Gerhard Goos, Juris Hartmanis, and Jan van Leeuwen

T0214965

Yusuf Pisan   Nikitas M. Sgouros
Tim Marsh (Eds.)

Entertainment Computing – ICEC 2014

13th International Conference, ICEC 2014
Sydney, Australia, October 1-3, 2014
Proceedings

 Springer

Volume Editors

Yusuf Pisan
University of Technology, Sydney, Australia
E-mail: yusuf.pisan@gamesstudio.org

Nikitas M. Sgouros
University of Piraeus, Greece
E-mail: sgouros@unipi.gr

Tim Marsh
Griffith University, Brisbane, Australia
E-mail: t.marsh@griffith.edu.au

ISSN 0302-9743   e-ISSN 1611-3349
ISBN 978-3-662-45211-0   e-ISBN 978-3-662-45212-7
DOI 10.1007/978-3-662-45212-7
Springer Heidelberg New York Dordrecht London

Library of Congress Control Number: 2014951520

LNCS Sublibrary: SL 3 – Information Systems and Application, incl. Internet/Web
and HCI

Typesetting: Camera-ready by author, data conversion by Scientific Publishing Services, Chennai, India

Printed on acid-free paper

Springer is part of Springer Science+Business Media (www.springer.com)

Preface

It is with pride that we present the proceedings of ICEC 2014, the 13th IFIP International Conference on Entertainment Computing, held for the first time in Australia. Australia, with the second-highest human development index in the world, is and will be one of the major players in shaping our global future. ICEC 2014 was held in Sydney, the financial, manufacturing, and economic powerhouse of Australia that many believe is the greatest city in the world.

Continuing the distinguished tradition of excellence of previous ICEC conferences, ICEC 2014 provided a leading international and interdisciplinary forum encompassing all aspects of entertainment computing including authoring, development, use and evaluation of digital entertainment artefacts and processes. The conference served to deepen our understanding and improve practice in this exciting and rapidly developing field.

The ICEC 2014 proceedings contain cutting-edge and insightful research articles. Overall we had 62 submissions, from which 20 were selected as full papers, six were selected as short papers, and eight were selected as posters. In addition, we had three demonstration papers and two workshops. All the submissions were thoroughly evaluated in a review and meta-review process by the ICEC 2014 Program Committee consisting of 58 distinguished experts from 23 different countries. We are grateful to all our reviewers and sub-reviewers for their hard, timely, and meticulous work that provided extensive and constructive feedback to all our submissions and had a decisive contribution to the success and high quality of this event.

The keynotes for ICEC 2014 were Leila Alem from Commonwealth Scientific and Industrial Research Organisation (CSIRO), Anaisa Franco, a New Media artist currently based in UK, and Stefan Greuter from RMIT University.

We thank our sponsors the University of Technology, Sydney (UTS), the Centre for Human Centred Technology Design (HCTD), and Griffith Film School, Griffith University, as well as our supporters. We also thank the IFIP TC14 Technical Committee for supporting ICEC 2014.

October 2014

Yusuf Pisan
Nikitas M. Sgouros
Tim Marsh

Griffith Film School

ICEC 2014 Workshops

Organization

Organizing Committee

Conference Chair

Yusuf Pisan   University of Technology, Sydney

Program Chairs

Nikitas M. Sgouros   University of Piraeus, Greece
Tim Marsh   Griffith University, Australia

Program Committee

Australia

Leila Alem	CSIRO
Erik Champion	Curtin University
Dennis Del Favero	UNSW
Sam Ferguson	University of Technology, Sydney
Stefan Greuter	RMIT University
Michael Hitchens	Macquarie University
Tim Marsh	Griffith University
Chek Tien Tan	University of Technology, Sydney
Stewart Von Itzstein	University of South Australia
Kok Wai Wong	Murdoch University

Austria

Helmut Hlavacs	University of Vienna
Gunter Wallner	University of Applied Arts Vienna

Belgium

David Geerts	University of Leuven

Brazil

Esteban Clua	Universidade Federal Fluminense

Bulgaria

Zlatogor Minchev	Bulgarian Academy of Sciences

Canada

Sidney Fels   University of British Columbia

China

Börje Karlsson   Microsoft Research Asia
Zhigeng Pan   Zhejiang University

Czech Republic

David Obdrzalek   Univerzita Karlova

Germany

Chris Geiger   University of Applied Sciences Düsseldorf
Jannicke Baalsrud Hauge   BIBA
Rainer Malaka   Bremen University
Maic Masuch   University of Duisburg-Essen
Marc Herrlich   TZI University of Bremen
Mike Preuss   TU Dortmund University

Greece

Konstantinos Chorianopoulos   Ionian University
Elpida Tzafestas   University of Athens

Italy

Luca Chittaro   University of Udine
Paolo Ciancarini   University of Bologna

Japan

Ichiroh Kanaya   Osaka University
Haruhiro Katayose   Kwansei Gakuin University

Korea

Sung-Bae Cho   Yonsei University
Kyung-Joong Kim   Sejong University
Hyun Seung   Yang KAIST

Netherlands

Sander Bakkes	University of Amsterdam
Rafael Bidarra	Delft University of Technology
Frank Dignum	Utrecht University
Anton Nijholt	University of Twente
Matthias Rauterberg	Eindhoven University of Technology

New Zealand

Christoph Bartneck	University of Canterbury

Norway

Monica Divitini	Norwegian University of Science and Technology
Letizia Jaccheri	Norwegian University of Science and Technology
Kristine Jørgensen	University of Bergen

Portugal

Luis Carriço	University of Lisbon
Nuno Correia	FCT
Joaquim Madeira	Universidade de Aveiro
Teresa Romão	DI/FCT/UNL

Singapore

Ryohei Nakatsu	National University of Singapore

Spain

Antonio J. Fernández Leiva	Universidad de Málaga
Pedro González Calero	Complutense University of Madrid

Sweden

Staffan Björk	Chalmers University of Technology and University of Gothenburg

Turkey

Selim Balcisoy	Sabanci University

UK

Marc Cavazza   University of Teesside
Kathrin Maria Gerling   University of Lincoln
Graham Kendall   University of Nottingham
Minhua Ma   Glasgow School of Art

USA

Christoph Borst   University of Louisiana at Lafayette
Jose Zagal   DePaul University

Table of Contents

Digital Games and Interactive Entertainment

Entertainment for Purpose and Persuasion

Computational Methodologies for Entertainment

Entertainment Devices, Platforms and Systems

Interactive Art, Performance and Novel Interactions

Short Papers

Digital Games and Interactive Entertainment

Trees of Tales: A Playful Reading Application for Arabic Children

Fatma Alaamri, Stefan Greuter, and Steffen P. Walz

GEElab, RMIT University
Melbourne, Australia
{fatma.alaamri,Stefan.greuter,steffen.walz}@rmit.edu.au

Abstract. In this study, we have developed a playful interactive reading and storytellng application called 'Trees of Tales'. The tablet application was designed to motivate Arabic children to read more for pleasure. 'Trees of Tales' was evaluated with 18 primary school children in Oman to investigate its effectiveness as an enjoyable reading tool. To assess the impact on usability and the children's experience of fun and reading preference, we conducted three reading sessions in which all participants read stories from 'Trees of Tales', non-interactive e-books and conventional printed books. This paper describes the design of the 'Trees of Tales' application as well as the results obtained with the 'fun toolkit'.

Keywords: Interactive Reading Application, Trees of Tales, Children e-books, Arabic children, Reading for pleasure.

1   Introduction

Islamic cultures, by the way of the Quran, emphasise that reading is quintessential to humankind. The first word of Quran sent to the Prophet Mohamed was the word 'Read', and it was repeated three times emphasising its importance (Quran, 96.1). Reading at home contributes to children's concentration abilities, social collaboration, and language development [2]. However, the huge decline in reading and publishing in the Arab world has been reported. The Arab Thought Foundation *Fikr* released in its fourth annual cultural development report in January 2012 that Arabic children read on average six minutes a year compared to the approximately 12,000 minutes western children are engaged in reading per year [1]. Arabic children often only read their textbooks and the Holy Quran as part of their educational and religious needs. However, they do not read for pleasure as much as wester people read despite the importance of reading that the Quran itself underlines.

Some Arabic countries such as the Gulf countries are often classified as high-income countries and often have a high literacy rates. Oman is listed within the best performing 35 countries in the world [21]. According to UNICEF statistics, literacy rates of children aged 15 years and older reached 97.4% for males and 98.2% for females in 2012 [22]. Literacy is therefore not the problem that is leading to the decline in reading.

Y. Pisan et al. (Eds.): ICEC 2014, LNCS 8770, pp. 3–10, 2014.
© IFIP International Federation for Information Processing 2014

Advanced technology is widely available in Gulf countries. In 2013, 181 mobile phones and 60 Internet users were registered for every 100 people in the area's population [22]. Despite the prevalence of technology however, there is limited access to reading materials for Arabic children. Particularly interactive e-books and apps in Arabic language are very rare.

Recent research indicated that interactive digital books provide children with enjoyment through interactivity, which motivates them to continue reading [10]. Animation in interactive storybooks was also linked to improved information recall [19]. However, as far as we know, there has not been any research on the effectiveness of interactive reading applications to motivate Arabic children to read. This paper compares and describes the experiences and opinions of Arabic children who read as part of three interventions that we compared: (a) an interactive reading application 'Trees of Tales', (b) a non-interactive e-book application 'Arabic Stories', and (c) traditional print books available in Omani Primary school libraries.

2   Reading for Pleasure

Research indicates that children, who enjoy reading, read more frequently and their reading proficiency increases. Several benefits result from reading for pleasure activities [6]. They include elevated levels of reading attainment, writing ability, text comprehension, grammar, breadth of vocabulary, positive reading attitudes, greater self-confidence, and pleasure reading in later life. The huge benefit of reading drives governments and organisations to encourage their people to read more [6].

Independent reading for pleasure is the most important indicator of the future career and social achievements of a child [11]. However, without motivation it is difficult to engage even the brightest children in reading or any other learning activities [15]. It was found that intrinsic motivation predicts an increase in the amount of reading for pleasure more than extrinsic motivation [7], [23]. Interest and challenge are the two main components of intrinsic reading motivation [9]. Therefore, it is important to foster the interest and curiosity of children through providing a range of reading topics that suits their ages and cultures.

3   Interactive E-books

E-book publishers and designers have attempted different approaches to use interactivity in e-books to motivate and engage children as well as increase their comprehension of the content [16]. Thus, research on how interactivity is used in e-books and how it can be used in an engaging and effective manner is important. Children need to be moved away from interactive e-books that merely entertain towards e-books that educate, whilst they entertain.

Most of the interactivity that occurs in e-books exists to improve the engagement of children with the application. Such applications are enjoyable and attractive for children and motivate them to continue interacting with the application. Recent evidence, however, suggests that children who read e-books with many interactive elements recalled significantly less narrative details than children who read print versions of the same books [5]. Conversely, Labbo and Kuhn [12] found that e-books, which integrated corresponding interactivity into the content of the story, were found to elevate the comprehension of children.

Additionally, it was found that features such as narration, sound effects and animation, which support the text, help to remove the effort from decoding individual words and allow children to focus on meaning [13, 14]. Digital books are known for their non-linear storytelling potential, which means "the telling of a story with an audience impact on the storyline, but not on the story goal or the end of the story" [3]. Therefore, one design approach to tap into this potential is to allow for the reader to intervene within storylines, and to try and match the content of the story to the visual elements. These audience-based actions may be resources for enjoyment and engagement and a method to reinforce the understanding of the story.

3.1 A Reading Application for Arabic Children (Trees of Tales)

The design of the reading application 'Trees of Tales' included Arabic traditional folktales in order to elevate the interest of Arabic children in the reading. Game elements are added to the application to provide playful experiences that encourage children to continue with the reading. Additionally, to provide flexibility of place and time for reading, we decided to use the iPad as a platform for the application.

'Trees of Tales' aims to provide Arabic children aged eight and above with a collection of interactive stories that motivate them to read for pleasure and that are based in their culture. The application also provides children with the option of creating new stories using the characters and backgrounds that are available in the existing stories. It includes interactivity such as dragging and dropping objects to the scene that aimed to keep children engaged. One of the main design considerations in Trees of Tales was to ensure that children were actually reading the stories while engaging with the interactive features available. To this end, children are asked to set the scene and manage a few actions in the story such as selecting and positioning the relevant pose of the character on the scene and adjusting the emotional state of the characters in correspondence with the text. Only if the scene is set in accordance with the text, the next page of the story will unlock.

Feedback was also provided to children when their choice of actions was wrong. For example, a selected character would not stick on the background and return to its previous position if moved to a wrong position. Similarly, when children looked for the hiding thieves in Joha's first story, a sad sound tune assisted children to recognise a wrong position. Ultimately, when the scene was completed according to the text, the Next Button appeared green and a jingle indicated that the child could proceed to the next page. Similar design elements and the Next Button existed on every page. Screen shots of a story page of 'Trees of Tales' showing the interactions are illustrated in Figure 1. If children changed a critical element that made the scene contradict with the storyline, the green button turned back to red again to indicate that there was something incorrect in the scene and the next page was locked again. However, children were able to be creative by adding other images or re-arranging the scene in a way that did not affect the storyline.

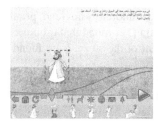

Fig. 1. Screen shots of a scene in 'Trees of Tales'

4   Experiment Design

This study evaluated 'Trees of Tales' (TT) as an enjoyable reading experience in comparison to two other reading interventions; non-interactive application (EB), and printed storybooks (PB). For the non-interactive application, we chose an iPad app named 'Arabic Stories' that we had found in the App store and that contained five Arabic stories. The printed books were 40 storybooks selected from the school library with the help of the librarian and children chose 3 to 4 of the books to read. Previous studies of children experiences with educational software found that both 'observed' and 'reported' fun are informative in user studies (Read, MacFarlane, & Casey, 2002). In this paper, we concentrated on the 'reported' fun, usability, and preference for reading.

An experiment of within-subjects counter-balanced design with the three interventions: TT, EB, and PB was performed. The sample comprised 18 children (9 boys, 9 girls) aged between 9 years and 10 years. The children were randomly selected from fourth grade of a public primary school in Muscat, Oman. To determine the order in which children used the three interventions, a counter-balanced design was applied (Foley, 2004). This approach required the division of the sample into six groups that read from the three interventions in different order.

The experiment was carried out over three weeks. One reading session was performed every week during the school's 25-minute break and in the library room. On the second and third weeks, the same children were allocated to a different reading intervention. Over the course of the three weeks, every child used each of the three interventions once.

4.1   Data Collection

The primary means of data collection was the 'fun sorter', which is part of the 'fun toolkit' [18]. The 'Fun Toolkit' is a data collection tool that assesses the opinions of children and their reaction to software, applications or games [20]. The 'fun sorter' required the children to rank the three reading interventions in order of preference on three separate criteria: (a) fun, (b) ease of use, and (c) how interesting the content was. The method provided each child with a form containing three spaces for each question and 'stickers' depicting the interventions. The pictures on the stickers were explained to them. The children were then asked to rank the three interventions by sticking the three stickers into the spaces on the form in the appropriate order. A question in the bottom of the form asked which intervention the children would choose to read again. For this particular question, the children could only choose one sticker to answer this question. All of the children completed the 'fun sorter' questionnaire and, from our observation, seemed to enjoy the activity (Fig. 2).

The 'fun sorter' instrument provided insight into the reading intervention the children enjoyed the most, the reading intervention children found the easiest to use and the reading intervention that contained the most interesting stories. Additionally, we found out which reading intervention children would select to read again.

Fig. 2. Images from the Experiment

5   Results and Discussions

The Fun Sorters completed by the children were coded in an ordinal manner 1–3 for each of the criteria Fun, Ease of use, and Best content. For example, 3 represented most fun and 1 least fun. The last question in the 'fun sorter' (I would choose to read from) was scored according to how many children chose that intervention. Table 1 shows, for each criterion, how many children ranked each intervention highest.

Table 1. Frequency each intervention was ranked first in the fun sorter

	TT	EB	PB
Fun	11	7	0
Ease of use	2	11	5
Best content	12	6	0
Child choice	13	5	0

The mean scores for fun were TT = 2.61, EB = 2.27, PB = 1.11. A Friedman test revealed statistical significant difference in perceived fun on the different reading interventions, χ^2= 22.33, p<0.0005. Post hoc Wilcoxon tests revealed the PB were ranked significantly lower than both TT and EB, but the difference between the EB and the TT was not significant. Children found 'Trees of Tales' the most enjoyable reading experience of the three interventions tested. This could be due to the visual and interactive elements in the application that encourages children to build the scene of the stories in a playful sense.

The mean scores for ease of use were TT = 1.83, EB = 2.39, PB = 1.78. A Friedman test revealed that there was no significant difference in perceived ease of use among the three interventions. However, table. 1 illustrates that only two children picked TT as the easiest to use, which indicates that the majority of children found TT not as easy to use as the other interventions. More than 50% of the children picked the non-interactive app as the easiest to use. This was expected as the application was direct and did not have interactivity that children had to complete except for picking a story and pressing next in each page.

The mean scores for best content were TT = 2.67, EB = 2.22, PB = 1.22. A Friedman test revealed statistical significant difference in perceived best content on the different reading interventions, χ^2= 20.81, p<0.0005. Post hoc Wilcoxon tests revealed the TT was ranked significantly higher on best content than PB, but the difference between EB and TT was not significant. This finding indicated that children found the stories in 'Trees of Tales' more interesting than the stories in the printed books. It is noteworthy to point here that the stories in 'Trees of Tales' were carefully selected from traditional folktales in Oman whereas the printed books were selected from the school library. Hence, providing children with stories and characters that relate to their culture, made it more interesting for them to read. This finding supports the view that interest is a factor of intrinsic motivation for reading [9]. School libraries should also consider providing interesting reading material to motivate children to read more.

The mean scores for children choice for each of the interventions were TT = 0.72, EB = 0.27, PP = 0.00. A Friedman test revealed that there was a statistical significant difference in children choices of the interventions to read. Post hoc Wilcoxon tests revealed that the significant difference was between the PB and TT. The difference in children choices between the PB and EB and between the EB and the TT was not significant. Interestingly most children in the sample preferred to read from the 'Trees of Tales' app although it was not easier to reading from. However, more research is needed to find out what aspect of 'Trees of Tales' children liked the most and what the most interesting features of the stories were. More information about the difficulties the children encountered while using 'Trees of Tales' would be interesting to inform the future development of the application.

The results presented here reveal that the decision whether or not to use an interactive reading application is based on how much fun it is perceived to be. Children's own reports of how much fun the interventions were to use and the most interesting content they found were correlated to their choices of the reading interventions they would like to continue using. However, their perceived ease of use did not correlate with their choice of intervention to read again. This could be due to their preference for challenge at this age and calls for further research. Challenge is one of the intrinsic motivation factors that influence reading for pleasure [9]. However, it is important for the application designers to balance challenge with abilities if we want children to continue reading in the future.

6   Conclusion

This study investigated the effectiveness of designing and developing an interactive reading application specifically for Arabic children. 'Trees of Tales' was designed with the purpose motivating Arabic children to read for pleasure. The 'fun sorter' was used to canvas the opinions of the 18 children regarding the different reading interventions including 'Trees of Tales'. Participants indicated that they enjoyed reading from 'Trees of Tales' more than the e-book or the printed books. They revealed that the stories included in 'Trees of Tales' were more interesting than the stories in the printed books. However, the children found 'Trees of Tales' the most difficult to use out of the three interventions. The preliminary results indicate that 'Trees of Tales' has a positive impact on Arabic children's reading behaviour.

Overall, this experiment shows that using technology such as tablet PCs for pleasurable reading offered children more enjoyment than the existing reading media in schools such as printed books. Although there was no significant difference in perceived fun and best content between the non-interactive e-book stories and 'Trees of Tales', the children indicated that they would read 'Trees of Tales' again, which supported our suspicion that interactive media has an advantage over the static media in this case.

Obviously, the analysis of children 'reported' experiences, needs to be connected with the 'observed' situations to complete the picture and develop a conclusion on the effectiveness of 'Trees of Tales' [18]. Additionally, the collected data raised questions about the specific features of 'Trees of Tales' that children enjoyed the most or found difficult, which calls for a further investigation of the video recordings that were conducted during the experiment. Future work will include analysis of the observational data collected in the reading sessions.

References

1. Al-Yacoub, I.: Sum of All Fears: Arabs read an average of 6 pages a year, study reveals (2012), http://english.alarabiya.net/articles/2012/07/14/226290.html (retrieved)
2. Beauchat, K.A., Blamey, K.L., Walpole, S.: Building preschool children's language and literacy one storybook at a time. Reading Teacher 63, 26–39 (2009)
3. Blythe, M.A., Monk, A.F., Overbeeke, K., Wright, P.C.: Funology: From Usability to Enjoyment. Kluwer Academic Publishers (2006)
4. Breakwell, G.M., Hammond, S., Fife-Schaw, C.: Research methods in psychology. SAGE, London (2000)
5. Chiong, C., Ree, J., Takeuchi, L., Erickson: Print Books vs. E-books: Comparing parent-child co-reading on print, basic, and enhanced e-book platforms. The Joan Ganz Cooney Center at Sesame Workshop, New York (2012)
6. Clark, C., Rumbold, K.: Reading for Pleasure: A research overview, vol. 30. National Literacy Trust, London (2006)
7. Cox, K.E., Guthrie, J.T.: Motivational and Cognitive Contributions to Students' amount of Reading. Contemporary Educational Psychology 26, 116–131 (2001)
8. Foley, H.: Counterbalancing. In: Lewis-Beck, M.S., Bryman, A., Liao, T.F. (eds.) The SAGE Encyclopedia of Social Science Research Methods, pp. 206–207. Sage Publications, Thousand Oaks (2004), doi:http://dx.doi.org/10.4135/9781412950589.n180

9. Guthrie, J.T., Wigfield, A.: Engagement and motivation in reading. In: Kamil, M.L., Mosenthal, P.B., Pearson, P.D., Barr, R. (eds.) Handbook of Reading Research, 3rd edn. Longman, New York (2000)
10. Hsu, M.C., Chen, C.P.: Analysis of Motivation Triggers in Interactive Digital Reading for Children. International Journal for Infonomics (IJI) 6(½) (2013)
11. Kirsch, I., de Jong, J., Lafontaine, D., McQueen, J., Mendelovits, J., Monseur, C.: Reading For Change: Performance and Engagement Across Countries. In: Organisation For Economic Co-operation and Development, OECD (2002)
12. Labbo, L.D., Kuhn, M.R.: Weaving chains of affect and cognition: A young child's understanding of CD-ROM talking books. Journal of Literacy Research 32, 187–210 (2000)
13. Lewin, C.: Exploring the effects of talking book software in UK primary classrooms. Journal of Research in Reading 23(2), 149–157 (2000)
14. Matthew, K.: Comparison of the influence of interactive CD-ROM storybooks and traditional print storybooks on reading comprehension. Journal of Research on Computing in Education 29(3), 263–275 (1997)
15. Metsala, J.L., Wigfield, A., McCann, A.D.: Children's Motivations for Reading. The Reading Teacher 50(4), 3 (1996)
16. Pearman, C.J.: Independent reading of CD-ROM storybooks: Measuring comprehension with oral retellings. Reading Teacher 61(8), 594–602 (2008)
17. Read, J.C.: Validating the Fun Toolkit: an instrument for measuring children's opinions of technology. Cognition, Technology & Work 10(2), 119–128 (2008)
18. Read, J.C., MacFarlane, S.J., Casey, C.: Endurability, engagement and expectations: Measuring children's fun. In: Interaction Design and Children, vol. 2, pp. 1–23. Shaker Publishing, Eindhoven (2002)
19. Seyit, E.I.: The impact of interactive storybook on elementary school students' recall. US-China Education Review, 140–146 (2011)
20. Sim, G., MacFarlane, S., Read, J.: All work and no play: Measuring fun, usability, and learning in software for children. Computers & Education 46(3), 235–248 (2006)
21. The World Bank. World Development Indicators (WDI). Data by country (2011), http://data.worldbank.org/country/oman (retrieved)
22. UNICEF, Country statistics (2013), http://www.unicef.org/infobycountry/ oman_statistics.html (accessed on January 20, 2014) (retrieved)
23. Wang, J.H.Y., Guthrie, J.T.: Modeling the effects of intrinsic motivation, extrinsic motivation, amount of reading, and past reading achievement on text comprehension between U.S. and Chinese students. Reading Research Quarterly 39, 162–186 (2004)
24. Wigfield, A., Guthrie, J.T., Tonks, S., Perencevich, K.: Children's Motivation for Reading: Domain Specificity and Instructional Influences. The Journal of Educational Research 97(6), 299–309 (2004)

Gamicards - An Alternative Method
for Paper-Prototyping the Design of Gamified Systems

Lauren S. Ferro, Steffen P. Walz, and Stefan Greuter

School of Media and Communication
Games and Experimental Entertainment Laboratory (GEElab)
RMIT University, Melbourne, Australia
{lauren.ferro,steffen.walz,stefan.greuter}@rmit.edu.au

Abstract. This paper introduces an early prototype concept known as *Gamicards,* for use in the design of gamified systems. With the popularity of gamified approaches and the varying knowledge of designers of these systems, not enough resources exist that can assist to guide designers through the process, ensuring important elements (such as motivation) are considered. *Gamicards* are an early prototype deck of cards that are designed to provide a resource for designers from a range of different backgrounds and knowledge of gamified design, with the intention to develop more meaningful gamified approaches.

Keywords: gamification, paper prototyping, game design, motivation, brainstorming, idea generation, personalization.

1   Introduction

Gamification is the application of game elements and game mechanics to make an ordinary task more engaging and enjoyable [1]. It has become popular across varying contexts from education, business, marketing, and social collaboration. The term engagement in this paper refers to the amount of time spent interacting with the gamified application, often with an increase after the implementation of a gamified approach. Gamification can use game elements and mechanics (i.e. badges, achievements) with the aim of increasing motivation to perform certain tasks, and is often successful. Motivation in the context of this paper refers to the users willingness to engage with the gamified application (this can be either extrinsic or intrinsic motivation)[1]. Whether it is to improve product engagement, customer loyalty, [1], [2] or to develop a more enjoyable way of interacting or completing tasks such as keeping organised or productive, gamification can be a favourable strategy.

The implementation of a gamified approach has been evident in many situations such as marketing strategies (i.e. loyalty programs such as Fly Buys[2]) and educational

---

[1] It should be noted that the intention of this gamified intervention; the intrinsic motivation of the user is the primary focus.

[2] https://www.flybuys.com.au

Y. Pisan et al. (Eds.): ICEC 2014, LNCS 8770, pp. 11–18, 2014.

institutions (i.e. gold stars, house points) and online educational platforms (i.e. Khan Academy[3], *DuoLingo*[4] and *Memrise*[5]), giving children a reward for completing household chores or good behaviour (i.e. Chore Wars)[6] . If you consider social activities such as Scouts, gamification is present in the form of collecting badges for acquired skills and completed tasks, social recognition, all playing a part in the development of a Scout [3]. It is through recent times that the term of "gamification" has become a buzzword and a favourable approach to "engaging" clients with new and exciting design schemes to maintain interest and promote a more enjoyable and ideally "fun" product [2]. Additionally, gamification can exist both in a physical sense (i.e. gold star stickers) as well as in a digital sense (i.e. badge and point reward systems) as an effective way to motivate and engage users. However, while the desire to modify and encourage specific user behaviour can be the trigger for using a gamified approach in the first place and that implementing a more enjoyable approach to ordinary tasks will make it more engaging; and while this is often successful, its success is not always long-term nor is the approach fresh.

2   Who Are Designing These Systems?

While, gamification approaches have been implemented across an array of areas, the designers who are creating these experiences may not have a background in game design, or gamification. The main difference between game design and a gamified approach is that the gamified approach is used for the design of real world situations, not artificial ones. Therefore, it is important that the designer is aware that such an approach produces outcomes that have real world effects and impacts the users motivations and behaviour - such as customer loyalty or productivity. Ultimately to what extent can only be viewed after users have engaged with the approach. However, these desired outcomes may be set by the designer, or stem from company objectives such as increased employee motivation which can be both positive and negative.

In some cases the thought of turning tasks into a gamified experience, can be an exciting process and the array of game elements and mechanics that can be used by the designer can be alluring. In some instances, the options of what game elements and mechanics to use may become overwhelming with designers opting for typical elements such as points and badges. This can become a problem if they are implemented without a meaningful purpose, as this may add an additional layer to a process that may interfere with the quality of user's engagement and enjoyment (if the points or badges become the driver of the task) if not taken into deeper consideration.

However, while people designing these systems can vary from inexperienced to experienced designers. Having two ends of the spectrum can be an important consideration in acknowledging that the designer's knowledge of using game elements and mechanics within a gamified approach varies as well. Therefore it is important to consider the diversity of design objectives as well as to provide adequate

---

[3] www.khanacademy.com

[4] Available online and as an application on smart devices. www.duolingo.com

[5] Available online and as an application on smart devices. www.memirse.com

[6] http://www.chorewars.com

resources so that amateurs do not develop bad habits early on in the process, or to suggest alternative approaches for more experienced designers.

For instance, in an educational context, teachers may design and implement gamified strategies into a classroom activity with the intention to increase behaviours such as the timely submission of assignments or the productivity on assignment tasks in the way of gold stars or house points. A more recent example of this is with the not-for-profit online educational organisation, *Khan Academy*. As evident in Figure 1, the *Khan Academy* have implemented a range of different badge types for completing various types of assessment or loyalty such as returning to *Khan Academy* to complete more tasks. However, while students generally enjoy receiving rewards, a focus on receiving rewards can distract the student of the initial aim. For example, if you provide students with a badge for completing an essay, the quality of the essay may not be the focus, but rather completing the essay to get the badge. Students may accumulate a lot of badges, perhaps to compete with others, but it raises the question about what kind of impact has the badge had on the students understanding of essay writing. Implementing badges that reflect behaviours such as no grammatical errors, may fix this situation – thus encouraging students to proof read their work.

Fig. 1. Khan Academy badge types (left to right: Meteorite, Moon, Earth, Sun, Black Holes, Challenge Patches)[7]

3   Resources for Designing Gamified Systems

At present, few resources exist that can assist individuals to design a gamified approach as opposed to the design of games [4]–[6] most notably, *Jesse Schell's deck (and book) of lenses* [7]. However, while there are specific resources available such as *GameOn!: Gamification Toolkit*[8], *GameGame* [8], *Playful Experiences (PLEX)* [9], [10] or simpler as *Grow-a-Game*[9] and *PlayGen*[10], there still needs to be a more concentrated resource for the design of gamified approaches aimed at both inexperienced and experienced designers. These resources provide support and assistance, while being diverse and open to many possible design options. While having the freedom to design any type of gamified approach can be a positive thing, it may become overwhelming to an inexperienced designer. Furthermore, if the design is based heavily around extrinsic and/or meaningless rewards, it may harm the longevity, user motivation and engagement with the gamified approach [11], [12].

---

[7] Badge icons taken from: https://www.khanacademy.org/badges
[8] http://www.gameonlab.com/toolkit/
[9] Also available as an app on the App Store on iTunes.
  http://www.tiltfactor.org/grow-a-game/
[10] http://gamification.playgen.com/

Fig. 2. (From left) Schell's deck of lenses, Grow-a-Game, PlayGen Deck

3.1   The Need to Provide Resources for Non-game Designers

Designers of gamified systems can range from educators to entrepreneurs with the vision of creating a more engaging approach to their given context. Having a diverse range if designers, also comes with a variation in knowledge and experience of gamified systems. With this in mind, it is important that if these systems are being implemented into contexts that cross over with real life expectations (i.e. improved academic performance) that they are carefully designed - much like the design of educational curriculum or a marketing strategy. Furthermore, the idea of what a game is may influence the general understanding of what is a gamified system. Industry experience has identified that individuals outside of a concentrated gaming and sometimes technology culture tend to perceive gamified approaches as either a waste of time or a potentially useful approach. Often the former, end up comparing gamified approaches to the idea of playing a game. Sometimes, the assumption is that a gamified approach is based entirely around that - a game. Therefore, it is important that there is an availability of adequate resources to provide support and an understanding of gamified systems and what it means to create a gamified approach - that it is not necessarily "a game". The aim here is that by developing such an understanding this stigma centred on gamified design will be broken.

4   Gamicards

Gamicards are an early prototype deck of cards that are designed to provide a resource to assist individuals in the development of gamified approaches. It forms part of a larger project that is investigating the relationship between personality types and gamified experiences [13]. The cards aim at covering the fundamental and core considerations for developing more meaningful and personalised gamified approaches. Additionally, developing a vocabulary and awareness of the other types of elements that are available to use – making designers aware that they stem beyond the more popular: badge, achievements and points. By having resources with aspects focusing specifically on user considerations, it will keep the gamified approach focused, without being restricting.

At present, *Gamicards* include five types of cards: (1) Game elements and Mechanics (2) User considerations (3) Context Cards (4) Motivation (5) Mystery Cards - for designers wanting to develop their own elements. Based on current data analysis from earlier work by Ferro et al. [13] the user considerations are expected to become more focused and inline with the development of a taxonomical relationship between users and associated game elements and mechanics. This taxonomical relationship aims to improve and strengthen a more meaningful interaction between the designer's choice of elements and mechanics, and the users experience with the gamified approach.

4.1   Game Elements and Mechanics

These cards consist of common elements and mechanics that are commonly found among various lists of game elements and mechanics [7], [14]–[16]. They range from rewards, badges and achievements, to other elements and mechanics such as leaderboards, points and status. Each card features a description that provides a brief outline about what the card is. This provides designers, who are unfamiliar with the terms, the ability to understand the element and to think about its potential in their gamified approach. The aim of providing a detailed resource is so designers can become aware of not only other existing game elements and mechanics but also be encouraged to think about ways to implement them.

4.2   User Considerations

These are the considerations that are most important when designing gamified experiences. They include the demographics of the user (i.e. who are they, where are they from, what are their intentions, etc.) objectives and outcomes (i.e. what is it that you want your users to achieve in a gamified system). User considerations can range in age, gender and location - which may influence, for example, the types of rewards administered or even virtual currency. While demographics tend to provide insight into the design of gamified approaches, the aim is to have a card specific to Users will help to place emphasis on this area of focus.

4.3   Context

Designers need to identify in the beginning, the context in which a gamified approach is targeting. For example, is the design within the context of education or is it within the context of business or marketing. The way that you would design an approach to motivate and engage student to submit homework on-time will vary in comparison to maintaining customer loyalty with purchasing certain brands. Furthermore, the motivation will also differ. In the case of loyalty programs consumers are often choosing to be a part of these gamified experiences. Where on the other hand, students are already participating in the educational curriculum and must complete their objectives to reach the defined outcomes; therefore the gamified approach is not so voluntary. This is an important consideration in the design of the gamified approach, as it is likely to be influenced by the context of which it is trying to be applied in.

4.4   Motivation

The motivation of a user can influence the design of a gamified approach two-fold. For instance, the designer must determine if the gamified application is providing the source of motivation by extrinsic incentives or is it facilitating and encouraging intrinsic motivation. While the latter is harder to design for, determining whether the motivation of the users will be intrinsic or extrinsic can not only affect and influence the users motivation to begin with but also the longevity of the gamified approach. This has been evident with the implementation of unnecessary rewards for already motivating tasks [17]. For example, [17] outlines a study of children who were already intrinsically motivated to draw. However, when the children were introduced with a reward for drawing – a task that they were already intrinsically motivated to do, their desire to draw reduced. Therefore, if the motivation is focusing heavily on extrinsic rewards, the design approach may need to be reconsidered and the users identified in more detail, especially if the approach is aimed at a long-term behaviour change (i.e. healthier lifestyle). When designing a gamified approach to be applied within a learning context, considering if the chosen element and mechanics are encouraging extrinsic motivation is another example that may be an area of concern. As mentioned previously, this could be the difference between providing a badge to be purely obtained and collected by a student as opposed to linking it to behavior like checking for grammatical errors, thus encouraging more thorough proof reading.

4.5   Mystery Cards

These cards can be used for any other elements that the designer wishes to incorporate as part of the gamified approach.

Fig. 3. Paper (left) and wooden (right) prototype

To use these cards together, a designer would first select the *User Considerations* cards and identify their target audience (i.e. basic demographics such as age, gender, location). Secondly, the designer would identify the *Context* of which their approach is to take place such as business, marketing, education, professional/personal development etc. Next, they would select the *Motivation* card and determine what kind of motivation that they aiming for such as long-term or short-term, to develop the user (i.e. healthier lifestyle) or to modify their behaviour (i.e. customer loyalty). Lastly they will identify what kind of elements and mechanics they would use to design the experience keeping the aforementioned details in mind and identifying if the choice of these elements and mechanics adhere to desired interaction(s). The designer is free to choose any elements from the array, even propose alternatives via the *Mystery* cards, but still have the visual representation outlining their objectives, bringing them back to the focus of their gamified approach.

5   Discussion

While no empirical research has yet to be conducted, preliminary interactions with the *Gamicards* looks promising. Inexperienced designers grasped the concept and design process quickly, understanding the basic concept of gamified design, while more experienced designers considered a range of different aspects that they would not necessarily have thought or focused directly on without the use of the cards. Thus for experienced designers, it has provided a complementary framework to their pre-existing methods and knowledge and for inexperienced designers, these cards and resources have provided a foundation to develop their skills and understanding on how to implement game elements and mechanics into an experience. While *Gamicards* are very much in the early prototype stage, further testing and iterations are expected to provide more solid results. This is to be further reinforced with current research into the relationship between personality types and game elements and mechanics.

References

1. Deterding, S., Dixon, D., Khaled, R., Nacke, L.: From game design elements to gamefulness: Defining 'gamification'. In: Proceedings of the 15th International Academic MindTrek Conference: Envisioning Future Media Environments, New York, NY, USA, pp. 9–15 (2011)
2. Zichermann, G.: Gamification by design: Implementing game mechanics in web and mobile apps. O'Reilly Media, Sebastopol (2011)
3. L. to the Editor, "Boy Scouts of America had gamification down back in 1910." Letters to the Editor (2013)
4. Kultima, A., Niemelä, J., Paavilainen, J., Saarenpäa, H.: Designing 'Game Idea Generation' Games, Loading.. 3(5) (December 2009)
5. Alves, V., Roque, L.: A Deck for Sound Design in Games: Enhancements Based on a Design Exercise. In: Proceedings of the 8th International Conference on Advances in Computer Entertainment Technology, New York, NY, USA, p. 34:1–34:8 (2011)
6. Wetzel, R.: Introducing Pattern Cards for Mixed Reality Game Design. In: Third Workshop on Design Patterns in Games (2014)
7. Schell, J.: The art of game design a book of lenses. Elsevier/Morgan Kaufmann, Amsterdam, Boston (2008)
8. Järvinen, A.: Theory as Game: Designing the Gamegame. In: Changing Views: Worlds in Play (2005)

9. Lucero, A., Holopainen, J., Ollila, E., Suomela, R., Karapanos, E.: The Playful Experiences (PLEX) Framework As a Guide for Expert Evaluation. In: Proceedings of the 6th International Conference on Designing Pleasurable Products and Interfaces, New York, NY, USA, pp. 221–230 (2013)

10. Arrasvuori, J., Boberg, M., Holopainen, J., Korhonen, H., Lucero, A., Montola, M.: Applying the PLEX Framework in Designing for Playfulness. In: Proceedings of the 2011 Conference on Designing Pleasurable Products and Interfaces, New York, USA, pp. 24:1–24:8 (2011)

11. Deci, E.L., Ryan, R.M.: Handbook of Self-determination Research. University Rochester Press (2002)

12. Deci, E.L., Ryan, R.M.: The 'What' and 'Why' of Goal Pursuits: Human Needs and the Self-Determination of Behavior. Psychol. Inq. 11(4), 227–268 (2000)

13. Ferro, L.S., Walz, S.P., Greuter, S.: Towards Personalised, Gamified Systems: An Investigation into Game Design, Personality and Player Typologies. In: Proceedings of The 9th Australasian Conference on Interactive Entertainment: Matters of Life and Death, New York, NY, USA, pp. 7:1–7:6 (2013)

14. Adams, E., Dormans, J.: Game mechanics: Advanced game design. New Riders, Berkeley (2012)

15. Sicart, M.: Defining game mechanics. Game Stud. 8(2) (2008)

16. Badgeville Announces Gamification Toolkit for World's Leading Enterprise Cloud Platform | badgeville.com, http://badgeville.com/news/announcements/badgeville-announces-gamification-toolkit-world%E2%80%99s-leading-enterprise-cloud-platfo (accessed: April 01, 2013)

17. Lepper, M.R., Greene, D., Nisbett, R.E.: Undermining children's intrinsic interest with extrinsic reward: A test of the 'overjustification' hypothesis. J. Pers. Soc. Psychol. 28(1), 129 (1973)

Design for Creative Activity: A Framework for Analyzing the Creative Potential of Computer Games

Wilawan Inchamnan[1,2], Peta Wyeth[2], and Daniel Johnson[2]

[1] Information Technology Faculty, Dhurakij Pundit University, Thailand
[2] Faculty of Science and Engineering, Queensland University of Technology, Australia
wilawan.inn@dpu.ac.th, {peta.wyeth,dm.johnson}@qut.edu.au

Abstract. This paper describes a design framework intended to conceptually map the influence that game design has on the creative activity people engage in during gameplay. The framework builds on behavioral and verbal analysis of people playing puzzle games. The analysis was designed to better understand the extent to which gameplay activities within different games facilitate creative problem solving. We have used an expert review process to evaluate these games in terms of their game design elements and have taken a cognitive action approach to this process to investigate how particular elements produce the potential for creative activity. This paper proposes guidelines that build upon our understanding of the relationship between the creative processes that players undertake during a game and the components of the game that allow these processes to occur. These guidelines may be used in the game design process to better facilitate creative gameplay activity.

Keywords: Videogames, Creative gameplay, Behavioral analysis, Expert review.

1 Introduction

The research described in this paper examines the impact that the design of a game has on the potential for that game to engage players in creative activity. Creative thinking is an important aspect of problem solving and a valuable skill to acquire. While existing research demonstrates the effectiveness of some games in facilitating creativity [4], this study focuses on the impact that specific game elements (e.g., goals, actions) have on the creative problem solving processes that occur during gameplay. Assessing the creative potential of an experience requires a focus on how an individual responds to particular activities [9]. This research examines the activities provided within games though specific game elements and analyses how these activities may facilitate creative engagement. It identifies the key specific components of computer games that support creative activity. The outcome of the research is a set of guidelines that can aid game designers in the creation of games to facilitate people's creative thinking skills.

Y. Pisan et al. (Eds.): ICEC 2014, LNCS 8770, pp. 19–26, 2014.

2   Background

Interactive experiences within a game environment allow people to express their creativity and intentions [15]. Research on creativity has resulted in multiple definitions, perspectives and models. For example, creativity has been defined to consist of at least four components: (1) the creative process, (2) the creative product, (3) the creative person, and (4) the creative situation [3]. It has also been grouped using four definitions: product, person, press (the "press" of the environment), and process [13]. Our research concentrates on the creative process and, more specifically, the thinking processes employed during creative activity. The creative process is the result of sustained and complex mental effort over time [13] and consists of a step-by-step sequence of mental activities.

To identify the potential of games to engage players in creative processes, criteria related to activity undertaken need to be clearly understood. While we understand that games have great potential to support creative processes [11], it is not clear how we go about designing for creative activity. We know that creative ideas result from the novel combination of ideas [14], that creativity involves a process of convergent and divergent thinking [2], and that critical thinking plays an important role [5]. To develop interactive experiences that incorporate these valuable, educative processes, we need a clearer understanding of how different game elements may be combined to produce creative potential.

3   A Creative Potential Game Design Model

The creative potential game design model is based on two distinct studies. The first study was designed to measure the creative processes that occur during gameplay [6]. The conceptual method that was employed to assess creativity examined the extent to which factors that have been identified as playing an important role in creative processes – task motivation, domain-relevant skills and creativity-relevant skills – are present within gaming experiences. A behavioral and verbal protocol method that has been used previously to measure creativity in structure building activities, collage making and poem writing [12] was employed during this research. The study involved participants being observed while playing the three selected puzzle games: Portal 2, Braid and I-Fluid (Portal 2 is played from a first-person perspective and involves solving puzzles via the placement of portals within the environment; Braid is a platform style game that involves solving puzzles by manipulating time; and I-Fluid is a game where the player controls a drop of water and attempts to solve physics based puzzles). They played each game for 15 minutes. To examine the creative process, participants were video recorded while playing the games and a video coding scheme was used to capture the type and frequency of observable behaviors and participant verbalizations.

The second study [7,8] examined specific elements of the three games used in study 1 to determine which of these elements are important in fostering creativity. A heuristic checklist forms the basis of this study and experts used the items in this checklist to analyze each of the games. The items are structured into the categories identified as the key components of moment-to-moment gameplay. The three categories – identify goals, perform meaningful action and interpret outcome – map to a model of interaction that is based on cognitive processing. This model provides an important link between specific elements of games and creative problem solving activity. Fig. 1 provides an overview of the Creative Potential Game Design Model that links all of these concepts. To understand the interrelationship between gameplay and creative potential we have interpreted the results of the two studies that have been undertaken.

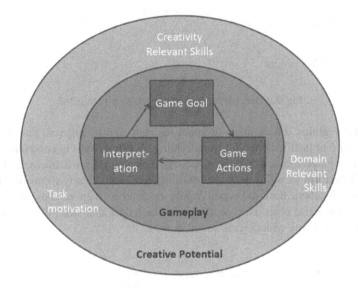

Fig. 1. Creative Potential Game Design Model

3.1   Analysis of the Play Experience

Our research has identified the extent to which each of the facilitating components of creative potential are present in each of puzzle games examined (Fig. 2). Results demonstrated that Portal 2 was best able to provide the task motivation and domain relevant skills necessary to engage in creative activity. Braid was the worst performer in both of these areas. Conversely, Braid was best able to provide the creativity relevant skills identified as important in creative processes and Portal 2 was least able to facilitate these skills. I-Fluid sat between Portal 2 and Braid for facilitating all three components.

Our more detailed analysis indicated that while the games were similar in many respects in relation to their ability to facilitate creative activity, there were areas where differences were evident (Fig. 3). Portal 2 was able to support task motivation through providing a greater number of tools to solve problems, offering more opportunities for players to use and freely manipulate a range of objects and providing options for players to playfully explore the world in their own time. Players had the time and resources to plan their approach and refine solutions to problems. Braid and I-Fluid limited the number of actions available to players and there were fewer pathways available that would lead to success.

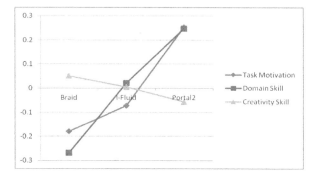

Fig. 2. Creative potential components for each game

A game's ability to facilitate domain-relevant skills centered on creating an environment that instilled confidence, providing clear pathways to complete tasks and ensuring that players understand the objectives they're trying to achieve. In the games that didn't perform as well on this component there were clearly times when players were uncertain about how the world would respond to their actions and how they could complete game objectives. Some of the challenges that arose for players related to difficulties working with objects and resources.

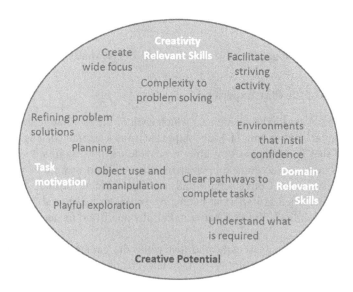

Fig. 3. Identified Means of Facilitating Creative Potential

From a creativity-relevant skills perspective our analysis indicates that overall frequency of players engaging in these types of activities were quite low. Areas identified as important in facilitating creativity-relevant skills included providing greater opportunities for players to take a wide focus when engaging in gameplay. This may be achieved through allowing activity that is future-oriented, letting players work through problems that require more than one step and facilitating interactions that enable players to develop their own goals. Problem solving needs to involve a player striving to achieve an outcome through overcoming challenging obstacles.

A tension has been identified between providing an experience that encourages striving (creativity-relevant skills) and producing gameplay where the player finds it straight-forward to understand what they are required to do and how they might go about doing it (domain-relevant skills). It appears that the ideal conditions for creativity are achieved within challenging environments where objectives are clear and consequences for exploration are positive. Given the focus within puzzle games on logical and conceptual challenges, experiences where players are able to develop their own goals or sub-goals is limited. Design for creativity involves opening up rule-sets, broadening the ways goals might be achieved and providing opportunities for non-goal directed behavior.

3.2   Analysis of Gameplay

The player's experience of the game derives directly from their interaction with the game environment and it is this environment that we analyze to determine where differences in creative activity occur. We apply the Seven Stages of Action [10], which details the process of executing and evaluating actions to achieve a particular goal, to moment-to-moment gameplay activity. Gameplay consists of the challenges and actions that a game offers the player and central to the experience is how the player addresses these challenges to achieve game objectives [1]. The three key components of game activity – goals and challenges, action and interaction, and interpretation –can be mapped to Norman's seven stages of action. Expert analysis of Portal 2, I-Fluid and Braid provides insight into how each game provides challenges that players must address to achieve goals, the effectiveness of the actions and interactivity available, and the quality the feedback presented so that players can assess their progress [8].

To determine how the components of game activity influence creative potential we firstly examined the expert review of Portal 2. Given that Portal 2 performed well in the task motivation and domain-relevant skills categories for creative potential, it is useful to identify the game activity components in which it performed better than Braid and I-Fluid. Analysis demonstrated that Portal 2 most effectively provided mechanisms that allow the player to succeed at particular challenges. Expert review found that the game challenges effectively allowed for cognitive and logical thinking and strategic planning, that there were multiple types of challenges available that players could approach in their own way and at their own pace, the level of challenge was well matched to player skill level, and that narrative mechanisms guided challenges and supported progress towards goals. Portal 2 did well at offering players interesting options and choices, allowing the player to perform a range of actions to address a challenge and the story was particularly well integrated with the gameplay. The game actions provide a good sense of control over interactions and they allow players to feel that they have a significant impact on the game world. The review found that the interface to Portal 2 was easiest to learn, use and master and that the game had good input control. In terms of feedback, analysis of results demonstrated that Portal 2 performed well at providing output that allowed the player to assess the state of gameplay at any given time. The feedback mechanisms provided positive reinforcement which enhanced free-choice and self-awareness.

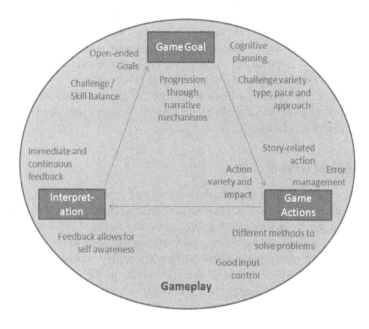

Fig. 4. Analysis of Game Activity Components for Creative Gameplay

Given that Braid performed slightly better than both I-Fluid and Portal 2 in terms of providing activities to support creativity-relevant skills, it is helpful to examine expert review data for its game activity components. Braid did well at supporting players in recovering from errors and at minimizing errors that are detrimental to gameplay. Compared to the other two games, Braid provides the most effective mechanisms for players to interpret the outcome of actions through mechanisms that give immediate and continuous feedback. Fig. 4 illustrates this analysis of game activity components and identifies areas of strength that may contribute to the ability of a game to facilitate creative activity.

4   Guidelines for Creating a Game with Creative Potential

As a first step towards producing guidelines that will aid in the development of games that facilitate creative problem solving, we have mapped game activity components (Fig. 4) to the mechanisms identified as facilitating creative potential (Fig. 3). These prelimary guidelines are outlined below, with the creative component facilitated included in brackets:

- Ensure that the game includes open-ended goals that allow players to develop their own sub-goals (wide focus, playful exploration)
- Create narrative mechanisms that allow players to understand their progress towards achieving goals and that clearly link to choices in the game (understand what is required, clear pathways to complete tasks)
- Create challenges that require logical thinking and strategic planning (complexity in problem solving, planning, refining problem solutions)
- Ensure that there is variety in the type of challenges provided and that these challenges can be perceived and approached in different ways by players (wide focus, complexity in problem solving, facilitate striving activity, playful exploration, object use and manipulation, planning)
- Implement challenges that develop at an appropriate pace and match a player's skill level (facilitate striving activity, environments that instill confidence)
- Implement rules that offer freedom of choice, where players have options about actions to use to solve a problem (wide focus, object use and manipulation, planning)
- Ensure that player actions have an impact on and shape the game world (wide focus, object use and manipulation, playful exploration)
- Ensure that actions available to the player relate to the overarching story/setting of the game and that feedback makes sense within this context (understand what is required, clear pathways to complete tasks)
- Manage player errors by allowing support for recovery from errors and ensuring that the impact is minimal (facilitate striving activity, environments that instill confidence)
- Ensure that the player has a sense of control of interactions through creating a game interface that is easy to learn, use and master (environments that instill confidence)
- Provide mechanisms that allow players to receive immediate and continuous feedback on their actions (environments that instill confidence, understand what is required, clear pathways to complete tasks, refining problem solutions)
- Ensure that feedback provided to the player positively reinforces good choices and allows for free choice and self-awareness (facilitate striving activity, understand what is required, refining problem solutions)

5   Conclusion

In this paper we map the results of our analysis of players engaging in creative problem solving during puzzle game play to the expert review of the components of these games. We have used data to better understand how in-game activities influence a player's engagement in creative activity. We have developed preliminary guidelines that consider the specific ways we can align game goals and challenges, actions and interactivity and interpretation/feedback mechanisms to support creative problem solving processes. Future work will investigate the applicability of the Creative Potential Game Design Model across different game genres. Furthermore, the guidelines produced will be applied and evaluated in the development of a game to support creative activity.

Acknowledgments. The authors would like to thank Games Research and Interaction Design Lab team, Queensland University of Technology for their support and cooperation during this study.

References

1. Adams, E.: Fundamentals of Game Design. Pearson Education (2013)
2. Amabile, T.M.: Creativity in Context. Westview Press Inc., Boulder (1996)
3. Brown, R.T.: Creativity. In: Handbook of Creativity, pp. 3–32. Springer (1989)
4. Catala, A., et al.: Exploring tabletops as an effective tool to foster creativity traits. In: Proceedings of the Sixth International Conference on Tangible, Embedded and Embodied Interaction. ACM (2012)
5. Clark, C.M., Veldman, D.J., Thorpe, J.S.: Convergent and divergent thinking abilities of talented adolescents. Journal of Educational Psychology 56(3), 157 (1965)
6. Inchamnan, W., Wyeth, P., Johnson, D., Conroy, D.: A method for measuring the creative potential of computer games. In: Herrlich, M., Malaka, R., Masuch, M. (eds.) ICEC 2012. LNCS, vol. 7522, pp. 270–283. Springer, Heidelberg (2012)
7. Inchamnan, W., Wyeth, P., Johnson, D.: Behavioural Creative Components Analysis of Puzzle Gameplay. In: Proceeding of the 5th International IEEE Games Innovation Conference, IGIC 2013, Vancouver, British Columbia, Canada, September 23-25 (2013)
8. Inchamnan, W., Wyeth, P.: Motivation during videogame play: Analysing player experience in terms of cognitive action. In: Proceedings of The 9th Australasian Conference on Interactive Entertainment: Matters of Life and Death. ACM (2013)
9. Kaufman, J.C., Kaufman, S.B., Lichtenberger, E.O.: Finding creative potential on intelligence tests via divergent production. Canadian Journal of School Psychology 26(2), 83–106 (2011)
10. Norman, D.A., Draper, S.W.: User centered system design; new perspectives on human-computer interaction. L. Erlbaum Associates Inc. (1986)
11. Paras, B., Bizzocchi, J.: Game, motivation, and effective learning: An integrated model for educational game design (2005)
12. Ruscio, J., Whitney, D.M., Amabile, T.M.: Looking inside the fishbowl of creativity: Verbal and behavioral predictors of creative performance. Creativity Research Journal 11(3), 243–263 (1998)
13. Santanen, E.L., Briggs, R.O., de Devreede, G.-J.: Toward an understanding of creative solution generation. In: Proceedings of the 35th Annual Hawaii International Conference on System Sciences, HICSS 2002. IEEE (2002)
14. Spearman, C.: Creative Mind (1930)
15. Sweetser, P., Johnson, D.: Player-centered game environments: Assessing player opinions, experiences, and issues. In: Rauterberg, M. (ed.) ICEC 2004. LNCS, vol. 3166, pp. 321–332. Springer, Heidelberg (2004)

Conceptual Model and System for Genre-Focused Interactive Storytelling

Börje F. Karlsson[1] and Antonio L. Furtado[2]

[1] Microsoft Research, Beijing, China
[2] Departamento de Informática, PUC-Rio, Rio de Janeiro, RJ, Brazil
borjekar@microsoft.com, furtado@inf.puc-rio.br

Abstract. This paper describes a conceptual model for the definition of a genre in the context of Interactive Storytelling and its implementation in LogTell-R, a system for the interactive creation of stories. This work builds on a previous system and experiments with plan recognition and discusses the foundations of our model to allow the creation of varied and coherent stories within a genre.

Keywords: storytelling, conceptual model, genre, plan generation / recognition.

1 Introduction

Schank [17] writes that humans understand the world in terms of stories. Arguably, the human brain has a natural affinity not only for enjoying narratives, but also for creating them [19]. Thus, the dynamic and interactive generation of stories is an interesting problem. However, the generation of stories that are coherent and interesting, while accounting for authors, and audience interactions remains an unsettled issue. A wide range of approaches has tried to integrate storytelling and interactive entertainment (narrative and gameplay), with limited success, mostly by overly restricting user interaction options. While this may be a pragmatic attempt to simplify the problem space, we feel that more generative approaches are required if the field is to become truly successful. One of the main open problems in the generative craft of stories resides in how stories may be generated and told. While it is probably not possible to define an ideal general model for good stories, we claim that sound methods to organize and combine events must be considered to confer enough dramatic power to narratives. Some approaches do make use of special narrative functions that enforce narrative principles in the context of the whole story (like raising tension, introducing dilemmas, or some mechanism to "move the story forward") [10], but while these efforts improve user engagement they still do not guarantee diversity of experience. A possible avenue for the development of more generative systems that can create interesting stories is related to the **definition of a genre**. Once a genre is specified with some rigour in a constructive way, it becomes possible not only to determine whether a given plot is a legitimate representative of the genre, but also to generate such plots. To tackle the problem of creating a more generative model to support the production of stories, we draw on previous

Y. Pisan et al. (Eds.): ICEC 2014, LNCS 8770, pp. 27–35, 2014.

system-building experience and on the four master tropes identified by semiotic research, namely: metaphor, metonymy synecdoche, and irony (which are the basic rhetorical structures by which we make sense of experience [2, 5]). By offering mechanisms derived from event relations connected to these tropes, we intend to augment the expressiveness of the narrative model.

This paper describes a conceptual model used to represent plots in a given genre and presents extensions to better support event relations and enhance the space of possibly interesting stories in the context of a plot generation system. We outline how an intended genre (to whose conventions the plots must conform) can be modelled and describe LogTell-R [10], an extended version of LOGTELL [4]. This new system uses **plan recognition** and **plan generation** in the creation of stories and a **plot algebra** to help define the story space. We then show how the new system works on the basis of the identified event relations, also indicating what is done to narrow the gap between the conceptual model and the implementation while helping to construct the possible plots. Finally, we offer some remarks on the results obtained.

2   Story Generation Systems

Story generation systems (SGSs) employ different strategies to configure their story models, which can be broadly classified as character-based, plot-based, and user-experience models. In character-based models, the storyline results from the interaction among virtual agents. Their main advantage is the ability for anytime user intervention, but, while powerful in terms of interaction, such interference level may lead the plot to uncharacteristic situations. Additionally, there is no guarantee that narratives emerging from the interaction between agents will create interesting drama. By contrast, in plot-based models, characters should follow more rigid rules, specifying the intended plot structure. User intervention is thus more limited, but it is usually easier to guarantee coherence and a measure of dramatic power. Lastly, SGSs with user-experience models, focus on the user by addressing individual preferences via user profiling and measuring the interestingness of story pieces.

We feel that an approach that fits in between plot-based and character-based is the best option, given that plots and characters are interlocking elements that cannot exist without each other [7]. Specifically, we try to conciliate both. User-experience concerns can be dealt with at later stages; as long as we can guarantee that enough variety of stories can be generated, possibly while considering changes in dramatization / presentation of story events. Even though it is argued that the key aspect of an interactive narrative is the story representation used to encode the author's vision of the experiences (story space [12]), little attention is given to what qualities such space should have. Most approaches to plot-influenced storytelling models consider only stories formed by sequences of events using their inherent temporal characteristics or simple causality relations, which are clearly not enough to guarantee interesting and varied stories. Other approaches use dilemma-inducing or tension-raising events, paying no attention to the relations between events in the plot model. Few efforts dedicate enough attention to relations between events. Three relevant exceptions are [15], [11], and [14]. Pinhanez [15] deals with a temporal model of events, providing mechanisms to handle their interlacing temporal relations. Building on the same principle, the Joseph system [11] claims to provide a formal framework to relate story components to one another. In it, a story is modelled as having two sub-components, a setting and an episode list, both of which have temporal intervals associated with them and information about event relationships is specified in its rules. The Joseph system is (to our knowledge) the first system constructed from an explicit, formal model for stories. ISRST argues that relations determined by the rhetorical context of events is key [14] and introduce an ontology model based on the organization of events. In ISRST, a relation is a binding between two entities, which refers to a specific rhetorical function. They further claim that "its use is impractical for the purpose of content creation, since most human beings make use of a more limited set of relations to construct and remember stories" [14]. To match this limitation, a reduced set of nine relations is considered. However, their ideas are not implemented in a concrete system.

Lastly, content creation tools in place to make the underlying complexity of the knowledge base transparent to authors is paramount, especially if the representation uses complex models or specialized programming languages. For example, although Façade has been a successful experiment, its architecture requires a great effort from authors. It uses four different content languages and took two years to author a game with only one scene, two characters, and that takes about 20 minutes to complete [13].

3   The LOGTELL Plot Composition Model

In summary, LOGTELL is a logic-based tool for the interactive generation and dramatization of stories via the use of a plan-generation system. The main difference between its conceptual model and similar planning systems is that it does not assume the existence of one goal for the story as a whole. Instead, at the beginning of the plot (and after each planning phase), goal-inference rules are used to consider new goals induced for the various characters. Its design borrows notions from narratology, in particular, the distinction of three levels in literary composition: fabula, story, and text [1]. At the fabula level, the characters in the narrative are introduced, as well as the narrative plot - corresponding to a chronological sequence of events. The story level concerns a different representation specific to these events and how they are narrated to an audience, be it through a temporal re-ordering of the events or other narrative techniques. The last level relates to the medium used to tell the story, such as natural language, movie, or any other communication medium.

When breaking down the IS problem into its smaller sub-parts, a similar separation is observed between the story generation and narration phases [10]. In SGSs, this breakdown means that different modules handle the two parts. In discussing the conceptual model behind the story space in LOGTELL, we are interested only in the fabula level, within its Plot Manager, where the narrative plot being manipulated consists of a partially-ordered set of events. Here we should recall that plot managers, in general, are interactive story generators that receive as input an already created piece of story (initially empty) and present as output a suggestion on how to continue the story. Their main function is to effect corrections so the story plot can develop correctly. If some inconsistency is detected in the input, the manager intervenes in order to ensure that the original goal can be reached, satisfying all the necessary constraints.

To model a chosen environment to which the plots to be composed should belong, it is necessary to specify at least: a) what can exist at some state of the underlying world; b) how states can be changed; and c) the factors driving the characters to act.

Accordingly, LOGTELL defines three schemas: static, dynamic and behavioural, representing, respectively: a) **Storyworld:** the world description takes the form of a set of facts (state), introducing the characters and their initial situation (relationships and attributes); b) **World State Changes:** narratives are composed of events and an event is a transition from a valid world state to another, which should also be valid; and c) **Character's behaviour:** to model the reasons for each character's actions, LOGTELL uses goal-inference rules specifying (in a logic formalism) the motivations of these agents when certain situations occur.

State transitions consist of a limited repertoire of pre-defined domain-oriented operations. A similar notion has been proposed by Vladimir Propp [16]. LOGTELL equates the notion of event with the state-change brought about by the execution of an operation by some agent. The dynamic schema is thus composed of a repertoire of pre-defined operations (typical of the chosen genre) in which characters can take part.

The generation of a plot starts by inferring goals for the characters from the initial configuration. A planner inserts events in the plot in order to allow the characters to try to fulfill their goals. The result is then presented to the user. If the user accepts it, the process continues by inferring new goals. The process alternates goal-inference and plan generation until the user decides to stop or no new goal is inferred.

To further explore the possibilities of generating varied coherent stories in the given "fairy-tale genre", we enabled mechanisms also for plan-recognition. Experiments with the system demonstrate that combining plan-recognition/generation and user participation constitutes a promising strategy towards the production of plots which are both diverse and coherent, as it helps guide the user [8]. However, that does not guarantee dramatic power. Sound methods to combine events must be considered to accomplish this goal; which led to the necessity to further extend the utilized model. We do not claim that the present effort is sufficient to create a fully immersive experience. We endeavour, as a more limited objective, to explore the possibilities of generating a large variety of stories by applying this strategy over a given genre.

4   Event Relations in Plot Composition

Many narratologists agree that the most important relation between events is the causal one. Nevertheless, this is not the only relation taken into consideration when human beings try to create story patterns in their minds [14]. The impact on the audience very much depends on how events are combined. Furtado [6] suggests that at least four concerns are involved in plot composition: a) the plot must be formed by a coherent sequence of events; b) for each position in the sequence, several alternative choices should apply; c) non-trivial interesting sequences must permit unexpected shifts along the way; and d) one may need to go down to details to better visualize the events or, conversely, to summarize detailed event sequences. These concerns have led to the identification of four relations between pairs of events that play a basic role in a story, and to the introduction of a fourfold perspective of plot composition in the context of IS. The four relations are: a) **syntagmatic** - the occurrence of the first leaves the world in a state wherein the occurrence of the second is coherent. The syntagmatic relation between events induces a weak form of causality or enablement, which justifies their sequential ordering inside the plot; b) **paradigmatic** - the events can be seen as alternative ways to accomplish a similar kind of higher-level action, so that both achieve the same basic effect in a significantly different way; c) **antithetic** - the events oppose or contradict each other, since the occurrence of each of them implies a radically different context; and d) **meronymic** – referring to the decomposition of an event into lower-level events, thus providing a more detailed account of the action on hand.

The first two relations were already handled in LOGTELL. To extend its functionality, we included the use of a hierarchy of (generalized) events and plan-recognition mechanisms during the plot composition phase [8]. This hierarchy consists of a conveniently structured library containing sequences of events with partial order relationships between them, which can be adapted if necessary to specific circumstances. The typical plans (also called complex operations) stored in the library result from meronymic relations between other operations (Propp-inspired). Complex operations formed by generalization are also represented, branching down to specialized operations corresponding to alternative ways to reach the same main effects.

Transgressive plots based on antithetic relations can add a dramatic impact, by introducing unexpected turns in the narrative, e.g. by the sudden recognition of a wrong belief, or by a radical change of fortune (Aristotle's "discovery" and "reversal"). If his beloved princess is abducted, the hero would normally rescue her – but the antithetically related capture event would be justified if she unexpectedly falls in love with the captor (the so-called Stockholm syndrome). Mechanisms to support this kind of dramatic change must be provided, one of the possibilities being to allow arbitrary user interventions at certain points (recalling the *deus ex-machina* device).

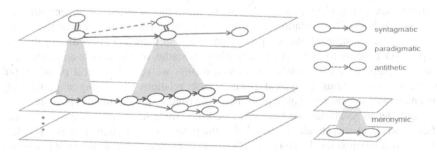

Fig. 1. Relations between events in the story space [6]

4.1   Genre as Story Space

Finding an answer to the question of what constitutes a given literary genre should allow one to determine whether or not a story can be classified as belonging to it. However proving that a conceptual model **M** for specifying a genre **G**, formulated as discussed in this paper, can fully capture how the genre is understood by a literary expert can be an over-ambitious effort. Yet, a useful approximation is attainable, taking the form of a definition by extension. If a system can generate stories according to the specified conceptual model **M**, the space of plots that can be generated might be regarded as constituting a genre G^M defined by the model, where plot has the usual meaning of sequence of events. It would be left to the designer of **M** the task of refining the model specification in order to achieve increasingly closer matches between the intuitive view of **G** and G^M. This is basically the role of the presented conceptual model. As argued, it determines the genre of the stories to be generated in correspondence to the story space of a system that uses that model. Such definition of genre as the set of stories that can be generated from a model is consistent with the way game designers discuss/describe genres by example [19].

While the story space of our example scenario refers to a simple medieval fantasy genre, our conceptual modelling method should be able to cope with an ample variety of genres of higher complexity. The structure of each story space thus specified is determined by the observed event relations. From an informal viewpoint (cf. Figure 1), events can be seen as nodes and syntagmatic, paradigmatic relations as connecting edges drawn over a plane, while meronymic relations appear as projections of events into event sequences over another plane. Antithetic relations between nodes can be seen as specifying constraints crosscutting the story space. Recall that paths formed by syntagmatic relations correspond to plots, whereas paradigmatic relations indicate alternatives – whose choice may entail, as signaled by antithetic relations, the exclusion of certain other alternatives branching from subsequent nodes.

Supporting the identified relations also brings extra benefits. Plot libraries can be organized as combined is-a and part-of hierarchies, which is a convenient way to deal with plots by taking advantage of the similarity or analogy among situations. While the part-of links result directly from meronymic relations, denoting in consequence composition / decomposition, the is-a links express the notion of generalization / specialization. If two or more events stand in a paradigmatic relation, their main effects should coincide, although they may differ with respect to less important side-effects. For instance, *abduction* and *elopement* can be seen as alternative forms of *villainy*. This justifies the introduction of a new event, which might be named *villainy* (or some more specific term), and its placement in a hierarchy above the other two one-event plots, i.e. it generalizes both. These relations contribute to the hierarchical structure of the library and, once it is constructed, its component patterns can then be reused during the plot composition process to help create new plots. Because our approach employs plan-generation/plan-recognition while composing a plot, we regard "typical plots" in our context as synonymous to typical plans. These relations also bring a particularly convenient way to deal with entire plots, helping visualize their dramatic structure.

Finally, let us recall that we have addressed the fabula level only, where one simply indicates which events should be included in the plots. One especially complex problem to be faced at the next level – story/narration, where the concern is how to tell the events – is how to properly convert the events into forms adequate for dramatization.

5   LogTell-R

To implement this model we extended LOGTELL's interaction modes and dynamic schema level, i.e. the set of operations that can transform the storyworld, to take into consideration the four relations previously presented. As mentioned before, the Plot Manager module originally dealt only with the syntagmatic and paradigmatic axes. The changes introduced in our new prototype now allow meronymic relations by introducing complex operations, and antithetic relations, by employing motifs.

When dealing with support for antithetic relations, since we emphasize interactive composition, we considered the possibility of user interventions that can result in some sort of discontinuity being produced.   If we see a disruption not as a discontinuity in one context, but as an attempt to put together two originally incompatible contexts, then the notion of blending [3] immediately comes to mind, as the technique or artisanship of conciliating the pending conflicts, which often requires a great deal of creativity. Incompatibilities between events – which we have been characterizing in terms of antithetic event relations – are usually induced by some factor involving the current value of a property or the beliefs of a character. A genre can in general be seen as a contract between author and audience [7] – in the sense that the audience knows what to expect – even if some event almost crosses the borderline of plausibility. Fortunately, blending can be achieved in a convenient way by resorting to folktale motifs [18], which often encode ingenious solutions to contradictions or dead-ends in a tale, while seeming to fit with the conventions of their encompassing genres. In order to support this mediation, LogTell-R permits the insertion of a motif at an appropriate position in the plot. This motif must come from a pre-defined set, and takes the form of a special (pseudo-)operation. Motifs are associated with either a goal specification or a set of post-conditions. In our proof-of-concept, we selected a set of genre-suitable motifs (e.g. life token - that allows to do without the unrealistic assumption that characters are omniscient). Motifs also act as dramatization tools, providing the audience a convincing explanation of why certain events must ensue. In our prototype, a motif is associated with a script defining the behaviour of the involved characters when dramatizing it.

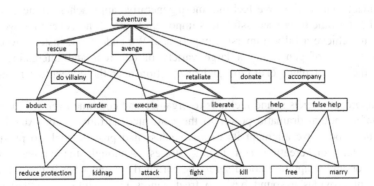

Fig. 2. Hierarchy of typical plans used in most of our experiments

Support for complex operations in plan recognition and the use of the hierarchy of typical plans can be seen as a complement to generation. The benefits of the plan library structure itself are twofold: it helps better visualize story structure, showing how to adequately chain events into a narrative scheme (like the three-parts classic structure [10]); and it helps in more easily understanding and analyzing the space of stories that can be generated. In LogTell-R, plot generation still happens in a step-wise fashion. A new way of choosing alternatives is enabled by selecting events and asking the plan-recognizer to retrieve generalizations containing them. Exploiting the meronymic axis at different levels of detail, plausible alternatives may be located by essentially walking up and down over the hierarchy. Instead of asking the system for suggestions, the user may also simply find it helpful to visually inspect the library of typical plans associated with the genre (Figure 2), and use it as inspiration to guide the composition of a plot.

As our approach is centered on the concept of hierarchies of typical plans and given that conceptual models tend to remain too far removed from system implementations, we narrow this gap with the help of an intermediate logical design stage. The approach utilized is a plot manipulation algebra (PMA) [9] for the creation of the hierarchy of typical plans. An added benefit of using PMA (supported by the planner to check pre- and post- conditions of operations) in the knowledge base editor is that one can more easily experiment with different ways to chain the events, and use this knowledge to revise the specification so as to improve the system's story space. Starting with the set of operations relevant for the genre (e.g. abduct, murder, liberate), algebra operands are applied to define the necessary relations between events (e.g. generalizations or placement of constraints on undesired event combinations). At each step, the user can visualize how the typical plan hierarchy is "grown".

6   Concluding Remarks

Few approaches to IS address the problem of what is a proper story space or the characteristics of events pertaining to a plot, preferring to focus on more controlled environments and stories. We feel that more generative approaches are necessary for the field to become truly successful. It is important to stress, however, that we do not propose to achieve a fully immersive experience. We endeavour, instead, to explore the possibilities of generating a large variety of coherent and interesting stories through the use of plan-generation and recognition over the conceptual model of a genre.

Our approach targets sound methods to organize and combine events, in ways that may confer enough dramatic power to the generated narratives. By extending our conceptual model, we augment its expressiveness and provide tools to prospective authors intent on creating and telling stories. Although the process of plot composition and adaptation could surely be enriched beyond what is presented here, our system provides a sound basis to treat genres that exhibit a good degree of regularity.

Having authorial tools make the complexities of the model transparent to authors is a major goal, primarily to reduce the burden on authors using the system, but also to guide them in the creation of interesting stories. Creating an interactive environment that behaves as expected is a tiresome task, as it is performed mostly by trial and error.

References

1. Bal, M.: Narratology. University of Toronto Press, Toronto (2002)
2. Burke, K.: A Grammar of Motives. University of California Press, Oakland (1969)
3. Casanova, M.A., et al.: Generalization and Blending in the Generation of Entity-Relationship Schemas by Analogy. In: Proceedings of ICEIS, Spain (2008)
4. Ciarlini, A.E.M., Pozzer, C.T., Furtado, A.L., Feijó, B.: A Logic-based Tool for Interactive Generation and Dramatization of Stories. In: Proceedings of ACE 2005, Spain (2005)
5. Culler, J.: On Deconstruction. Cornell University Press, Ithaca (1983)
6. Ciarlini, A.E.M., Barbosa, S.D.J., Casanova, M.A., Furtado, A.L.: Event Relations in Plan-Based Plot Composition. ACM Computers in Entertainment 7, 4 (2009)
7. Glassner, A.: Interactive Storytelling: Techniques for 21st Century Fiction (2004)
8. Karlsson, B., Ciarlini, A., Feijó, B., Furtado, A.L.: Applying the Plan-Recognition/Plan-Generation Paradigm to Interactive Storytelling. In: ICAPS 2006 Workshop on AI Planning for Computer Games and Synthetic Characters, Lake District, UK (2006)
9. Karlsson, B., Barbosa, S.D.J., Furtado, A.L., Casanova, M.A.: A Plot-Manipulation Algebra to Support Digital Storytelling. In: Natkin, S., Dupire, J. (eds.) ICEC 2009. LNCS, vol. 5709, pp. 132–144. Springer, Heidelberg (2009)
10. Karlsson, B.: A Model and an Interactive System for Plot Composition and Adaptation, based on Plan Recognition and Plan Generation. PhD Thesis, PUC-Rio, Brazil (2010)
11. Lang, R.R.: A Declarative Model for Simple Narratives. In: AAAI Fall Symposium (1999)
12. Magerko, B.: A Comparative Analysis of Story Representations for Interactive Narrative Systems. In: Proceedings of AIIDE 2007, USA (2007)
13. Mateas, M., Stern, A.: Façade: An Experiment in Building a Fully-Realized Interactive Drama. In: Game Developers Conference, pp. 4–8 (2003)
14. Nakasone, A., Ishizuka, M.: ISRST: An interest based storytelling model using rhetorical relations. In: Hui, K.-C., Pan, Z., Chung, R.C.-K., Wang, C.C.L., Jin, X., Göbel, S., Li, E.C.-L. (eds.) Edutainment 2007. LNCS, vol. 4469, pp. 324–335. Springer, Heidelberg (2007)
15. Pinhanez, C.: Interval Scripts: A Design Paradigm for Story-Based Interactive Systems. In: Proceedings of CHI 1997, Atlanta, USA (1997)
16. Propp, V.: Morphology of the Folktale. S. Laurence (trans.). Univ. of Texas Press (1968)
17. Schank, R.C., Colby, K.: Computer Models of Thought and Language. Freeman (1973)
18. Thompson, S.: Motif-Index of Folk-Literature. Indiana University Press, USA (1989)
19. Wallis, J.: Making Games that Make Stories. In: Second Person. MIT Press (2007)

Workflow Patterns as a Means to Model Task Succession in Games: A Preliminary Case Study

Simone Kriglstein[1], Ross Brown[2], and Günter Wallner[3]

[1] Vienna University of Technology, Vienna, Austria
kriglstein@cvast.tuwien.ac.at
[2] Queensland University of Technology, Brisbane, Australia
r.brown@qut.edu.au
[3] University of Applied Arts Vienna, Vienna, Austria
guenter.wallner@uni-ak.ac.at

Abstract. Over the last decade, people involved in game development have noted the need for more formal models and tools to support the design phase of games. In this paper we present an initial investigation into whether workflow patterns – which have already proven to be effective for modeling business processes – are a suitable way to model task succession in games. Our preliminary results suggest that workflow patterns show promise in this regard, but some limitations, especially with regard to time constraints, currently restrict their potential.

Keywords: Game Design, Design Tools, Workflow Patterns.

1 Introduction

Over the last decade, people involved in game development have repeatedly voiced the need for more formal models and tools for designing games. The traditional, and still used, game design document, a detailed and mostly textual description of all aspects of a game design (cf. [1]) has been criticized for several drawbacks. The design document is time-consuming to create, while at the same time being rarely read by members of the development team (see, e.g., [2]) and needs constant maintenance to keep the information up-to-date with highly iterative game development processes (cf. [2, 3]). Kreimeier [4], in a survey of game design methods, noted that the informal discussion of game design makes it difficult to put *individual insight into a context of established knowledge*. Therefore, formal visual languages have been proposed to more effectively express, abstract and communicate gameplay concepts or relationships between them (e.g., [2, 5–7]).

In a related context, Nelson and Mateas [8] point out that game development lacks tools to visualize and reason about systems of game mechanics on an abstract level. However, game designers agree that prototyping is essential for verifying design ideas (cf. [1, 9]). Yet, prototyping can be a time-consuming and costly process. On that account, researches have therefore proposed prototyping

Y. Pisan et al. (Eds.): ICEC 2014, LNCS 8770, pp. 36–41, 2014.

tools to visually model and simulate different aspects of game design on an abstract level (see, e.g., [3, 10, 11]).

In this paper we present an investigation into whether the widely supported workflow patterns [12] are a suitable way to model the succession of tasks players have to perform in a game. In a similar manner to Van Der Aalst et al. [12], we have sought to use a pattern analysis approach to identifying recurring structures within lists of activities performed by players in computer games. Such a pattern approach provides independence from the underlying game implementation environments, and the underlying theoretical languages used to describe such flows of activities. A workflow patterns approach enables us to specify abstractly the tasks to be performed by players within game environments, as the tasks given to players may share similarities in structure to tasks in business systems. The future benefits of such an approach are thus the ability to define such gameplay activity patterns in a rigorous and formal manner (drawing from the Petri net formalisms of workflow patterns) giving us both the power to deeply analyze their correct execution, and then execute them in Petri net based systems.

2   Related Work

To date a lot of work has been conducted to establish a common design vocabulary, for instance, in the form of design patterns used to *express clearly intentions, analyses, and opinions regarding gameplay* [13].

While design patterns are usually expressed in natural language, some game researchers have argued for more visual models to more clearly and compactly express and communicate ideas about game design (see the recent survey of Almeida and Silva [1] for a discussion on this subject). For example, Koster [5] presented a graphical notation system as a complement to classic game design documents to better communicate the game design. Bura [6], building upon the work of Koster [5], proposed a visual grammar which was influenced by Petri nets resembling data-flow representations of processes (whereas we are concerned with a control-flow perspective). Araújo and Roque [10] also applied Petri nets to model games and emphasized that the formal semantics of Petri nets can be leveraged to formally analyze and simulate game design elements already in an early design stage (e.g., to detect unwanted behavior).

Recently, Dormans [3] developed the *Machinations* tool, a graphical notation framework to express the rules of and simulate game economies in order to balance a game's economy or to prevent dominant strategies. While borrowing concepts from Petri nets, *Machinations* diagrams are aimed to be less complex and more accessible to designers. The work has been later extended by Klint and van Rozen [11] to allow not only for simulation but also for formal analysis of game designs. While the above mentioned works aim at expressing game mechanics, Cook [7] focused on the player experience and proposed *skill chain diagrams* to visually represent how players learn and acquire skills.

Workflow software technology has been applied to games by Brown et al. [14] who used a workflow language to script game tasks.

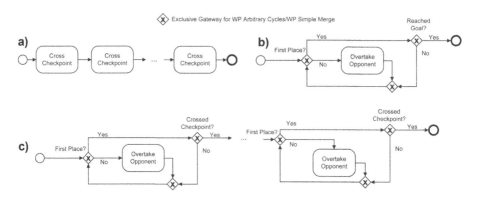

Fig. 1. The general three workflow patterns for the four main race events of NFS illustrated using the BPMN 2.0 visual grammar [15]: a) Pattern for checkpoint race event, b) pattern for sprint and for rival race event, and c) pattern for battle race event

3   Use Cases

For our initial investigation we have chosen two gameplay distinct action games, *Need for Speed: The Run* and *Half Life 2*.

Need For Speed: The Run (NFS): NFS is an action racer where the player takes part in a race across the US. The complete race is broken down into stages with each stage again divided into different race events. These events can roughly be divided into: a) checkpoint races, b) sprint races, c) rival races, and d) battle races. In case of a checkpoint race, a sequence of checkpoints has to be crossed. In workflow terms this can be described with a *Sequence* pattern (Workflow Pattern #1 [17]). This is illustrated in Fig. 1a.

A bit more complex is the workflow pattern for the sprint race event (see Fig. 1b), where the player has to overtake a number of opponents and to cross the goal line in first position. The task to overtake multiple opponents can be described as a cycle that repeats until the player is on the first place (WP #10 - *Arbitrary Cycles* [17]). However, overtaking all opponents and reaching the first place is not enough to win the race, the player also has to maintain the lead until the goal line is reached. This is modeled with a second arbitrary cycle. The *Simple Merge* pattern (WP #5 [17]) is used to merge the outgoing branch of the Overtake Opponent node and the false branch of the second arbitrary cycle.

The rival race event is technically the same as the sprint race event except that the player has to race against specific drivers that are part of the storyline. It can therefore be modeled the same way as the sprint race.

The battle race is a slight modification of the sprint race, where the player has to overtake an opponent and keep the lead until a checkpoint is reached after which the player races against another opponent until the next checkpoint. This repeats several times during a single battle race. The basic structure of the workflow pattern for a battle race event is therefore similar to the workflow

Fig. 2. Examples of the major tasks performed in an FPS – from left to right: Kill Agent, Use Resources (ammunition, healing items) and Open Door

pattern for a speed/rival race event with the difference that it repeats several times in sequential order (see Fig. 1c).

Half Life 2 (HL2): HL2 is a single player first-person shooter (FPS). Like a number of first person shooters, you acquire weapons and health packs in order to defeat non-player characters (NPCs) and traverse levels. Analysis of the levels in the game indicate a number of workflow patterns. First of all, entrance to a level triggers instancing of gameplay tasks (WP #6 - *Multi-Choice* [17] in combination with WP #8 - *Multi-Merge* [17]). We group these into three major task types, viz. Kill Agents, Use Resources, Open Doors (see Fig. 2). Kill Agents is the destruction, by whatever means, of other agents in the game. Open Door tasks are a general description of having to remove a physical impediment to progress spatially, for example, opening a door, destroying an oil drum, or killing a blocking NPC. These sequences are embedded within a set of multiple tasks that may be ignored. For example, you do not have to kill all agents to progress through a level. This killing of agents and collection of resources is often up to the discretion of the player. A subset of the tasks require a certain sequence (WP #1 [17]) for them to be completed.

In the level *Routekanal1* there are certain sequences that must be performed before progression can occur. For example, you clear out an area of NPCs with a mounted machine gun (Kill Agents) and come to an oil drum that has to be destroyed (Open Door) before you can traverse to the next location and enter a tunnel. Note, it is possible to avoid shooting the NPCs if you are skilled enough in traversal, but you must shoot the oil drum. Therefore, this is an example of an enforced sequence within multi-choices. Once the level is traversed, a final door opening task is completed to exit the level; left over tasks are removed from the list allocated to the player. You cannot go back to the level to finish the other remaining tasks, you must recommence the level in order to begin again, or, you must go to a save point in the game to recommence the level at the same state. This is an example of the *Canceling Discriminator* pattern (WP #29 [17]).

Combining these four workflow patterns together, we construct an overall FPS workflow pattern shown in Fig. 3 (left). We argue that this pattern, in slight variations, forms the structure of a number of FPS games. Thus designs for other FPS games can be configured from an executable form of such a pattern.

In addition, there is further detail in the tasks being performed in the cancellation region. In a similar manner, such tasks may be devolved into a split

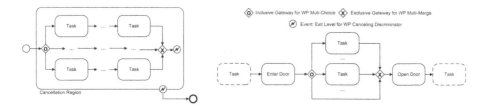

Fig. 3. Left: General FPS workflow pattern for HL2. Right: Exploded BPMN view of tasks in the left image, illustrating how the door opening tasks are key to enforcing particular orderings of tasks in HL2 as an FPS

upon opening a door and entering a region of a level. We define that a level is broken up into regions of gameplay, with door opening choke points, that enforce a sequence, but contain within them multi-choices and merging, as per Fig. 3 (right). Note that this pattern has no cancellation upon entering a new region. So the tasks in the split can be circumvented at the discretion of the player.

4   Discussion

In the presented use cases we focused on the description of the succession of tasks which players have to perform to successfully complete a level, but we did not consider implications of failure. However, modeling the consequences of failing a task can be equally important in game design (e.g., what happens if a checkpoint in a racing game is not reached). Workflow patterns may also be suitable for this task, for example, the WP #4 - *Exclusive Choice* [17] can be used to describe branching depending on if the previous tasks were completed successfully or not.

Workflow patterns can be used to describe tasks on different levels of abstraction (e.g., opening a door could be described simply as `Open Door` or in more detail by modeling what actions are necessary to actually open it, for instance, `Pull Lever` followed by `Turn Knob`). Furthermore, a combination of the different abstraction levels can be used, for example, to provide a high-level overview with more detailed descriptions on demand.

One of the biggest limitations of the original control flow workflow patterns [12] for modeling task succession is perhaps their limited support of time aspects, e.g., time spans or timeouts. However, time aspects play a very important role in games. For example, in the above NFS use case the player has to reach the checkpoints within a predefined time limit. Future work can focus on analyzing how new time-based patterns (e.g., [16]) can be used to describe time critical game tasks.

5   Conclusions

In this paper we investigated the applicability of workflow patterns for modeling task succession in games. For this purpose we have chosen two different games as initial case studies. Our first results suggest that workflow patterns show some promise, but that there are also some limitations that currently constrain their potential in regard to games and which need further investigation, in particular, the ability to model winning and losing conditions and time aspects. Further case studies will be necessary to confirm our preliminary observations.

References

1. Almeida, M.S.O., da Silva, F.S.C.: A systematic review of game design methods and tools. In: Anacleto, J.C., Clua, E.W.G., da Silva, F.S.C., Fels, S., Yang, H.S. (eds.) ICEC 2013. LNCS, vol. 8215, pp. 17–29. Springer, Heidelberg (2013)
2. Librande, S.: One page designs. Presentation at the Game Developers Conference (2010)
3. Dormans, J.: Engineering Emergence: Applied Theory for Game Design. PhD thesis. Amsterdam University of Applied Sciences (2012)
4. Kreimeier, B.: Game design methods: A 2003 survey (2003), http://www.gamasutra.com/view/feature/2892/game_design_methods_a_2003_survey.php (accessed: February 2014)
5. Koster, R.: A grammar of gameplay: Game atoms: can games be diagrammed? Presentation at the Game Developers Conference (2005)
6. Bura, S.: A game grammar (2006), http://www.stephanebura.com/diagrams/ (accessed: February 2014)
7. Cook, D.: The chemistry of game design (2007), http://www.gamasutra.com/view/feature/129948/the_chemistry_of_game_design.php (accessed: February 2014)
8. Nelson, M.J., Mateas, M.: A requirements analysis for videogame design support tools. In: Proc. of the 4th International Conference on Foundations of Digital Games. ACM (2009)
9. Neil, K.: Game design tools: Time to evaluate. In: Proc. of 2012 DiGRA Nordic. University of Tampere (2012)
10. Araújo, M., Roque, L.: Modeling games with petri nets. In: Atkins, B., Kennedy, H., Krzywinska, T. (eds.) Breaking New Ground: Innovation in Games, Play, Practice and Theory: Proc. of the 2009 DiGRA Conference. Brunel University (2009)
11. Klint, P., van Rozen, R.: Micro-machinations: A DSL for game economies. In: Erwig, M., Paige, R.F., Van Wyk, E. (eds.) SLE 2013. LNCS, vol. 8225, pp. 36–55. Springer, Heidelberg (2013)
12. van der Aalst, W.M.P., ter Hofstede, A.H.M., Kiepuszewski, B., Barros, A.P.: Workflow patterns. Distrib. Parallel Databases 14(1) (July 2003)
13. Björk, S.: Game design patterns 2.0, http://gdp2.tii.se (accessed: February 2014)
14. Brown, R., Lim, A., Wong, Y., Heng, S.M., Wallace, D.: Gameplay workflow: A distributed game control approach. In: Proc. of the 2006 International Conference on Game Research and Development. Murdoch University (2006)
15. Object Management Group: Business process model and notation version 2.0 (2011), http://www.omg.org/spec/BPMN/2.0/ (accessed: April 2014)
16. Niculae, C.: Time patterns in workflow management systems. Technical Report BPMcenter.org (2011)
17. Workflow Patterns Initiative: Control-flow patterns (2010), http://www.workflowpatterns.com/patterns/control/ (accessed: April 2014)

Spheres and Lenses: Activity-Based Scenario / Narrative Approach for Design and Evaluation of Entertainment through Engagement

Tim Marsh[1] and Bonnie Nardi[2]

[1] Griffith Film School, Queensland College of Art, Griffith University, Australia
t.marsh@griffith.edu.au
[2] Donald Bren School of Information & Computer Sciences, University of California, Irvine, US
nardi@ics.uci.edu

Abstract. Building on A.N. Leontiev's original activity theory, we propose extensions to bridge conceptual gaps to operationalize an activity-based scenario / narrative approach leading to a universal framework to inform design and reason about the user experience of entertainment through engagement in task-based, as well as improvised, extemporaneous and serendipitous interaction and gameplay.

Keywords: activity theory, design, analysis, engagement, user experience, interaction, gameplay, improvisation, interactive storytelling, scenario, narrative.

1 Introduction

Engagement infers positive characteristics, synonymous with quality of user experience in interaction and gameplay [1, 18, 19]. In this paper we focus on engagement as a means to reason about and assess quality of the user experience of entertainment, whether positive, fun and exciting, through stimulating and thought provoking, to difficult, scary, or darker experiences that are either pleasurable or a necessary part of a wider whole cultural experience [15]. While engagement typically implies flow-like interaction and gameplay with one application or game on a single platform, observation of real-world technology use also reveals additional and alternate patterns of engagement in interaction and play (figure 1). In the real-world people typically engage with a range of digital platforms appropriate to the situation, process or task at hand, shifting between applications on one or more platforms, and even pausing momentarily to reflect, while still appearing to remain engaged. This is especially so with the younger digital native generation who appear to seamlessly navigate and interweave between a variety of platforms, applications and services. While multi-platform/application use has not gone unnoticed, it is invariably described under the broad label of multitasking, for example engagement in browsing and online multitasking [10], and/or typically reflecting concurrent application/platform use and with other tasks (e.g. driving). In addition, observation in

Y. Pisan et al. (Eds.): ICEC 2014, LNCS 8770, pp. 42–51, 2014.

studies with games for entertainment and games for learning in natural environments (e.g. classroom, video games clubs) have long identified behaviours that don't entirely connect with flow-like engagement between players and digital games but identify behaviours that extended beyond the game-world whereby players momentarily reflect and/or interact with other users-players out-of-game in the real-world. Rather than having a detrimental effect, extending engagement beyond the game world improved the overall experience for users-players [11, 16, 20].

Fig. 1. Interaction and gameplay: one application/game on one platform (left), through to more than one application on one (middle) or more platforms (right)

In addition to multitasking and task driven interactions, we emphasize a more free-spirited, unconstrained, non-linear, improvised and extemporaneous nature of interaction and gameplay for entertainment or stimulation. Where users-players craft their own narratives, in-game and between applications and platforms, by playing, selecting, searching, and creating, that is driven by and appropriate to, their own tastes, interests, preferences, desires and individual/group cultures and sub-cultures. In this respect, users-players have been likened to editors, curators, authors and composers [3, 13]. A perspective that is similar in many respects to the "cut-up" technique (attributed to Dadaists) practiced by artist writer Brion Gysin and William S. Burroughs [2] and various musicians (David Bowie, Kurt Cobain) whereby narratives, storylines, lyrics and points of view are created, cut-up into pieces and arranged "any which way" (figure 2). In addition, in contrast to interruption/disruption as potentially negative characteristics in design and evaluation of interactive technology and media, paradoxically interruption from email, SMS or social media, etc. are positive characteristics that provide anticipation and experience that heighten engagement. In many ways the "cut-up" and interruption are similar to techniques used in filmmaking styles alternate to Hollywood (e.g. French New Wave, Russian montage), and Brechtian and improvisational theatre, in which devices are used at unpredictable moments in a production/performance to surprise, shock, startle, create juxtapositions, etc. and encourage reflection in an audience/participants. Our concern in this paper is not only to inform design of interaction and gameplay from such devices per se [12], but also to view users-players as designers, authors, curators, composers and editors creating their own narrative, texts and experience through interaction and gameplay, within, between and across applications/games and platforms.

In order to analyze such engagements in interaction and gameplay with one or more applications/games on one or more platforms, we need an approach, method or framework that can model, support and represent both in-game/application and switching between apps and platform. While evaluation typically incorporates a mixed methods approach with outcomes providing different but complementary results, there's little in the way of an underlying theoretical model or framework to inform, guide and connect design, development and evaluation. Activity theory is one such approach that has long been identified as "a powerful and clarifying descriptive tool" [17] and widely used in analysis of work-related organizations, systems, and human-computer interactions (HCI). However, as suggested by Kaptelinin & Nardi (2006), activity theory needs to evolve in order to move forward towards being a more practical and theoretical approach for design and evaluation for user experience. In order to support more than one activity, application and platform, we revisit A. N. Leontiev's (1981) original work on activity theory to illuminate and extend important concepts, leading to the proposal of a universal framework for the evaluation (and inform design) of the user experience of entertainment through engagement in interaction and gameplay. This paper is structured as follows. In the next section we provide a brief history of activity theory, describe the activity-based scenario/narrative approach, its extension to a universal framework, and describe its application to interaction and gameplay with multi-platform and multi-application use.

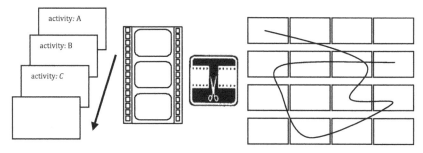

Fig. 2. Schematic showing (left to right) analogy of sequential ordering of activities to film frames, and through interaction, improvisation or "cut-up", users-players can be considered similar to editors, curators, authors, designers creating their own narratives, texts & experiences

2   Activity Theory

Originating from Soviet psychology, two versions of activity theory currently co-exist: A. N. Leontiev's (1959/1981; 1975/1978 - Russian and English translations) original hierarchical framework of activity and Engeström's (1987; 1990) expanded triangle incorporating collective activity (figure 3). While essentially developing from similar roots found in the work of Vygotsky, the two approaches are different and even have "different views" of the same concepts (e.g. "object") - refer to Kaptelinin & Nardi (2006) for informed discussion. While interest has primarily been on Engeström's (1987; 1990) version (e.g. CSCW, HCI) largely because of its expansion to analyze social/collective activities, in this paper we focus on Leontiev's (1981) activity theory approach and in particular, on his first book publication [9]. This is because it incorporates a hierarchical framework and powerful concepts that define activity, and as described in the following sections, provide the means to reason about engagement in interaction and gameplay for the user experience of entertainment.

In activity theory, the smallest unit of analysis is activity. However, identification of activity and associated processes, which is crucial for analysis, has been a major hurdle and stumbling block for analysis that has arguably constrained its wider adoption and use. In his psychology and framework, Leontiev (1959/1981) elegantly captured one of the central ideas in Marxist philosophy on the alienation of worker in capitalist production, while at the same time helping to demonstrate the contented (or self-actualized) worker in the Soviet Union (USSR/CCCP) through consideration of the defining concepts of activity, "motive" and "object" (or "objective"). Motive is the intention driving an activity and objective characterizers the activity as a whole and includes all actions or processes carried out toward the fulfillment of motive. By using the original version of activity theory proposed by Leontiev (1981), the problems of identification are minimized. In addition, the same concepts to identify and understand activity provide a means to reason about engagement in interaction and gameplay. While in his second book, Leontiev (1978) joined "motive" with "object" by stating that object of activity is "its true motive", like Kaptelinin (2005), we also find the coupling of "motive" with "object" problematic and argue for considering them as separate, but related concepts. Given that "motive", one the defining concepts of activity, was joined with object (Leontiev 1978), it seems unsurprising then that dealing with, and identifying where activity starts and ends is "notoriously difficult" for researchers and academics who exclusively refer to Leontiev's (1978) second book. While Engestrom's expanded version of activity theory provides a framework to reason about people's collective activity towards an object, because there is no equivalent to the concept motive, we have no explicitly named concept or means to reason about people's level of interest or engagement in activity. Hence, using Engestrom's expanded version of activity theory may be carrying out analysis on people who may be disinterested or unengaged in the collective activity under observation. So in the words of Marx, they are alienated from their work.

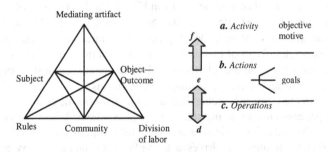

Fig. 3. Two Versions of Activity theory: Engeström's (1987; 1990) expanded triangle (left) and A. N. Leontiev's (1978; 1981) original hierarchical framework of activity (right)

There are two ways to reason about the relationship between objective outcome and motive. The first and widely published way using Leontiev's (1981) original activity theory is the degree to which the outcome from objective "coincides" with motive. When the outcome from objective coincides with motive, it is fulfilled or complete and the activity ends, and as Leontiev (1981) states, this identifies "activity proper". The second alternative way to assess the relationship between objective outcome and motive identified through re-examination and focused analysis of Leontiev's (1981) original activity theory, is the degree to which objective outcome *merges* with motive which we argue also identifies "activity proper". This reading and interpretation of the relationship between objective outcome and motive has to our knowledge received very little if any attention nor has it been previously used in the assessment of activity. Merges implies two important aspects, firstly, the actions or processes undertaken are heading in the right direction and secondly, merges doesn't necessarily suggest an end point (i.e. objective outcome coincides with motive) but suggests that as long as actions are contributing to the merging, then motive is being fulfilled or satisfied. So for example, if a motive to interact or play with technology is to be entertained or stimulated and the outcome from carrying out/performing processes provides just that, then the objective outcome merges with or towards motive. If this condition is maintained then users-players could hypothetically continue to be engaged in interaction or play indefinitely (or at least until some other need arises, from disruption or fatigue, etc.).

2.1   Lenses: Activity-Based Scenario / Narrative Approach

An activity-based scenario/narrative approach and framework was proposed [14], building on Leontiev's (1981) activity theory, to plan, model, describe, develop and evaluate scenarios and narrative of interaction and gameplay. In reference to figure 3, central to this is the hierarchical framework of activity composed of: activity, actions and operations and characterized respectively by objective, goals and conditions. The hierarchical structure is dynamic with shifts between activity, actions and operations orchestrated according to activity theoretical concepts and determined by situations and circumstances (of interaction and gameplay). Its power comes from its lens-like ability to focus on any level of abstraction from high-level descriptions of activities to zoom in to any level of detail/complexity. So providing a flexible and dynamic framework that supports design, development and analysis of interaction and gameplay. However, the focus of this earlier work was on individual activities dealing with one application/game on one platform [14]. In the next section we extend this to deal with one or more activities, applications and platforms.

Activity is directed towards achieving an objective (as denoted by "a"). The objective is a process characterizing the activity as a whole. When the objective is fulfilled the activity ends. The objective is closely related to motive, and the motive is the intention that stimulates and drives a user-player to interact / play a game. In activity theory, the objective's outcome and motive have to be considered in the analysis of "activity proper" [9]. While in previous work [14] this has been used to provide a way to frame and reason about the degree to which work/play has been successful through the objective outcome of activity coinciding with the motive that stimulates a player to activity ("a"). Herein we extend how we assess and design for the user experience of entertainment through engagement in interaction and gameplay by considering "activity proper" through how objective outcome and motive merge or are merging. Activity is made up of a combination of actions ("b"). The action level contains the heart of the narrative/scenario, using text, graphics, storyboards, etc. to describe the game environment (e.g. settings, surroundings, circumstances), the game mechanics, game rules and the gameplay. Actions are performed with conscious thought and effort, and are planned and directed towards achieving a goal. While actions have been considered similar to what the HCI literature refers to as tasks [17], Leontiev (1981) also refers to actions as processes. Herein we refer to actions as processes to provide a wider view of actions beyond tasks or task-based so that the goal of processes can be considered as experience or entertainment. Actions/processes may themselves be made up of sub-processes directed towards sub-goals, and sub-processes can be made up of sub-sub-processes, and so on. This depends on the level of complexity in a narrative, scenario of interaction/gameplay. Actions are performed by a combination of operations. Operations are performed with little conscious thought or effort in the use of physical interactive and virtual in-game artifacts triggered by conditions of actions ("c"). Players' shifts in focus between action and operation levels provide an indication of learning and reflection. For example, the early phases of using an artifact will have been performed with deliberate and conscious attention. At this point they are actions. When they become well practiced and experienced, actions become routine. That is, they do not need to be planned and at such a point are performed with little conscious thought or effort. In this way, actions become operations as represented by the downward pointing vertical arrow ("d"). This provides a way to reason about the mastery of (in-game, interface, virtual, real) artifacts/tools. Conversely, operations become actions when something goes wrong, impedes interaction, or is associated with user-player learning represented by the upward pointing lower vertical arrow ("e"). This provides a way to reason about "focus shifts", "breakdown", learning and opportunities for design [21].

2.2   Sphere of Engagement through Motive in Activity

Considering the relationship between objective and motive provides powerful ways to reason about people engaged in activity. If the outcome from objective coincides or merges with motive (that stimulated users-players to perform actions/process of an objective), then they are engaged in activity (see section 2 and 2.1). Activity should not be considered as a holder or container for action/processes and operations, but is defined by objective and motive that identifies user-player engagement in activity – we refer to this as sphere of engagement as illustrated in figures 4 to 7.

During interaction with a computer-based platform (tablet, notebook, desktop, smart phone), activities are created, ended, fulfilled or postponed. Users-players can become engaged in several applications (on-line, social media, game) in an interactive session/encounter. If the motive for interacting/play with each application is different, then activities representing each application are separate as depicted by the spheres of engagement in figure 5. But if the overall motive that stimulated a user-player to interact-play with a computer-based platform is shared between applications/activities (e.g. entertainment, stimulation) then they may dip-in and out of, switch or shift between applications/activities while at the same time remaining engaged (irrespective of kinds of user experience or types of entertainment). Here the sphere of engagement encapsulates more than one application/activity, as in figure 6.

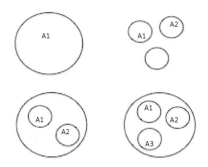

Clockwise from top left - Sphere(s) of engagement: **Fig. 4.** User-player engaged in activity (A1). **Fig. 5.** Engaged in separate activities (A1-A3). **Fig. 6.** Encapsulating one or more application/platforms (A1-A3). **Fig. 7.** In-game activity (A1) and out-of-game activity (A2)

It's easier to appreciate sphere of engagement with many apps each represented by an activity that share a motive and are supported on one platform (tablet, notebook, desktop, smart phone) but what about applications (on-line, social media, games, video calls) supported on more than one platform. Likewise, we argue that if each activity share a motive such as to be entertained or stimulated, etc. then the user-player can remain engaged in interaction /gameplay switching between apps and platforms and likewise a sphere of engagement is created/develops (figure 6). As mentioned in the introduction, as observed in studies in games clubs and schools, user-players switch between in-game play to interacting with fellow user-players/students out-of-game/off-game. Rather than have a detrimental effect, this behavior appeared to heighten experience and engagement. Here the sphere of engagement encapsulates the real-world environment where the game is situated (figure 7). This perspective has implications for analysis of blended learning whereby in-game and off-game learning activities are connected through sphere of engagement. In design, learning activities can be designed so that in-game and off-game motives are connected and are encapsulated within a sphere of engagement. Activities can be the same or different for in-game and off-game. For example, while in-game play could be to learn about some topic in history, a user-player's attention could be diverted to an off-game activity to undertake a mathematical exercise. Here an action or process in the history game is either shared with/leads an activity to undertake a mathematical exercise in the real-world or an action transforms into an activity to undertake a mathematical exercise in the real-world. Similarly, the sphere of engagement illustrated in figure 7 also represents gameplay for entertainment undertaken between in-game and out-of-game activities.

2.3   Creation of Narrative, Scenario, Improvised Story and Experience

As described in section 2.2, the activity-based narrative/scenario approach and associated concepts, provide a flexible framework for analysis and design of user-player interaction and gameplay with one or more application on one or more platforms. It's not difficult to see how the framework can support a variety of multi-application and multi-platform use (as described in section 1) in our analogy of user-player as editor, curator, composer, director, author, etc., creating their own narrative, texts and experience through interaction and gameplay, within, between and across applications/games and platforms. For example, as discussed in section 1, user-players construct their own narratives of user experience and entertainment by shifting from app to app on one or more platforms according to tastes, interests, preferences, individual and group cultures and sub-cultures, as well as serendipitous and improvised on-the-fly interaction, the activity-based narrative/scenario approach provides a hierarchical framework and concepts to model, describe, reason about and trace such interactions and gameplay. In addition, the activity-based narrative/scenario approach can also provide support for future interactions and gameplay. For example, recently, we have become more and more aware of the increased interest from leading computing, software and social media corporations (Google, Facebook) in the once novel technological products and platforms and novel interactions that have not seen daylight outside of research labs and associated conferences for the last few decades. In particular, the focus of interest has been on emerging wearable platforms (e.g. VR headsets, iGlass, etc.) that can provide support for many apps on one platform. While the activity-based narrative/scenario approach provides a hierarchical framework and concepts to model, describe, reason about and trace user-player interactions and gameplay with such platforms (as outlined in section 2.2), it can also inform design for transitions between applications. For example, Apple is already alert to similar design opportunities as demonstrated through iPad's use of audio fades (in-and-out) and visual dissolves in response to undetermined or random user-player "cut-ups"/"mash-ups"/switches between apps and services. Extending this idea, the activity-based narrative/scenario approach could be used to inform the design of devices for orchestrating or persuading user-player "cut-ups"/"mash-ups"/switches between apps and services to heightened experiences and engagements.

3   Discussion and Conclusion

In this paper we have proposed an approach and framework to reason about the user experience of entertainment through engagement in task-based, as well as improvised, extemporaneous and serendipitous interaction and gameplay. Towards this we have explored the original writing of A. N. Leontev (1981) and proposed extensions to bridge conceptual gaps to operationalize an activity-based scenario/narrative approach [14] leading to a universal framework. Its power comes from two main approaches, lens and spheres: firstly, its lens-like ability provides a way to focus on any level of abstraction from high-level descriptions of activities to zoom in to any level of detail/complexity; secondly, considering activity through the relationship between "objective" and "motive", and by the degree to which they coincide and merge provides powerful ways to reason about people engaged in activity through the user experience of entertainment and captured in the term sphere of engagement provides concepts to deal with one or more activities, applications and platforms.

References

1. Boyle, E.A., Connolly, T.M., Hainey, T., Boyle, J.M.: Engagement in digital entertainment games: A systematic review. Computer in Human Behavior 28(3), 771–780 (2012)
2. Burroughs, W.S., Gysin, B.: The Third Mind (1978)
3. Danzico, L.: The Art of Editing: The New Old Skills for a Curated Life. Interactions XVII(1) (January/February 2010)
4. Engeström, Y.: Learning by Expanding: An activity-theoretical approach to developmental research. Orienta-Konsultit, Helsinki (1987)
5. Engeström, Y.: Activity Theory and Individual and Social Transformation. In: Engeström, Y., Miettinen, R., Punamäki, P. (eds.) Perspectives on Activity Theory-Learning in Doing Social, Cognitive and Computational Perspectives, Part 1: Theoretical Issues, pp. 19–38. Cambridge University Press, Cambridge (1999)
6. Kaptelinin, V., Nardi, B.: Acting with Technology: Activity Theory and Interaction Design. MIT Press (2006)
7. Kaptelinin, V., Nardi, B.: Activity Theory in HCI Research: Fundamentals and Reflections. Morgan & Claypool, San Rafael (2012)
8. Leontiev, A.N.: Activity, Consciousness, and Personality. Prentice-Hall (1978)
9. Leontiev, A.N.: Problems of the Development of the Mind. Progress, Moscow (1981)
10. Lehmann, J., Lalmas, M., Dupret, G., Baeza-Yates, R.: Online Multitasking and User Engagement. In: ACM International Conference on Information and Knowledge Management (CIKM 2013), San Francisco, USA (2013)
11. Manninen, T.: Virtual Team Interactions in Networked Multimedia Games - Case: "Counter-Strike" – Multi-player 3D Action Game. In: Proceedings of PRESENCE 2001 Conference. Temple University, Philadelphia (2001)
12. Marsh, T., Nitsche, M., Liu, W., Chung, P., Bolter, J.D., Cheok, A.D.: Film Informing Design for Contemplative Gameplay. In: ACM SIGGRAPH, Sandbox Symposium on Video Games (2008)
13. Marsh, T.: Users as editors and curators: Activity framework for cultural media interaction design. In: 9th International Conference on Entertainment Computing, Cultural Computing: Art, Culture and Technology, Workshop, ICEC 2010, Seoul, South Korea (2010)
14. Marsh, T.: Activity-Based Scenario Design, Development and Assessment in Serious Games. In: Gaming and Cognition: Theories and Practice from the Learning Sciences. IGI Global (2010)
15. Marsh, T., Costello, B.: Experience in serious games: Between positive and serious experience. In: Ma, M., Oliveira, M.F., Hauge, J.B., Duin, H., Thoben, K.-D. (eds.) SGDA 2012. LNCS, vol. 7528, pp. 255–267. Springer, Heidelberg (2012)
16. Marsh, T., Sim, J.J., Chia, D.: Entertainment and Language Learning: Voice Activated Digital Game and Interactive Storytelling Trials in Singapore Schools. In: Pisan, Y., Sgouros, N.M., Marsh, T. (eds.) ICEC 2014. LNCS, vol. 8770, pp. 217–219. Springer, Heidelberg (2014)

17. Nardi, B.: Context and Consciousness: Activity Theory and Human-Computer Interaction. MIT Press, Cambridge (1996)
18. O'Brien, H.L., Toms, E.G.: What is user engagement? A conceptual framework for defining user engagement with technology. Journal of the American Society for Information Science & Technology 59(6), 938–955 (2008)
19. Schoenau-Fog, H., Louchart, S., Lim, T.: &Soto-Sanfiel, M.T.: Narrative Engagement in Games – A Continuation Desire Perspective. In: Foundations of Digital Games (2013)
20. Seay, A.F., Jerome, W.J., Lee, K.S., Kraut, R.E.: Project Massive: A Study of Online Gaming Communities. In: Proceedings of the SIGCHI Conference on Human Factors in Computing Systems, CHI 2004. ACM Press (2004)
21. Winograd, T., Flores, F.: Understanding Computers and Cognition: A New Foundation for Design. Ablex Publishing Corporation, Norwood (1986)

Interactive Storytelling in a Mixed Reality Environment: The Effects of Interactivity on User Experiences

Marija Nakevska, Anika van der Sanden, Mathias Funk, Jun Hu,
and Matthias Rauterberg

Department of Industrial Design Eindhoven University of Technology, P.O. Box 513,
5600 MB Eindhoven, The Netherlands
{m.nakevska,m.funk,j.hu,g.w.m.rauterberg}@tue.nl,
m.j.v.d.sanden@student.tue.nl

Abstract. Interactive storytelling in a mixed reality environment merges digital and physical information and features. It usually uses an augmentation of the real-world and physically-based interaction to create an immersive experience that corresponds to the dramatic storyline of the interactive narrative influenced by the actions of the user. Immersiveness is a crucial aspect of such an installation, and can be influenced by multiple factors such as video, sounds, interaction and, finally, the density of all combined stimuli. We used one of the stages from our interactive ALICE installation to investigate immersiveness and its contributing factors in a between-group design with a special focus on the effects of interactivity, and the feedback and feedforward stimuli of the environment on the users' experiences. The study was carried out with 41 participants and the results showed that immersiveness not necessarily depends on the modality of stimuli, but instead on their time-density.

Keywords: interactive storytelling, mixed reality, immersiveness.

1 Introduction

Interactive storytelling in a mixed reality environment merges digital and physical information and features. It usually uses an augmentation of the real-world and physically-based interaction. The dramatic storyline of the interactive narrative is influenced by the actions of the user. The participants are engaged in an interaction taking place in a real physical environment that does not involve direct use of a computer and interaction devices.

Dow [6] addresses three experiential pleasures of immersive and interactive stories: presence, agency and dramatic involvement. The features of the medium that can be manipulated by the design are: perceptually immersive interfaces, interactivity, and narrative structures. The terms immersion and presence often are used together, immersion describes a set of physical properties of the media technology that may give rise to presence [9]. Presence in a storytelling environment is defined as the feeling of being in a story world, while dramatic involvement is the feeling of being caught up in the plot and with characters of a story [6].

Y. Pisan et al. (Eds.): ICEC 2014, LNCS 8770, pp. 52–59, 2014.

Interactivity refers to the degree to which users of a medium can influence the form or content of the mediated environment. While, agency refers to the empowerment of the user to take meaningful actions in the world which effect relate to her intention [10]. The motivation for a user to act in an interactive narrative may be very different from common interaction with a product or in gaming. In interactive storytelling, source for agency may be the ability to navigate and to influence the environment, to interact with characters or to have an effect on the course of events and outcome of the narrative. Feedback and feedforward are one of the most common used design principles in interaction design. Through feedback the user receives information about the effectiveness of her action, whereas feedforward communicates what kind of action is possible and how it can be carried out.

We use the third stage "Eat me, drink me" from the ALICE project [2], to explore the challenges in designing an interactive narrative. The ALICE installation consists of six consecutive stages, creating an experience based on selected parts from the novel "Alice's Adventures in Wonderland" by L. Carroll [3]. The user takes the role of the character Alice and experiences the sequence of emotional and behavioral states as Alice did in the narrative. In this paper we present the technical and storytelling mechanisms and we study the effects of interactivity on the user experience. A between subjects experiment was conducted to explore potential differences in sense of presence, agency and satisfaction with different levels of interactivity. The independent variable was the interaction environment. We hypothesize that an interactive setting should lead to higher levels of presence, agency and satisfaction.

After reviewing relevant research, we present the experimental setup and results regarding the relation between these variables of interactivity, presence and agency, resulting in several conclusions in the last paragraph.

2   Related Work

Existing physically interactive spaces usually implement full body interaction, augmentation of a physical space or manipulation of real, physical objects. The MIT Media Lab created several physically interactive story environments, that used a "less-choice, more responsiveness" approach to engage physically the users as characters in a story; concluding that "compelling interactive narrative story systems can be perceived as highly responsive, engaging and interactive" [8]. Dow et. al., present results of a qualitative, empirical study by using augmented reality(AR) interactive drama AR Facade [5], which showed that "immersive AR can create an increased sense of presence", and "increased presence does not necessarily lead to more engagement" [4]. The multimodal mixed reality installation, Synthetic Oracle, is used for an empirical research that indicates the importance of the choice of interaction mode and shows that "the activity level and behavior of users modulates their experience, and that in turn, the interaction mode modulates their behavior" [1]. This empirical research suggests that the interactivity and interaction type can have an impact on the behavior and the personal experience of the user. It is important to further evaluate and quantify the experiences from empirical perspective. In the next section we describe the setup of the "Eat me, drink me" stage and the results from the experiment that involved 41 participants.

3   Experiment

3.1   Eat Me, Drink Me

The "Eat me, drink me" stage is designed to induce similar experience to the one described in the original narrative. Following is the summary from the narrative [3]: *"Alice enters a room with doors all around that differ in size. She finds a key that unlocks one small door, but she is too big to fit through it. After she drinks and eats, she undergoes several changes, she grows and shrinks. Eventually she has the right size and the key from the small door."*

The participant finds herself trapped in a cube room, to continue further out of this room, the user needs to find the right relation between her size and the room and to have the key to "open" the door. Since the ALICE installation has six stages in total, the participant has to go through each stage in a limited amount of time. We aimed the interaction design to support each participant to move on to next stage in three to five minutes.

Spatial Design. The 5-sided Cave Automatic Virtual Environment (CAVE) is 3x3x3 meter cube made of white semi-translucent canvas, see Figure 1. The floor has pressure sensors to measure the position of the participant in the room. On each wall of the room, a virtual (VR) door (Fig. 2b) is projected, on the sliding side is projected a white VR door smaller than the others and features a doorknob (Fig. 2c) as a character from the story.

Physical Props. On one side of the room on a table the participant finds a cookie box labeled "Eat Me" and in the other corner is a bottle labeled "Drink Me"(Fig. 2a). These objects contain sensors to register interaction accordingly. The box is equipped with an IR sensor that detects movement when the participant takes a cookie. The bottle contains a wireless connected tilt sensor which detects if the participant is drinking from the bottle. Behind one of the tables, a physical key with a label "Take me" is hidden.

Interaction Design. When the participant performs an action, takes a cookie (eats) or drinks, the projected room becomes smaller; and on the second eat/drink action the room becomes bigger. Both actions feature an appropriate sound, which emphasizes the impression that the participant is getting smaller or bigger. During the experiment we observe if the participant takes the physical key, and with Wizard of Oz method we indicate in the system, which is coupled with a virtual key that appears at the doorknob featuring VR sparkles and a piano "fantasy" sound. Each step on a pressure sensor results in a cracking sound played on loudspeakers. The cracking sounds are different depending on the previously taken actions. If the participant is "big", the cracking sound of the floor is heavier, and vise versa, the cracking sounds are shorter and lighter. An ambient sound is played in the background that consists of fantasy music and dropping water. The "water drop" sound features a different echo depending of the relative size of the VR room.

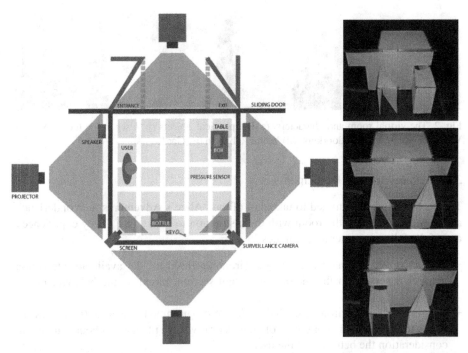

Fig. 1. Overview of "Eat me, drink me" stage. (a) left, the schematic overview of the physical setting (b) right, the scale model of the CAVE, from top to bottom: (1) the entrance is opened, (2) the entrance and exit are closed, (3) the exit is opened

The interactive doorknob gives hints for participant's actions. When the participant comes closer to the VR door (Fig. 2c) and is too big to fit through, the doorknob says: *"Sorry! You're way too big."* When the participant approaches the door and has no key with her, the doorknob says: *"No use. Haha! I forgot to tell you. I'm locked."* If the participant approaches the door and has the key in her hand, the virtual door will open. If the VR door opens the participant sees the White Rabbit in a beautiful garden waving and saying: *"Oh, dear! Oh, dear! You will be late"* (Fig. 2d).

A narrator voice gives guidance based on the participant's behavior. As the participant moves around in the environment, the number of triggered pressure sensors is counted. When the number of steps passes eight the narrator voice says: *"Are you just moving around in here, will you ever find the way out?"* If standing on the same position is detected the narrator voice says; *"Oh dear! You are just standing here!"* To facilitate the progress through the story, we introduced explicit feed-forward hints from the interactive doorknob, like *"Alright, try the bottle"*, *"Now try the box on the table"*. After three minutes, the doorknob gives the appropriate guidance, depending on the last taken action from the participant and waits for the participant to finish it.

Fig. 2. The virtual room and characters. (a)The physical objects (b) User inside the CAVE (c) VR door with interactive doorknob (d) White Rabbit in the Garden

3.2   Procedure and Participants

The participants were invited to take part of the "Alice's Adventures in Wonderland" and they were led into the room with the instruction to "have fun". They experienced one of the following interaction modes:

— Interactive environment (IE): The environment used all the available interaction features described in the interaction design section, based on the behavior of the user.
— Non-interactive environment (NIE): A pre-programmed scenario (that uses 10 from the described features) of the narrative is played without taking in consideration the behavior of the user.
— Non-interactive with minimum stimuli (NIMS): A pre-programmed scenario (that uses 4 features) of the narrative is played without taking in consideration the behavior of the user.

Forty-one participants joined the study, all university students from 18 to 33 years old (13 female, 28 male, mean age 23 with a standard deviation of 3). Twelve participants joined the IE setting; sixteen joined the NIE and thirteen the NIMS setting. All experimental sessions took less than 20 minutes including the experience about 4 minutes and a survey about 15 minutes.

3.3   Measurements

Presence. Participants were administered with the ITC-Sense of Presence Inventory (ITC-SOPI) to evaluate their levels of physical presence [7]. The ITCSOPI is a validated 44-item self-report questionnaire that was used in this study to measure how physically present and involved the users feel in the storytelling environment through four factors: spatial presence, engagement, ecological validity and negative effects.

Agency. We measured the subjectively perceived agency based on the perceived proficiency, the perceived responsiveness and technical aspects of the environment and how much the participants are aware of their influence on the events in the environment. The following items were created: *"I felt proficient in my actions with the environment during the experience"*, *"I was aware of my influence on control mechanisms in the environment"*, *"I felt that the environment was responsive to my* *behaviors"*. Since, agency is achieved when the actions of the user are causing the intended effect on the mediated world; we added items to check if the user's intention and the hints from the environment match. *"I knew what actions I should take to do to go out"*, *"I knew what I should do because the environment gave me a hint"*, and *"The physical objects were obvious hint for interaction"*.

Satisfaction. We also measured how much the participants appreciated the experience. They were asked to rate the experience on several scales: *"The experience was: terrible, okay, good, great, best thing of entertainment experiences, best thing in my life"*, *"I have really enjoyed myself during this experience"*. And to choose on a 5-points Likert scale between: *"Very dissatisfied"* - *"Very satisfied"* and *"Terrible"* - *"Delighted"*.

We also observed the users' behavior via video records from the surveillance system. The actions of the users recognized by the sensing mechanisms (pressure sensors, IR and tilt sensors) were recorded in a text file.

4   Results

Figure 3 illustrates the means of the factors generated by the ITC-SOPI questionnaire, the agency and satisfaction questionnaires. Differences between the means for the three conditions for presence, engagement, naturalness, negative effect and satisfaction were examined for significance using a one-way ANOVA for independent groups design. The results showed no significant differences between the three conditions for presence, engagement, naturalness, negative effect and satisfaction.

A one-way between subjects ANOVA was conducted to compare the effect on agency for IE, NIE and NIMS conditions. There was a significant effect on agency for the three conditions [$F(2, 38) = 8.209$, $p = 0.001$]. Post hoc comparisons using the Tukey HSD test indicated that the mean score for the IE condition ($M = 3.56$, $SD = 0.54$) was significantly different than the NIE condition ($M = 3.02$, $SD = 0.54$) and the NIMS condition ($M = 2.71$, $SD = 0.49$). The NIE condition did not significantly differ from NIMS condition.

Taking the data from the sensing mechanisms, we counted the number of actions (eat, drink, trigger feedback) that were triggered by the users. We compared the number of actions by the participants in each setting for the IE, NIE and NIMS conditions with one-way ANOVA. There was a significant difference for the three conditions [$F(2, 25) = 6.237$, $p = 0.006$]. Post hoc comparisons using the Tukey HSD test showed that the mean score for the IE condition ($M = 5.08$, $SD = 2.46$) was significantly different than the NIE condition ($M = 9.06$, $SD = 4.14$). The NIE condition is significantly different from the NIMS condition ($M = 4.66$, $SD = 3.44$). However, the number of actions from the participant in the IE condition does not differ significantly from the NIMS condition.

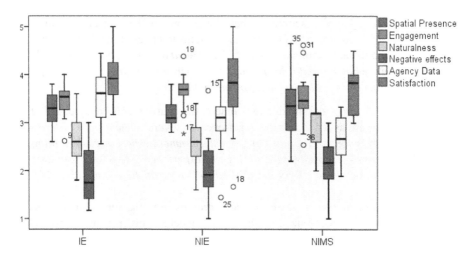

Fig. 3. Dimensions of the presence (spatial presence, engagement, naturalness, negative effects), agency and satisfaction by treatment conditions: IE, NIE and NIMS

5   Discussion

The results showed that the interaction types did not influence the feelings of presence and the satisfaction from the experience. We originally expected that the presence factors of the interactive environment will be significantly higher than that of NIE and NIMS environment. We assume that the CAVE as a strongly immersive environment, contributes for high feelings of presence even when the environment is not responsive to the actions of the user.

Through observation of the actions of the users and by quantifying the number of actions we noticed differences in the users' behavior. The participants that were immersed in a not responsive environment (NIE) were more active and tried out more interaction possibilities (touch, walk, look around). The participants who experienced minimum stimuli in a non-interactive environment (NIMS) did not performed as many actions; instead they would rather stand and look around. The participants in the non-interactive environment (NIE) more often showed confusion and frustration, while the participants in the interactive environment (IE) seemed satisfied every time they discovered an interaction asset. The stimuli provided from the environment evoke different behavior and with that also a different personal user experiences.

In the interactive setting (IE) everyone had slightly different experience depending on the triggered stimuli and the actual context. Not everyone would reveal all of the events from the narrative, e.g. the virtual garden was visible only if the participant approached the small VR door and had the key. The order in which they would discover the events or the pace in which the story would be played different for different participants. The events from the story were context related and they would trigger only if the person was at the right place on a right time.

6   Concluding Remarks

This paper has described the fully realized interactive story "Eat me, drink me" inspired by one of the chapters from the narrative "Alice's adventures in Wonderland". We present the interactive story, the technology and design decisions that went into building the system. Furthermore, we investigate the user interaction and the overall experience. The study contributes to our knowledge about the design of interactive and mixed reality spaces, and how the responsiveness and the amount of stimuli induce or bias behavior and experiences. We have to point out that results obtained with the different settings over short durations of time have to be taken with precaution since its effects may vary over longer time periods. One limitation of this study is the usage of subjective post hoc measures of experience such as ITC-SOPI, where presence and engagement are measured based on the overall perception of the immersive environment. Further studies would explore the user experience in an enriched interactive setting that implements more challenging scenario of the interactive narrative.

References

1. i Badia, S.B., Valjamae, A., Manzi, F., Bernardet, U., Mura, A., Manzolli, J., Verschure, P.F.J.: The effects of explicit and implicit interaction on user experiences in a mixed reality installation: The synthetic oracle. Presence: Teleoperators and Virtual Environments 18(4), 277–285 (2009)
2. Bartneck, C., Hu, J., Salem, B., Cristescu, R., Rauterberg, M.: Applying virtual and augmented reality in cultural computing. IJVR 7(2), 11–18 (2008)
3. Carroll, L.: Alice's adventures in wonderland. Broadview Press (2011)
4. Dow, S., Mehta, M., Harmon, E., MacIntyre, B., Mateas, M.: Presence and engagement in an interactive drama. In: Proceedings of the SIGCHI Conference on Human Factors in Computing Systems, pp. 1475–1484. ACM (2007)
5. Dow, S., Mehta, M., Lausier, A., MacIntyre, B., Mateas, M.: Initial lessons from ar facade, an interactive augmented reality drama. In: Proceedings of the 2006 ACM SIGCHI International Conference on Advances in Computer Entertainment Technology, p. 28. ACM (2006)
6. Dow, S.P.: Understanding user engagement in immersive and interactive stories. ProQuest (2008)
7. Lessiter, J., Freeman, J., Keogh, E., Davidoff, J.: A cross-media presence questionnaire: The itc-sense of presence inventory. Presence: Teleoperators and Virtual Environments 10(3), 282–297 (2001)
8. Pinhanez, C.S., Davis, J.W., Intille, S., Johnson, M.P., Wilson, A.D., Bobick, A.F., Blumberg, B.: Physically interactive story environments. IBM Systems Journal 39(3.4), 438–455 (2000)
9. Riva, G., Davide, F., IJsselsteijn, W.: 1 being there: The experience of presence in mediated environments. In: Being There: Concepts, Effects and Measurements of User Presence in Synthetic Environments, pp. 3–16 (2003)
10. Wardrip-Fruin, N., Mateas, M., Dow, S., Sali, S.: Agency reconsidered. Breaking New Ground: Innovation in Games, Play, Practice and Theory. In: Proceedings of DiGRA 2009 (2009)

A Tool for Evaluating, Adapting and Extending Game Progression Planning for Diverse Game Genres

Katharine Neil[1,2], Denise de Vries[2], and Stéphane Natkin[1]

[1] CEDRIC-CNAM, Paris, France
katharine.neil@gmail.com, stephane.natkin@cnam.fr
[2] Flinders University, Adelaide, Australia
denise.devries@flinders.edu.au

Abstract. Game progression design is a demanding, data-intensive design activity that is typically performed by game designers without even basic computational support. To address this, a concept for tool-supported "progression planning" has been proposed and implemented by Butler, Smith, Liu & Popovic for the design of their educational puzzle game *Refraction*. *Refraction* is a game that has relatively undemanding progression design needs. Further tool development and practice-based evaluation is needed to establish whether – and if so, how – a generic, tool-supported progression design process can address the diverse range of often complex progression design challenges that game designers find themselves engaging with. In this paper we describe how we used three game design case studies in contrasting game genres to inform the development of a tool that adapts and extends the progression planning approach.

Keywords: game design, progression planning, design tools.

1   Introduction

Designing game progression, commonly understood as a structure consisting of serially introduced unique challenges [1], can be a demanding task for a game designer. To design a game's progression is to design the way that game is experienced by the player over time; the way gameplay elements are introduced is largely responsible for its aesthetics of pacing, challenge and variety.

Currently computational support is not used for this task, despite the increasing importance and sophistication of progression within game design. In response to the need for tools to aid progression design thinking, Butler, Smith, Liu & Popovic have proposed a general architecture for "progression planning" tools which they have implemented within their level authoring tool for their educational game *Refraction* [2]. As a demonstration of this concept, the Refraction tool ably hints at its potential. However, its strength as a tool to help solve challenging progression design problems remains largely untested; as Butler et al acknowledge, Refraction game's genre and scope as a puzzle game with modest progression design needs limits its applicability to other games.

Y. Pisan et al. (Eds.): ICEC 2014, LNCS 8770, pp. 60–65, 2014.

We have sought to implement, evaluate and build upon this progression planning approach, by orienting it towards more demanding and more varied progression design problems. To this purpose we used three game design case studies in contrasting genres, all at the early progression design phase of their development: a top-down shooter with puzzle elements, a casual strategy game and an adventure game. In this paper we describe how we adapted and extended Butler et al's progression planning concept to support progression design for these games.

2   Research Objectives

We have two main research goals for this work. The first is to evaluate and explore how *Refraction*'s progression tool approach can be applied to the progression design challenges of games other than *Refraction* – particularly its universality in terms of servicing the needs of games of contrasting genres. The second, which foreshadows the first, is to discover and reveal the ways in which Butler et al's approach requires adapting or extending in order to apply it. This paper focuses on the results of our second objective.

2.1   Our Approach

There exists a wide gulf between the primitive document-editing and non-standardised diagramming practices that many game designers currently use and the advanced automated design and reasoning based research being applied to the problem of game design tools in the research community. While mixed initiative game design research is exploring the potential of computers to participate in design thinking and serve not merely as "tool" but as collaborator or   expert [3][4], practitioners still do their design thinking typically without any computational support.

With a "first, do no harm" philosophy in mind, it is the "low-tech" elements of Refraction's progression planning tools - its simple constraints editing and visualisations – that interest us the most. We see them as a possible first step forward from the nascent formal approaches being explored within current practice, in that they support what many designers are more or less already doing. In building upon this aspect of the Refraction tool we also serve our aim of working at a sufficiently generic level so as to adapt the approach to other games. Accordingly, when implementing Refraction's approach we have in certain cases chosen to simply visualize the data and allow the designer to conduct their own analysis and policing of design moves (as done with pen and paper) rather than add computational support, choosing and thereby necessarily restricting the form that support should take.

3   Method

It was not practical to use the *Refraction* progression planning tool itself as a starting point for our work, as it is integrated with the game's level editor and generation system. We began, therefore, by building our own progression planning tool based on *Refraction*'s approach. We then adapted and extended our tool with a view to simultaneously servicing the specific needs of three game design case studies. These case studies were all at the early progression design point of their design cycle. The games have been under development by the primary author of this paper for between six months and three years. The designs represent three game genres: a casual strategy game, an adventure game and a top-down shooter. Usefully, these genres vary quite markedly in the nature of their progression. Servicing these contrasting design needs helps enforce a degree of universality in our tool design. Our games cannot be representative of all game genres, however, and like *Refraction*'s system, the design of our tool was inevitably driven by the needs of specific games rather than the needs of all possible games. Intuitively, the progression planning requirements of all three of our games go beyond the concept-based progression units used for the *Refraction* game. Most notably, unlike *Refraction* the games are all, to some degree, non-linear in their progression structure. This feature invokes the challenge of how to plan progression that does not take the form of linear sequence.

4   System Model

Here we describe our tool and how it builds upon, modifies and extends the model used by Refraction's progression planning tool.

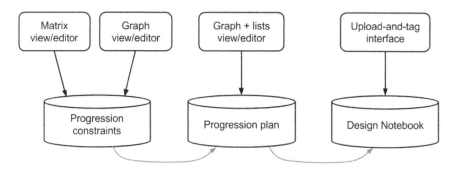

Fig. 1. System model

Our system, inspired by *Refraction*'s, comprises constraints, plan and idea repository components (see Fig. 1). While our system performs a similar role, our differing workflow approach is manifest in some important functional differences. *Refraction*'s system uses its simple constraints calculations to drive generative features and analyze design moves, generating the progression plan and, optionally, the levels themselves. Our system removes the generative features and much of the automated analysis performed by their system, and instead focuses on presenting and organizing the results of our calculations to the designer. Most notably, our system, created to serve all three of our case studies, does not include a procedural level generation system or an integrated level editor. We have replaced this component with a designer's notebook style feature for storing and tagging ideas, design patterns and work-in-process levels, which can then be filtered according to data created in the progression plan component. We have also extended the constraints and progression plan components, adding additional calculations and visualization features, including a graph traversal algorithm to the progression plan component in order to apply constraints to non-linear level progressions.

4.1   Progression Constraints Component

As in *Refraction*'s tool, our progression constraints component allows the game designer to create game elements and constraints by defining some elements as explicit prerequisites and co-requisites of other elements. An element can be as concrete and quantifiable as an ammo pickup, for example; or a quality the level might contain like "intense combat". As well as providing a matrix-style editor, the tool automatically infers transitive prerequisites (as does *Refraction*'s tool). This is a non-trivial calculation for a designer to perform manually.

Graph and Matrix Interfaces
To this component we have added an editable graph-based view as an alternative to the matrix view. We chose to include a graph-based view upon discovering that the progression plan for our adventure game could be in fact better described and supported by taking the form of progression constraints, leaving the progression structure itself for managing the higher level episodic narrative. As in matrix view, graph edges are automatically added when constraints are transitively inferred by the tool. This kind of computational support is useful for managing the binary but complex progression logic of an adventure game.

4.2   Progression Plan Component

Graph Interface
The most signification modification we have made to *Refraction*'s approach is expanding the progression plan out from their linear table form into a graph-based editor and analyzer. A graph allows for games that have a non-linear progression structures to be modeled. The designer uses the graph interface to create levels or mission stages as nodes and define connections between them as edges. He or she can select a node in the graph to edit the properties of the associated level.

Game Elements List
Alongside the graph interface we display a list of all game elements. Any element in the list may be selected and added to the level's game elements list. The elements in the list are displayed differently, according to their eligibility for use in the currently selected level: eligible, ineligible and potentially eligible. Eligibility is based on the

constraints defined using the Progression Constraints component: it is calculated using a graph traversal algorithm (our progression plan analyzer) to determine whether a given element satisfies the constraints governing the level. The inclusion of the "potentially eligible" type is due to the non-linear progression structure. It services the case where one or more, but not all, paths leading to the level satisfy the constraints associated with the listed element. Being "potentially eligible" may render the element appropriate or inappropriate for inclusion in the selected level, depending on the nature of the game or the element itself. The designer is left free to make an informed decision as to whether they wish to include the element based on this contextual information.

Level Game Elements
The level's game elements list is where the designer defines the contents of the level, using game elements from the game elements list.   The designer may simply indicate the presence of a concept used (e.g. "ranged combat") or they may specify the number of instances of the element in the level (e.g. 5 ammo pickups).

Progression Histories
A designer may wish to know which game elements the player has experienced or has potentially experienced by the time they reach the selected level, based on the content of the levels that may or must be completed prior to it. This can be viewed for all possible paths to the level, or for a single path selected in a "Paths to selected level" list. For example, the designer might see that the player has encountered a minimum 4 ammo pickups but potentially a maximum of 16. Selecting a path also highlights all the levels along that path in the graph view.

Graph Element Visualization
Refraction's tool includes a constraint editor and visualizer that plot the density and frequency of elements in the progression plan, in order to regulate progression considerations such as game pacing. In line with our approach, our tool computes this for the purpose of visualization only: we highlight all nodes of the progression graph that contain a selected game element, thus affording the designer a broad overview of where instances of a given element are used in their game.

4.3   Filtered Design Notebook Component

Our third component of the system, as noted above, is an alternative to Refraction's integrated level editor. Design process is commonly understood to be notoriously non-linear.[1] Here we provide a home for level design fragments or design patterns that do not yet have a home within the progression plan itself. Ideas can be tagged with one or more of the game elements it includes, and the notebook can be filtered

---

[1] According to Donald Schon, "unpredictability is a central attribute of design - it is not necessarily the defining one, but it is important. It means that there is no direct path between the designer's intention and the outcome"[5].

by the level's game elements list to display all ideas that contain only the game elements relevant to that level.

5   Conclusion

We have found that is possible to apply, adapt and extend Butler's progression planning approach to other game genres, by using three contrasting case studies with concrete progression planning challenges to discipline and inform this process. It being unlikely that we have anticipated all the needs of our three design case studies, further additions and modifications will probably need to be made during this process. Our next step is practice-based evaluation: we will integrate the tool into the progression design process of our three case studies, and diarize the experiences of the designer for analysis. This analysis will then be used towards developing a generic tool-supported progression design process that can be refined and tested with a wider group of designers and design cases.

References

1. Juul, J.: The open and the closed: Games of emergence and games of progression. In: Mäyrä, F. (ed.) Computer Games and Digital Cultures Conference Proceedings, pp. 323–329. Tampere University Press (2002)
2. Butler, E., Smith, A., Liu, Y., Popovic, Z.: A mixed-initiative tool for designing level progressions in games. In: ACM Symposium on User Interface Software and Technology (2013)
3. Khaled, R., Nelson, M.J., Barr, P.: Design metaphors for procedural content generation in games. In: Proc. SIGCHI Conf. Hum. Factors Comput. Syst., CHI 2013, p. 1509 (2013)
4. Smith, G., Whitehead, J., Mateas, M.: Computers as design collaborators: Interacting with mixed-initiative tools. In: Proc. Work. Semi-Automated ...(2011)
5. Winograd, T.: Bringing design to software. ACM Press (1996)

The Active Use of Online Presence, Movies and Gameplay to Improve Classroom Engagement

Sean Costain and Dale Patterson

Queensland College of Art, Griffith University, Gold Coast, Australia
{s.costain,d.patterson}@griffith.edu.au

Abstract. The online world is filled with rich interactive games, spaces, motion pictures and personas. Despite a rapid growth in online education, the tertiary classroom looks quite different to the entertaining online world it exists within. The design of mobile online resources, both official and unofficial, plays a key role in student engagement and learning. From the teachers perspective designing an online presence and in particular engaging online learning resources, is critical to the success of the learning environment. This project looked at the use of popular forms of online materials, including gameplay, movies and social media, and whether the application of entertainment centered tools enhanced the learning environment. The results of the 9 year, 984 participant study indicate that the increased and active use of the entertainment based tools had a significant positive effect in terms of student engagement and a significant positive effect on learning outcomes for international students.

Keywords: online learning, student engagement, gameplay, social media.

1 Introduction

The online environment, available today to students, offers resources on an enormous scale. Unfortunately the reliability of these resources is less clearly indicated. Prior to the widespread use of the web, the learning and teaching environments used in tertiary education were significantly simpler, both in terms of technology, scale of information and reliability of information. With the addition of mobile online learning resources, online course delivery and social media communications, the tertiary education space is a very different place to that which existed just 25 years ago [1,2]. Today students have immediate access to the pool of rich online resources in a range of interactive forms. Knowledge of facts has become less relevant to these students as they have 24 hour a day, seven day a week, access to information at their fingertips.

The ability to discern valuable information, as compared to the less reliable information, from the mix that exists on the web, becomes a critically important skill for the student [3,4]. Aside from pure informational resources, the web also offers a range of richer and more engaging options. These include social media, chat as well as online video and audio tutorials and advice on "how to" complete numerous tasks.

These more interactive and visually richer forms of accessing information appeal to students on many levels, including personal engagement as well as simply being a more entertaining way to obtain the required information [5,6].

Y. Pisan et al. (Eds.): ICEC 2014, LNCS 8770, pp. 66–73, 2014.

For teaching staff, and those designing learning resources and programs, it is critical to design learning resources that are relevant and effective for the student in this online learning space [1], [7], [8], [9]. To achieve this it would seem logical that the teaching staff would look to using the common forms of online resources that students are seeking out, including short entertaining videos, social media interaction and others, as a means to deliver their resources and knowledge.

This research project implemented a study over a nine year period to identify whether the increased use, by teaching staff, of popular forms of entertainment, in the form of movies, interactive gameplay and social media had an impact on the effectiveness of the learning environments they created.

2 Online Learning Resources

Learning resources come in a range of possible forms and formats. For the purpose of this study the focus was in the online delivery of resources based on popular forms of entertainment. This approach included the use, and comparison of the effectiveness of, several types of formats for this content. Key formats included, long and short video and audio clips, interactive gameplay (in both game and social media platforms) as well as the active and passive use of social media.

The short movie format, was a critical element in the trial as these items became the most viewed and used (with more than three times the amount of interaction from participants than any of the other forms). Each of these movies was designed to be much like a short movie trailer only containing key and quite specific pieces of knowledge. These clips were constrained to being no longer than five minutes in length and were designed to be as informal as possible (including showing minor errors and corrections). Several critical additions to each of these resources included the removal of official branding, the inclusion of the person (teaching staff member) in the clips themselves and the publication in personal (non official) locations on the web. The intent of these elements was to help break down the barriers between staff and student and reinforce the links and build rapport between the student and staff.

The same approach was applied to developing the interactive gameplay scenarios and social media interactions. The focus being on short, very specific and helpful "tips" being delivered in a non official format but by a person with whom the student is comfortable, and has trust in the reliability of their information. Interestingly the feedback from the study regarding the interactive gameplay indicated that the teaching staff members willingness to engage in such "play", outside of the content and teaching scope, was the most highly rated item listed in the question asking "Which activity helped you get to know your teacher better?" with 44 percent of participants questioned listing gameplay as the most effective experience. This demonstrated the power of interaction in building relationships, but also shows the ability of a game, though the focus on a separate, and in these cases a shared task, to remove many fears and barriers to communication. The focus on the game play allows communication channels to open (about and in the game) and from that better understanding and ongoing communication was most effectively generated.

With the web itself having so many unreliable information sources, generating trust is critical to the success of this system. Where the textbooks of the past were a known entity with reliable information, the web contains information that is not edited and in many cases is simply incorrect. This leads to a more information wary student. One who seeks the ready accessibility of the Internet resources, but also questions their true value. In reality, this web based collection of information is what the student often consults first, but due to their uncertainty in the information, they will often cross check with multiple sources. Essentially they perform a simple form of peer review before giving trust to the information obtained.

Developing this level of trust in the teaching staff members "unofficial" content is one of the key challenges. Participant feedback from the study indicated the fact that the staff member was open on a personal level, thus enabling students to make the link between their personal "unofficial" identity and their true real world identity made them more confident in the truth and personal reliability of the teaching staff members virtual persona. With confidence transferred to the reliability of the tips and tricks provided through the short videos of that persona. In simple terms there appears, based on the studies findings, value in truth in virtual personas and also value in more personal detail and engagement.

3   Online Teaching Presence and Persona

The learning environment populated with students today is a rich and highly technology based world. For many teaching staff this in itself is challenging. In many cases students are more comfortable with the technology and communication systems than the staff themselves [7, 8]. The question of how important, in the modern era, an online presence is for an effective teacher is challenging. At its core, teaching involves assisting the student to obtain the knowledge and skills required to understand and successfully deal with challenges. For the modern teacher this means being there to assist with personal face-to-face learning, but also being there to assist with independent learning through online presence, interactive communication and the delivery of engaging learning resources. For the teacher, this makes their online presence a critical element of their professional persona. In the world of online study, a teacher's online presence is often more heavily accessed and utilized than the interpersonal face-to-face engagements. Managing this virtual professional teaching presence, in its many forms and including the use of entertainment techniques to engage and inspire the students, is a skill that has become a valuable skill to all teachers involved in the fast growing online education environment.

The 24/7 nature of online environments makes it almost impossible for any member of teaching staff to be available at all times to students. One of the key techniques pursued in this research was the use of personal entertainment oriented media as a means to capture key elements of knowledge and present them in an engaging and personal online form to students.

One of the key issues with online delivery of materials is the sense of detachment that students feel [9,10]. This research experimented with differing levels of "person" in the online personas of teaching staff. The objective was to understand what level of personal link is beneficial in building effective forms of communication. To understand and measure the importance of different features of the staff members online presence, the study developed three levels of online teaching resources or presence.

The first level, the control group, contained staff who had no online presence and delivered learning materials in a classic face-to-face teaching manner. Students knew them as a teacher in class but had no additional "personal" information.

The second level, passive virtual presence, contained staff who had an online presence, delivered materials online, but did not actively engage in the online community or use specific targeted personal short videos, interactive games or active use of social media. Students knew them as a teacher in class and also had a limited amount of additional "personal" information through their professional media profiles.

The third level, the active virtual presence, contained staff that had an online presence, delivered materials online and actively engaged in the online community including the use of specific targeted personal short videos and interactive games scenarios. They also pursued active use of social media to communicate with students. Students knew them as a teacher in class and also had a significant amount of additional "personal" information and contact through their detailed personal social media profiles.

3.1   Mixing Online Teaching Presence and Learning Resources

Most professional personas link closely to the topic of the professional work being carried out. In these professional scenarios the separation between the individual's persona and the content of the work can often be blurred. For virtual teaching presence this soft boundary between content and person provides an interesting platform for delivering learning materials. Initially the content builds confidence in the online identity, and draws students to it. Over time the identity becomes trusted and the identity itself can actively drive students to resources.

This research project sought to understand the role of the human element or "person" in the virtual teaching presence. Specifically to experiment with different levels of "person" relative to "content" in the virtual personas and to critically review the impact, positive or negative, that these changes caused. The goal being to identify mechanisms through which improvements could be made to a virtual teaching persona's ability to function as an effective teaching tool.

4   Experimentation and Analysis

To gain a better understanding of the type of resources that were most effective, an experimental study was carried out using variations on teaching presence (these differing levels incorporate different types of learning resources used). The key purpose of the observational study was to identify whether the entertainment oriented learning resources (movies, games and social media as included in the active virtual presence) had an impact on the learning outcomes or engagement of students when compared to the control and passive presence groups.

The experimental work involved a randomized control trial comparing the different types of teaching presence. The trial involved four teaching staff and 984 students across a period of nine years. The participants were all students involved in tertiary level classes, and were engaged in the study for six-month periods. Participants ranged in age from 17 to 54 years. They came from a range of cultural backgrounds and were taught in the English language (a second language for many of them).

The trial began with each participant being surveyed and then randomly allocated to one of the three levels of teaching presence (control, passive virtual or active virtual). Each participant then undertook their course/project, using the method as appropriate for their group. Interacting with staff, fellow participants and course materials, submitting appropriate assessment items as required. The topic/course content and assessment were consistent for all participants, thus keeping only the delivery method as the altered factor. During the trial they were also surveyed to gain insight into their feedback on how satisfied and engaged they were with the course and its delivery method. The final data element that was collected looked at how the students engaged with the online resources by recording the methods and times at which they accessed the online resources, providing information on which resources and personas were more or less effective in generating engagement and in driving use of the resources.

At the conclusion of the course an assessment was made of the students learning/creative outcomes in the form of examinations and project based work. These assessments were used to measure the effectiveness of the teaching method in terms of learning outcomes. Participant feedback was also collected as a means to measure participant satisfaction and engagement. From this data comparisons between the methods of teaching, with differing types of virtual personas, were developed.

4.1   Findings from the Study

The results from the study show that the use of an active virtual presence and in particular the level to which entertainment based techniques were applied, had positive results in terms of the participants experience when compared to the control group. Three key areas of interest were measured, those being learning outcomes, satisfaction and engagement. The active virtual presence group (which included the short movies, game play and social interaction) was significantly more successful in terms of engagement and satisfaction, and achieved positive improvements in learning outcomes for specific groups within the study.

In the key area of learning outcomes, the differing virtual presence did not cause a statistically significant difference across the full group. Overall the learning outcomes amongst students in the control group, averaging 64.7%, were similar to those amongst both the active, averaging 71.4%, and passive virtual presence groups, averaging 67.6%. When reviewed as 95% confidence intervals for the range of participants, these value ranges crossed indicating that there was no statistically significant difference between the learning outcomes from differing "presence" styles. This indicates that the use of entertainment focused learning resources did not cause any significant change to the learning outcomes of the students.

Although there was no statistically significant difference across the full group, there was a difference in learning outcomes for one specific sub group, participants with English as a second language. For participants with language/culture issues their results showed improvement going from 39% in control groups, to 43% in passive virtual presence groups, and most significantly up to 61% in active online presence groups. This improved ability to engage and transfer knowledge to these particular groups, through the use of online entertainment based methods was unexpected and offers potential. With international students playing such a large role in educational classes, these results were an important finding from this study.

In terms of engagement, two key measures were used. Firstly the quantitative data obtained from recording how and when participants accessed the resources. Secondly the feedback obtained in surveys. These results indicated that accesses to resources were higher in the active virtual presence group than any other group. In fact the activity itself played a key role in this. The study showed that an activity (engagement with resources), whether by staff or student, triggered a chain of interactive events. On average a single active interaction in the community learning space, led to an average of more than seven responses and interactions with information. Hence active engagement with the community led to an increase in the use of learning resources as well as increased communication amongst participants.

True identity also played a role, with the personas that incorporated the teachers identity (in a non threatening "unofficial" form) actively into the gameplay and movie content, gaining more engagement and more active response to interactions. Survey responses indicate that this related to a level of knowing the person and feeling a sense of trust and confidence with them. This confidence was critical as it allowed students to feel comfortable enough in the teaching staff, and most importantly the virtual presence of those staff members, to experiment and make mistakes. In simple terms the unofficial elements of the virtual presence gained more interaction, than the official. Participant feedback indicated it was unofficial and more of an open discussion forum which would not have an impact on results or perceptions of their work.

In one class, with 84 students, the social media unofficial group had 76 members join (90% of students in class optionally choosing to join group). During the 24 hours prior to the first assessment item, there were 62 active engagements compared to the average rate of just over one engagement per day. In contrast the number of participants who engaged with the official learning resources in that same 24-hour period was 32, almost half the rate. Clearly showing a preference for the unofficial social media group over the official online learning group. This was interesting as the resources represent contact with the same person, yet the format (of short more personal and unofficial movies) made them more accessible and desirable to participants.

This finding was reflected not only in regards to assessment and feedback but also in the key content items. Presentation of short video clips through the unofficial mechanism generated more than twice the amount of views and more than four times the amount of participant interactions than any other type of content item.

The other key area of analysis related to levels of participant satisfaction. In this regard, the control group showed higher levels of community satisfaction than the passive virtual presence group. Although they were learning and interacting, they didn't feel as engaged with the passive virtual presence. The active presence group however was significantly higher, than both the control and passive groups, in terms of satisfaction ratings. This once again indicates that the short videos and interactive games created a higher level of satisfaction amongst the participants.

The participant feedback was for the same course content, assessments, with the same member of teaching staff, with the only difference being a differing set of learning resources (more entertainment based in active group). The results highlight the fact that students in active groups found the online community, mixed with targeted short video, game play and social media interactions more engaging. As a result they were statistically significantly more satisfied than their counterparts in other groups.

5   Discussion and Conclusions

The results from this and other studies show that an effective virtual teaching presence can achieve more than just a presentation of the resources and a representation of the member of teaching staff [4,8,10]. With clever design, particularly through the use of entertainment based content design and delivery, the virtual presence can provide both an identity for the teaching staff member, and also, and perhaps most importantly, provide a mechanism for actively engaging the students in learning activities and delivery of learning resources [11]. To achieve this involves developing mechanisms to build trust, confidence and communication channels. As the participant responses demonstrated, establishing trust was strongly linked to the amount of true individual personal detail that features in the online presence as well as the early engagement of staff and students [5], [12]. Meeting the teacher in person and linking that back to the virtual identity/persona gave an increased level of confidence. The use of virtual presence in this regard also provides a less intimidating environment than the face-to-face classroom. For some groups, including international students, the ability to engage at a distance enables time to formulate responses and deal with the issues caused through language and culture. As a result international students performed much better in the active virtual presence groups.

Overall the results indicate that the communication channels that were most actively used throughout the study were those of an unofficial form in the format of short personal video tips and tricks delivered through social media platforms.

Teaching involves engagement with the student, helping them to see the relevance of the content to their world, and inspiring them to become passionate about the topic.

The somewhat distant and cold world of the Internet presents a challenging problem in terms of how to most effectively engage with students. The raw learning materials and information may be of the highest quality, but without an engaging mechanism to draw the students to them, they will be unsuccessful as teaching and learning tools. This is evidenced in studies such as those by Kim et al. that state, "media integration and instructors quality teaching were significant predictors of both social presence and learning satisfaction" [12].

Results from this study demonstrate that the active use of learning resources formatted along the lines of entertainment pieces, and delivered through trusted virtual presence that is "unofficial" in form, are more effective in terms of engagement and satisfaction. Specific groups were also more effective in terms of learning outcomes.

References

1. Allen, E., Seaman, J.: Going the Distance: Online Education in the United States. Sloan Consortium. PO Box 1238, Newburyport, MA 01950 (2011)
2. hKreber, C., Kanuka, H.: The scholarship of teaching and learning and the online classroom. Canadian Journal of University Continuing Education 32(2) (2013)
3. Harasim, L.: Learning theory and online technologies. Routledge, London (2011)
4. Hattie, J.: Visible learning: A synthesis of over 800 meta-analyses relating to achievement. Routledge, London (2013)
5. Junco, R.: The relationship between frequency of Facebook use, participation in Facebook activities, and student engagement. Computers & Education 58(1), 162–171 (2012)
6. Meyer, K.: The influence of online teaching on Faculty productivity. Innovative Higher Education 37(1), 37–52 (2012)
7. Palloff, R., Pratt, K.: Lessons from the Virtual Classroom: The Realities of Online Teaching. John Wiley & Sons, New Jersey (2013)
8. Baran, E., Correia, A., Thompson, A.: Transforming online teaching practice: Critical analysis of the literature on the roles and competencies of online teachers. Distance Education 32(3), 421–439 (2011)
9. Patterson, D.: Creativity in the Online Classroom: Findings from a Five Year Randomized Control Trial. In: Bastiaens, T., Marks, G. (eds.) World Conference on E-Learning in Corporate, Government, Healthcare, and Higher Education, vol. 2012(1), pp. 760–766. AACE (2012)
10. Shaikh, Z., Khoja, S.: Role of Teacher in Personal Learning Environments. Digital Education Review 21 (2012)
11. Patterson, D.: Using Interactive 3D Game Play to Make Complex Medical Knowledge More Accessible. Procedia Computer Science 29, 354–363 (2014)
12. Kim, J., Kwon, Y., Cho, D.: Investigating factors that influence social presence and learning outcomes in distance higher education. Computers & Education 57(2), 1512–1520 (2011)

Entertainment for Purpose
and Persuasion

A Focused Review and Initial Conceptual Design for Merging Exergame and Activity Monitoring Technologies

Reem Altamimi[1], Geoff Skinner[2], and Keith Nesbitt[2]

[1] The University of Newcastle, NSW, Australia
Reem.Altamimi@uon.edu.au
[2] The University of Newcastle, NSW, Australia
{Geoff.Skinner,Keith.Nesbitt}@newcastle.edu.au

Abstract. In an era of increasing technology use, it has been recognized that children and adolescents have become more sedentary and engage in less physical activity. Motivating children to be more physically active is not an easy task given their preference for seated leisure activities. Video games are a favorite leisure activity amongst children and adolescents. Exergames have been suggested as one form of game that may make children more active. Activity monitoring technologies are another proposed solution. This paper reviews literature in the areas of exergaming and activity tracking technology and proposes an initial design that involves merging the two areas. This work builds on our previous research in this area and makes an original contribution through the suggestion of added benefits that stem from the integration of exergames and activity tracking technologies. Furthermore, we plan to expand our research beyond the scope of this paper to propose a model based on this incorporation. Here we conclude that the careful integration of exergames and physical activity tracking technology provides the greatest potential to increase and maintain physical activity levels in children and adolescents.

Keywords: Physical Activity. Exergames. Activity Monitoring Technologies.

1   Introduction

Physical activity in children is an important issue that has previously been considered in the literature [1, 2]. The implication of physical activity on children and adolescents' health and development is the driving reason behind this interest. Regular participation in physical activity has been found to reduce the risk of many diseases including heart disease and diabetes and also improves physiological and psychological function [1]. Unfortunately, it has been identified that when indoors, children spend large amounts of their time engaged in sedentary or light level physical activities and when outdoors spend less that 15% of their time engaged in vigorous physical activity [3]. Another study confirmed that children approximately 20% of their time engaged in high-intensity physical activity [2]. Yet educating young children about the importance of regular physical activity remains a key in helping to reduce levels of inactivity in adulthood [1, 2].

Y. Pisan et al. (Eds.): ICEC 2014, LNCS 8770, pp. 77–83, 2014.

One factor that contributes to a healthy, active life-style is ensuring children adhere to the daily recommendations for physical activity which is 60 minutes of moderate to vigorous intensity physical activity for children and adolescents [1], [4]. Measuring levels of physical activity in this age group is therefore important [5]. Likewise it is important to study what motivates children and adolescents to exercise. Children between the ages of 8 and 18 spend numerous hours playing video games either on gaming consoles, handheld platforms or cell phones [6] on a daily basis [7]. The wide range of options in gaming platforms and game content is factor that contributes to the increased amount of time young people spend playing video games [6]. Unfortunately, most of the popular games increase screen time and led to more sedentary behavior amongst children and adolescents. However, a new generation of video games that involves physical exertion along with gameplay, called "Exergames", are being developed with the express aim of decreasing sedentary behavior and motivating active living.

It has been suggested that active video games provide an opportunity to improve physical activity levels in children and adolescents [8, 9]. Activity tracking technologies provide further potential for promoting exercise in children and adolescents as they can be used to track and monitor the intensity and level of physical activity [5].   Our research is designed to explore the best available technology-based solutions for physical activity promotion in children and adolescents. In this paper, we examine the use of exergames and activity monitoring technology with regard to their ability to promote and maintain exercise levels in children and adolescents. This paper reviews literature in these areas and proposes an initial design that combines exergaming and activity tracking technology.

2   Exergames and Activity Tracking Technologies

2.1   Exergames

Exergames have the benefit of motivating exercise by providing a safe, entertaining and engaging fitness experience. Exergames are important as they may encourage children to exercise and reduce the burden of obesity in this population [10]. However, it remains to be seen whether active video games really promote physical activity in children and adolescents. Some literature reports that active video games increase physical activity levels [11, 12] while other studies report that active video games have no effect on improving rates of physical activity [13, 14].

When developing applications for exergaming there is a spread of reports in the literature across broad age ranges from young children to adolescents, adults and even senior citizens. Indeed the age of targeted players is an important factor that games developers need to be aware of when developing games [15, 16]. Video games that attract younger players may not attract adolescents or adults due to the differences in their thoughts, perceptions and experience [15].

Exergame interfaces typically incorporate sensing devices that detect and track players' body motion during the game play. Examples of these devices include the Wii Remote Plus & Sensor Bar, the Wii Balance Board, the PlayStation Move Eye &

Motion Controller and the Xbox 360 Kinect sensor. There are several differences between the various exergame interfaces. For example, the Xbox 360 Kinect sensor uses both the player's body and voice as controllers while the Wii Remote involves a physical prop that needs to be held by the player [17]. In a study that developed an exergame prototype called "Wii!!! Soccer" [8], Wiimote technology is used to capture a player's foot motion for playing a game of virtual soccer. Although this game simulates a real life soccer experience, it limits players' movements as they have to strap an infrared sensor bar to their legs while playing the game [8].

2.2   Activity Tracking Technologies

Direct observation, questionnaires and technology-based monitors are examples of techniques that have been used to monitor physical activity in children and adolescents. Examples of technology-based monitors include accelerometers, pedometers, and health life wristbands. These tools can be worn, for example, on an individuals' wrist or arm or clipped to their belt or shoe in order to track and record their physical movements. Different accelerometer-based monitoring tools have been used to measure intensity, frequency, level, pattern and duration of physical activity in children and adolescents [2, 3], [18]. Some of these accelerometers have been validated for use in classifying sedentary behavior and levels of physical activity in children such as light, moderate and vigorous [18].

Pedometers are another example of wearable devices that have been investigated in the literature with regard to their ability to measure levels of physical activity. An early systematic review stated that, based on the literature, children between the ages of 8 and 10 were expected to take 12,000-16,000 steps/day and healthy young adults were expected to take 7,000-13,000 steps/day [19]. It has been shown that a pedometer can provide valid and reliable data [20]. Pedometers may prove useful in recording walking activities in free-living populations [20] and are simple and affordable [21]. Therefore, it has been suggested that pedometers are particularly useful for assessing physical activity and measuring daily activity in children [22]. Health life wristbands such as Nike+ bands, Fitbit FLEX and Jawbones Up are new examples of physical activity monitoring tools. They allow for regular self-monitoring and goal setting that provides essential feedback that serves to increase self-awareness that can lead to behavioral change [23] [24].

3   An Integrated Solution

Reviewing the literature in exergaming has revealed the potential of these types of games to increase energy expenditure [11], [25, 26] and therefore facilitate the increase of physical activity levels in children and adolescents [12], [27]. However, some challenges have been identified in the ability of exergames to motivate children to exercise. While exergame play alone does not meet the daily amount of exercise recommended for children and adolescents [25], [13], there is some evidence to suggest that the use of exergames can contribute significantly to meeting some of the daily requirements for physical activity [26]. An additional challenge is that some children and adolescents may lose interest in playing exergames over time [28]. Currently issues of motivation and sustained interest in exergame play are still under investigation and need to be assessed over longer periods of time. Another possible challenge with using this technology is the limited or restricted access to active video game play. These restrictions may result from the concern of children becoming addicted to active video game play which has the potential to negatively affect behavior and academic performance.

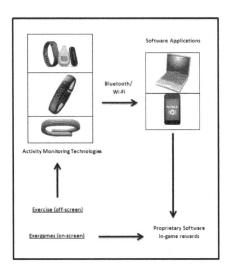

Fig. 1. The Integration Framework of On-screen and Off-screen Physical Activity (Activity monitoring technologies photos are adapted from [32] [33] [34])

Physical activity tracking technologies have been suggested as another method to increase individuals' motivation to exercise. These technologies are an effective means of increasing individuals' self-awareness through self-monitoring and goal setting. However, there is still concern about individuals losing motivation and interest over time, especially when goals associated with this technology are not achieved. An additional concern is that due to the variety of these technologies currently available, individuals may become confused about which is most appropriate for them. Inaccurate selection of an appropriate physical activity monitoring technology may result in a person giving up use of this technology.

Our previous work in this area has suggested the best solution involves the integration of active video game technology with physical activity tracking technology [29], [30], [31] to increase both on-screen exercise and off-screen exercise. The framework illustrated in Fig. 1 shows the two possible ways of exercising. Children are able to exercise in front of screens while playing exergames. In addition, their off-screen time exercising is also recorded by activity tracking devices and then this activity provides game rewards that are transferred through Bluetooth or Wi-Fi to the game software. Based on physical activity levels, the in-game or virtual rewards are applied and thus the more physically active the child is, the more in-game rewards and progress they make in the game. In this way, both on-screen and off-screen physical activity support in-game performance and associated rewards.

"MetaKenkoh" is an Internet-based adventure game for children that uses a similar integrated approach. In order to play this game, children need to wear a pedometer that records their off-game steps. Pedometer data are uploaded daily to an internet database by parents. Children's steps are then converted into energy units that are used in game play [27]. Likewise, "Fish'n'Steps" is a social computer game that uses a pedometer device to keep track of daily step counts in players. The participants are encouraged to take more daily steps as these steps are translated to the growth of their character in the game when data is uploaded [35]. 'ibitz' for Kids technology is developed by GeoPalz and includes a wireless pedometer and a free-downloaded application. Thorough the pedometer device, children's physical steps can be tracked and then synchronized to the app where their physical exertion translates to virtual rewards [36].

4   Conclusion

We certainly agree with the notion that combining the appeal and motivation associated with active video games and also encouraging free physical play provides the most benefit. The ability of children to complete challenges and accumulate rewards in both on-screen and off-screen play may help reinforce physical activity in both of these environments.

This foundational paper has been developed to explore the potential to implement technology-based solutions to promote physical activity amongst children and adolescents. Exergames and activity tracking technologies have multiple implications for increasing physical activity levels in children and adolescents. The integration of both of these technologies may have even greater implications for increasing levels of physical activity in young people. This paper discusses the feasibility of combining exergames and activity tracking technologies. Based on the literature we reviewed, a preliminary model that integrates these two technologies has been proposed. This model could potentially be utilised to test the feasibility of the integration of these technologies. This work complements work performed in our previous studies. Based on this review and our previous work, we plan to further investigate and consequently integrate these technologies as a method of increasing physical activity among children and adolescents.

Acknowledgements. The primary author is employed and sponsored by Taibah University, Madinah, KSA.

References

1. U.S. DEPARTMENT OF HEALTH AND HUMAN SERVICES, Centers for Disease Control and Prevention, National Center for Chronic Disease Prevention and Health Promotion, The President's Council on Physical Fitness and Sports, Physical activity and health: A report of the Surgeon General Executive Summary (1999)
2. Hoos, M.B., Kuipers, H., Gerver, W.-J., Westerterp, K.R.: Physical Activity Pattern of Children Assessed by Triaxial Accelerometry. European Journal of Clinical Nutrition 58, 1425–1428 (2004)
3. Kawahara, J., Tanaka, S., Tanaka, C., Aoki, Y., Yonemoto, J.: Daily Inhalation Rate and Time-Activity/Location Pattern in Japanese Preschool Children. Risk Analysis 32, 1595–1604 (2012)
4. Strong, W.B., Malina, R.M., Blimkie, C.J., Daniels, S.R., Dishman, R.K., Gutin, B., et al.: Evidence Based Physical Activity for School-Age Youth. The Journal of Pediatrics 146, 732–737 (2005)
5. Berlin, J.E., Storti, K.L., Brach, J.S.: Using Activity Monitors to Measure Physical Activity in Free-Living Conditions. Physical Therapy 86, 1137–1145 (2006)
6. Rideout, V.J., Foehr, U.G., Roberts, D.F.: Generation M: [superscript 2]: Media in the Lives of 8-to 18-Year-Olds. Henry J. Kaiser Family Foundation (2010)
7. Phillips, C.A., Rolls, S., Rouse, A., Griffiths, M.D.: Home Video Game Playing in Schoolchildren: A Study of Incidence and Patterns of Play. Journal of Adolescence 18, 687–691 (1995)
8. Cherabuddi, N.R.: Exergaming: Video Games as a Form of Exercise
9. Biddiss, E., Irwin, J.: Active Video Games to Promote Physical Activity in Children and Youth: A Systematic Review. Archives of Pediatrics & Adolescent Medicine 164, 664–672 (2010)
10. Kiili, K., Merilampi, S.: Developing Engaging Exergames with Simple Motion Detection. In: Proceedings of the 14th International Academic MindTrek Conference: Envisioning Future Media Environments, pp. 103–110 (2010)
11. Maddison, R., Ni Mhurchu, C., Jull, A., Jiang, Y., Prapavessis, H., Rodgers, A.: Energy Expended Playing Video Console Games: An Opportunity to Increase Children's Physical Activity? Pediatric Exercise Science 19 (2007)
12. Mhurchu, C.N., Maddison, R., Jiang, Y., Jull, A., Prapavessis, H., Rodgers, A.: Couch Potatoes to Jumping Beans: A Pilot Study of the Effect of Active Video Games on Physical Activity in Children. International Journal of Behavioral Nutrition and Physical Activity 5, 8 (2008)
13. Maddison, R., Foley, L., Mhurchu, C.N., Jiang, Y., Jull, A., Prapavessis, H., et al.: Effects of Active Video Games on Body Composition: A Randomized Controlled Trial. The American Journal of Clinical Nutrition 94, 156–163 (2011)
14. Baranowski, T., Baranowski, J., O'Connor, T., Lu, A.S., Thompson, D.: Is Enhanced Physical Activity Possible Using Active Videogames? Games For Health: Research, Development, and Clinical Applications 1, 228–232 (2012)
15. Baranowski, T., Buday, R., Thompson, D.I., Baranowski, J.: Playing for Real: Video Games and Stories for Health-Related Behavior Change. American Journal of Preventive Medicine 34, 74–82, e10 (2008)
16. Gerling, K.M., Schild, J., Masuch, M.: Exergaming for Elderly: Analyzing Player Experience and Performance. In: Mensch & Computer 2011, Germany, p. 401 (2011)

17. Tanaka, K., Parker, J., Baradoy, G., Sheehan, D., Holash, J.R., Katz, L.: A Comparison of Exergaming Interfaces for Use in Rehabilitation Programs and Research. The Journal of the Canadian Game Studies Association 6, 69–81 (2012)
18. Puyau, M.R., Adolph, A.L., Vohra, F.A., Zakeri, I., Butte, N.F.: Prediction of Activity Energy Expenditure Using Accelerometers in Children. Medicine and Science in Sports and Exercise 36, 1625–1631 (2004)
19. Tudor-Locke, C.E., Myers, A.M.: Methodological Considerations for Researchers and Practitioners Using Pedometers to Measure Physical (Ambulatory) Activity. Research Quarterly for Exercise and Sport 72, 1–12 (2001)
20. Bassett Jr., D.R., Ainsworth, B.E., Leggett, S.R., Mathien, C.A., Main, J.A., Hunter, D.C., et al.: Accuracy of Five Electronic Pedometers for Measuring Distance Walked. Medicine and Science in Sports and Exercise 28, 1071–1077 (1996)
21. Tudor-Locke, C.E., Myers, A.M.: Challenges and Opportunities for Measuring Physical Activity in Sedentary Adults. Sports Medicine 31, 91–100 (2001)
22. Rowlands, A.V., Eston, R.G., Ingledew, D.K.: Relationship between Activity Levels, Aerobic Fitness, and Body Fat in 8-to10-Yr-Old Children. Journal of Applied Physiology 86, 1428–1435 (1999)
23. Schnoll, R., Zimmerman, B.J.: Self-Regulation Training Enhances Dietary Self-Efficacy and Dietary Fiber Consumption. Journal of the American Dietetic Association 101, 1006–1011 (2001)
24. Wierenga, M.E., Browning, J.M., Mahn, J.L.: A Descriptive Study of How Clients Make Life-Style Changes. The Diabetes Educator 16, 469–473 (1990)
25. Graves, L., Stratton, G., Ridgers, N.D., Cable, N.T.: Energy Expenditure in Adolescents Playing New Generation Computer Games. British Journal of Sports Medicine 42, 592–594 (2008)
26. Straker, L., Abbott, R.: Effect of Screen-Based Media on Energy Expenditure and Heart Rate in 9-to 12-Year-Old Children. Pediatric Exercise Science 19 (2007)
27. Southard, D.R., Southard, B.H.: Promoting Physical Activity in Children with MetaKenkoh. Clinical and Investigative Medicine 29, 293–297 (2006)
28. Dixon, R., Maddison, R., Mhurchu, C.N., Jull, A., Meagher-Lundberg, P., Widdowson, D.: Parents' and Children's Perceptions of Active Video Games: A Focus Group Study. Journal of Child Health Care 14, 189–199 (2010)
29. Altamimi, R., Skinner, G., Nesbitt, K.: FITTER-A Framework for Integrating Activity Tracking Technologies into Electric Recreation for Children and Adolescents. International Journal of Medical, Pharmaceutical Science and Engineering 7 (2013)
30. Ilung, P., Altamimi, R., Skinner, G.D.: Exertainment: Designing Active Video Games to Get Youth Moving. In: Proceedings of the International MultiConference of Engineers and Computer Scientists (2014)
31. Pranata, I., Altamimi, R., Skinner, G.: An Adaptive Framework Allowing Active Video Games to Address Child Obesity. GSTF Digital Library (2014)
32. Fitbit, fitbit Products (2014), `http://www.fitbit.com/au`
33. NIKE, Nike+ (2014), `https://secure-nikeplus.nike.com/plus/`
34. Jowbone. UP (2014), `https://jawbone.com/up`
35. Lin, J.J., Mamykina, L., Lindtner, S., Delajoux, G., Strub, H.B.: Fish'n'Steps: Encouraging Physical Activity with an Interactive Computer Game. In: Dourish, P., Friday, A. (eds.) UbiComp 2006. LNCS, vol. 4206, pp. 261–278. Springer, Heidelberg (2006)
36. ibitz, ibitz™ kids and adult wireless pedometers (2014), `http://ibitz.com/`

Ora – Save the Forest! Designing a Social Impact Game

Hazel Bradshaw[1], E. Penelope Holland[2], and Mark Billinghurst[1]

[1] The Human Interface Technology Laboratory, Christchurch, New Zealand
Hazel.Bradshaw@canterbury.ac.nz,
mark.billinghurst@hitlabnz.org
[2] Landcare Research, Lincoln, New Zealand
HollandP@landcareresearch.co.nz

Abstract. Computer models for designing educational games need to have practical applications as well as underlying theoretical principles. In this paper, we present the Structural Playability Process (SPP), a new approach for designing and implementing serious games. Using the SPP designed game *Ora – Save the Forest!* as a case study, we describe the four SPP spaces: education, translation, design and engine. Ora is a forest-pest-management game based on scientific models and intended to inform players about the complexities of ecosystem management. Preliminary user study results show that SPP is an effective method of producing motivating and successful learning environments.

Keywords: Serious/Educational games, Game-design, Structural Playability (SPP), Flow, Motivation, Game-play.

1   Introduction

Computer games stimulate motivation, skill development and affect learning and knowledge acquisition [1,2]. There is a need for more empirical evidence supporting the effectiveness of games as learning environments [3], but game design is key in finding a balance between education and games [4]. Game design models bring structure to the design of educational games by applying motivation theories, among which Csikszentmihalyi's [5] Flow theory is prominent. Design models utilising Flow for educational game design [6,7,8] provide insight into how to align theory with game design, but rarely cover the practical implementation of a game.

This paper describes the design approach for "Ora - Save the Forest![1]" A social impact game designed using the novel Structural Playability Process (SPP) to meet the need for a practical methodology for educational game design. The SPP draws on several theories in psychology: skilled performance theory [9]; motivational theories [10,11] and optimal experience or 'Flow' [5]. Flow is an eight stage state of optimal experience, where the 'experiencer' is intrinsically motivated to continue engaging with the task at hand.

---

[1] http://www.playora.net/

Y. Pisan et al. (Eds.): ICEC 2014, LNCS 8770, pp. 84–91, 2014.

Theoretically, development of computer games which create conditions for 'Flow' [12] can produce 'intrinsic motivation' [11], inspiring the player to take on further challenges and drive their learning experience. Our research explores the connection between game design, Flow and learning gains. In the rest of the paper we first describe the Ora – Save the Forest! Game, focusing on the SPP methodology, then results from a user study conducted with the game, and finally conclusions and directions for future work.

2   Ora – Save the Forest!

At the heart of the SPP is the application of skilled performance theory, which structures the design of game mechanics to provide a scaffold upon which the experience of Flow can be developed. The four design and development spaces of the SPP are 1) Education, 2) Translation, 3) Design and 4) Engine. The primary advantage of this approach, over others, is that the gameplay process breaks down into spaces that can be engaged with by all stakeholders, from client to designer to programmer. The SPP spaces link learning outcomes to gameplay mechanics and offer a practical implementation method for structuring gameplay inside a game engine. In the rest of this section we describe how the SPP was applied in the design and development of "Ora – Save the Forest!".

2.1 The Educational Space (1) of the SPP drives game design by linking a complex problem to a narrative via learning outcomes. The designer works closely with the client to explore and contextualise the game concept. This requires defining a target audience, and their intrinsic and extrinsic motivations [5][11]. Understanding client and audience motivations helps establish the learning outcomes, learning objectives and objective tasks.

A Complex Problem – Pest control in New Zealand is a contentious issue: research indicating the consequences of management is not well understood by some members of the general public who have a stake in the process (e.g. land owners and managers, recreational land users). The public need to be engaged in order to make informed decisions about pest management on their land or communities. Academic papers are difficult to access for the layperson, and most scientific knowledge transfer to date has been via media releases, workshops or word of mouth. It is difficult to get a national scale audience engaged via these routes. Developing a game based on pest management research is a novel way to engage and inform the public with up to date science, and to help players gain a realistic appreciation that ecosystem management is a complex problem (the primary learning outcome).

Client and Target Audience - The client was Landcare Research, a NZ Crown Research Institute involved in terrestrial biodiversity management. The target audience was the NZ public with a core demographic of rural New Zealanders of both genders, with a tertiary education but not necessarily academics.

Defining motivations - Key outcomes for the game were; to provide an aid to public dialogue and engagement with a complex problem, scientific knowledge transfer, and innovative and engaging ways to implement and present research findings.

Intrinsic motivations come from the inside; for example, wanting to achieve the aspirational goal of maintaining and restoring New Zealand's forest ecosystem and biodiversity. This intrinsic motivation is shared between client and target audience, and became the learning objective for Ora. Extrinsic motivations come from the outside; for example, wanting to see the results of the learning objective. The client-centred extrinsic motivations were to control possum population dynamics temporally and spatially, with the aim of promoting understanding and awareness of the effectiveness of available possum control options. The game should therefore allow players to interact with the underlying science to experience this. The extrinsic motivators of the target audience were to see native bird and tree recovery and maintain a 100% NZ Pure perception. Therefore, the game-world, its narrative and rewards should display these results, following appropriate in-game actions.

Learning outcomes - Using learning outcomes for defining and assessing student performance is well established in higher education [13]. Learning outcomes and objectives ultimately define the primary game goals in the correct context. Considering the motivations of client and target audience allowed us to define the learning outcome and objectives for Ora: participants should be able to gain a realistic appreciation that management of an ecosystem is a complex problem. This learning outcome provided the educational design and directive for player achievement, and describes the scope of the activity for player and designer. The player's path to meet the learning outcome is via the application of learning objectives, broken down into objective tasks. Objective tasks guiding Ora gameplay design are to monitor the environment to assess tree health and possum impacts, and to manage the environment.

2.2 The Translation Space (2) is where learning objectives and objective tasks are embedded within a simple narrative, contextualising the gameplay for the player and the designer who aims to 'maximize the player experience through the planning, structure and execution of the key elements of Gameplay Progression (mechanics, duration, ancillary rewards, practical rewards and difficulty)' [14].

Narrative - Ora places the player at the heart of the action: You are the hero tasked with saving the beautiful but fragile native forest from the jaws of hungry invaders. The narrative was established to reflect client and target audience motivations. The setting is native NZ forest, invaded by Australian brushtail possums, the player is introduced to the game world by an omnipresent entity, the guardian of the forest, who enlists the player's help in returning the ecosystem to its former glory. A giant tree at the centre of the virtual forest is the physical embodiment of the forest guardian. This "control tree" houses the gameplay interface that the player uses to monitor, interact and control the underlying forest-pest-management models. It is here that we find the non-player character Liana, a scientist who acts as liaison between guardian, game-world and player. Liana provides the narrative context and acts as the gameplay mission delivery system, and is the player's main point of contact inside the game.

2.3 The Design Space (3) is where the educational content is mapped into gameplay. To meet the learning outcome, the learning objectives are translated into a set of primary game goals that guide gameplay development through skill stages. Skill stages are a core device of the SPP. They apply the skilled performance scaffold which elicits Flow conditions. In the SPP, there are three types of gameplay goals; Aspirational/long-term goals (intrinsic); Mid-range goals (intrinsic/extrinsic); and Short-term immediate goals (extrinsic).

The primary game goals result from the translation of learning outcomes and objectives filtered through the narrative. They reflect player motivations and form the basis of the narrative progression. In Ora, the primary game goals are (1): To repel an army of mammalian pests led by marauding possums *(immediate motivational goal and direct player action);* (2): To save the native flora and fauna *(mid-range goal and reinforcer of player action);* (3): To restore the forest ecosystem to its former glory *(success indicator and long-term aspirational goal creating opportunities for feedback on actions).*

The simulation model (sim) that underlies Ora provides the player with methods for achieving gameplay goals. It integrates models of possum birth, death and movement [15], impacts on tree health and mortality [16] and interactions with management tools such as traps [17] and poison bait [18], with costs (time and money) for executing monitoring or management. The sim allows players to set up "operations" comprising a series of actions such as choosing contractors, transport and equipment, setting trap or bait station layout, providing quotes, and implementing operations at the appropriate time, thus providing a basis on which to build gameplay mechanics.

Gameplay – The design plan for Ora has four levels, which deal with the challenges of using the available tools within limited budgets, ethical dilemmas and meeting the needs of concerned citizens. These are: (Level 1) Ground operations; (Level 2) Aerial operations; (Level 3) Managing stakeholders; (Level 4) Combination of levels 1-3. In this paper we focus on the gameplay development of Level 1 which comprises a 61 hectare area of forest enclosed by a predator-proof fence. The forest consisted of three native, palatable tree species (Kamahi, Southern rata and Hall's Totara) and the initial possum population was set at 20 per hectare with an equal sex ratio. Interactions between trees and possums were controlled by the sim, which allows the trees to grow and change over time while showing the impacts of possum browse on the forest canopy. In-game possums move around the gameplay area, with movements dictated by the position of their home ranges. Game time is moved at roughly one night per second of play, so 15 minutes of gameplay could equate to 2.5 years of forest time. The game needed to make player perception of involvement close to that of the client and/or other entities involved in implementing or directing pest control in NZ. We therefore developed a system of reward and feedback that enables players from the public, scientists and managers to perceive the value of each other's input.

Epic win and fail - The outcome for Level 1 was to establish good tree health and a healthy bird population, by reducing possum numbers in the fenced area. The Level 1 'Epic Win' state would see possums eradiated inside the fenced area and trees at 80%+ attainable health, and the release of a player-nurtured kiwi into the newly created sanctuary. The 'Epic Fail' state would be the opposite, with a healthy possum population, less than 20% tree health and an unhatched egg or unreleased kiwi. To achieve the level goal, the player must access ground-based pest control options in the sim: Tree Monitoring; Trapping; and Baiting. The in-game application of these operations form the goal orientated skill based tasks of level 1.

Skill stages - To manage task progression, gameplay was subdivided into four skill stages, drawing on the 'Three Phases of Skill Learning' [19] and the principles of achieving a skilled performance [9]. A skill stage has five components: the challenge to be undertaken, tasks contributing to the challenge, feedback on tasks, rewards for task completion, and progression to the next skill stage. This logical structure guides the pacing of goal orientated progression, by building on levels of complexity and challenge. Ideally, this progression creates Flow [5], as challenge and skill increase simultaneously to balance player anxiety and boredom. Level 1 is a tutorial level, sitting in the Cognitive or Early phase of skill learning, 'Where a learner tries to understand the task and what is being demanded of them' [9]. The design allows the player to learn the game interface, control system and ground-based management options. Within Level 1, skill stages progress in complexity and size. Skill Stage 1 starts with basic tree monitoring in 1 hectare of playable space, increasing to the complete tool box of ground control strategies across 61 hectares by Skill Stage 4 (Fig. 1).

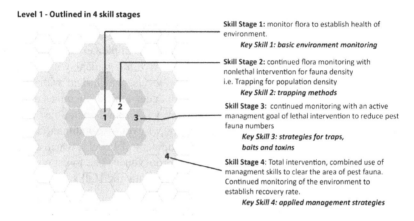

Level 1 - Outlined in 4 skill stages

Skill Stage 1: monitor flora to establish health of environment.
Key Skill 1: basic environment monitoring

Skill Stage 2: continued flora monitoring with nonlethal intervention for fauna density i.e. Trapping for population density
Key Skill 2: trapping methods

Skill Stage 3: continued monitoring with an active managment goal of lethal intervention to reduce pest fauna numbers
Key Skill 3: strategies for traps, baits and toxins

Skill Stage 4: Total intervention, combined use of managment skills to clear the area of pest fauna. Continued monitoring of the environment to establish recovery rate.
Key Skill 4: applied management strategies

Fig. 1. Map of skill stage tasks increasing in difficulty and spatial complexity

The User Interface (UI) - Supporting and contextual gameplay features were developed within the skill stages, using the narrative to tie them together. The UI was designed to deliver a cohesive user experience throughout the skill stages. From the control tree (see Translation Space), the player accesses game controls, sets out to explore a 3D forest environment, interacts with the feedback and reward system, and meets Liana, who guides the player through the gameplay missions (see Engine).

Rewards and Feedback – Feedback on individual tasks is delivered via the **Logbook**, giving feedback from the sim (e.g. tree health after a monitoring operation, number of possums trapped after a trapping operation), allowing players to interact directly with the underlying science. Indirect feedback is provided by updating the forest health status, which is tracked by in-game status graphs, and by visually updating the displayed trees to show possum browse and canopy recovery. The game also features a native birdlife **nurture system**. During level 1, the player is awarded a kiwi egg, which they must attempt to hatch and release into the sanctuary. Successful management intervention to complete a gameplay mission gives the player **science points**, which increase the hatching rate of the egg. This reward system focuses the player on the positive aspects of pest management (e.g. saving birds) rather than the negative (e.g. killing possums), and gives the player a simple scale of achievement to follow (e.g. get enough science points to hatch the bird).

2.4 The Engine Space (4) is where the game design is implemented in software. The *Design* space skill-stages become the gameplay missions that are coded in the engine mission system. Off-the-shelf game engines, such as Unity3D in this project, do not have built-in mission systems for implementing gameplay. The SPP, unlike more theoretical design processes [6,7,8] provides a practical means for creating a logic based, engine-side mission system, comprising of four, hierarchical steps: 1) Mission Control; 2) Mission Set; 3) Missions; 4) Mission Objective.

1. **Mission Control** has controls for setting gameplay parameters for the entire gameplay level (Fig 2, left). Mission Control initiates the sim and mission sets, checks for completion, then iterates a new set or ends gameplay. Nested within Mission Control is the:

2. **Mission Set**, which holds all related missions defined under the relevant skill stage. This follows the same pattern as Mission Control, checking and instantiating all missions linked to the Mission Set as needed. The Mission Set contains:

3. **Missions.** The Mission starts by triggering the onscreen mission delivery system (Fig 2. centre, Liana dialogue) and deeper levels of player guidance (by producing Journal entries). When the player completes their interaction with Liana, a:

4. **Mission Objective** is triggered. The Mission Objective houses gameplay tasks the player will undertake. On completion of the Mission Objective, the logic either starts the next objective in sequence or begins the mission completion sequence. The completion logic provides feedback dialogue to the player from Liana on the outcomes of the mission. It then triggers the reward and any other feedback systems that are linked to that particular mission (Fig 2. centre). The Mission is then flagged as complete and triggers the next Mission in the Set, or gameplay ends.

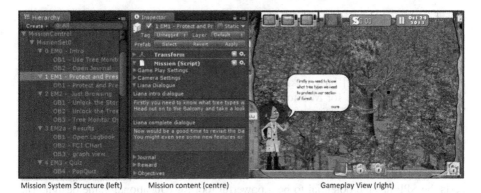

Mission System Structure (left)   Mission content (centre)   Gameplay View (right)

Fig. 2. SPP Engine Space mission system applied in (Unity3D) game engine

3   Results

The game design was tested using: (1) pre/post and follow-up tests measuring knowledge acquisition and (2) the EGameFlow [20] survey of participant enjoyment on Flow. We compared the Ora game (ORA) to a classroom experience of the sim (SIM), which shared the UI and 3D world environment of Ora, but did not include skill stage mapping and mission delivery (Liana). The hypotheses stated: (a) the SPP-designed ORA would provide a learning environment that better supported knowledge acquisition in SIM; and (b) ORA would better promote 'Flow' state conditions.

Participants were recruited (26 female and 26 male, 18-50 age range) from Canterbury, NZ. Survey answers for knowledge acquisition and Flow were summarized for each player to give a score per survey (pre/post/follow-up). We found that players of the SIM learned slightly more immediately after the user study (post) compared to before (pre), with the average degree of change between pre and post surveys equal to 22% for ORA and 27% for SIM.

However, knowledge retention after 4 weeks was higher for ORA than SIM: no significant change ($p = 1.0$) could be detected in the follow-up survey from pre-test levels for SIM players, but ORA players retained a significant amount of knowledge ($p < .003$) compared to pre-test levels. ORA players also had a more positive perception of the experience than SIM players: overall 56% of ORA players responded positively to experiencing Flow conditions compared to only 33% for SIM players. There was also a statistically significant difference between the two groups in the Flow conditions of Feedback (Mann-Whitney $U = 151$, $p < .001$) and Immersion (MWU = 231.5, $p < .05$), with the mean rank significantly higher for ORA in both instances. Overall this confirms our hypotheses that the Ora game better supported long-term knowledge acquisition when compared to the classroom taught SIM, and that ORA also better promoted conditions of a 'Flow' state.

4   Conclusion

The four spaces of the SPP (Education, Translation, Design and Engine) provide a practical way to translate a client 'problem' into an effective gameplay environment. The use of motivation theories [5][11] to define learning outcomes, objectives and tasks provides a framework for structuring narrative and gameplay goals. Use of skill performance theory [9] based skill stages [19] link the Design and Engine spaces. This provides structure for Mission Sets with their system of challenges, tasks, feedback and reward into effective gameplay that improves the occurrence of a Flow state.

Implementing the Mission Set structure into a game engine provides a system supporting player progression and gameplay goal achievement. The fact that Ora gameplay resulted in greater knowledge retention, induced a more positive perception of Flow showing significantly better Feedback and Immersion when compared to the sim, suggests the SPP has the potential to be a powerful tool for educational game design. The Design and Engine Spaces are practical, straightforward, and general enough to be applied to any serious game concept. However, considerable collaboration is required by designer and client to work through the Education and Translation Spaces. For a game designer not experienced in teaching methods, mapping learning outcomes could prove challenging. Future opportunities for further dissemination and testing would come through collaboration with other game designers and projects.

References

1. Dondlinger, M.J.: Educational Video Game Design: A Review of the Literature. Appl. Educ. Technol. 4(1), 21–31 (2007)
2. Connolly, T.M., et al.: A systematic literature review of empirical evidence on computer games and serious games. Comput. Educ. 59(2), 661–686 (2012)
3. O'Neil, H.F., Wainess, R., Baker, E.L.: Classification of learning outcomes: Evidence from the computer games literature. Curric. J. 16(4), 455–474 (2005)
4. Wei, T., Li, Y.: Design of Educational Game: A Literature Review. In: Pan, Z., Cheok, A.D., Müller, W., Zhang, X., Wong, K. (eds.) Transactions on Edutainment IV. LNCS, vol. 6250, pp. 266–276. Springer, Heidelberg (2010)
5. Csikszentmihalyi, M.: FLOW: The Psychology of Optimal Experience. Harper & Row (1990)
6. Kiili, K.: Towards a participatory multimedia learning model. Educ. Inf. Technol. 11, 21–32 (2006)
7. Finneran, C., et al.: A person-artefact-task (PAT) model of flow antecedents in computer-mediated environments. Int. J. Hum. Comput. Stud. 59(4), 475–496 (2003)
8. Cowley, B., Charles, D., Black, M., Hickey, R.: User-System-Experience Model for User Centered Design in Computer Games. In: Wade, V.P., Ashman, H., Smyth, B. (eds.) AH 2006. LNCS, vol. 4018, pp. 419–424. Springer, Heidelberg (2006)
9. Fitts, P.M., Posner, M.I.: Human Performance. In: Human Performance. Brooks/Cole Pub. Co., Belmont (1967)
10. Maslow, A.H.: A theory of human motivation. Psychol. Rev. 50(4), 370–396 (1943)
11. Deci, E., Ryan, R.: Intrinsic Motivation and Self-Determination in Human Behavior, pp. 1–5, 28–40. Plenum Press, New York (1985)
12. Oblinger, D.: Simulations, Games, and Learning. Educause 39, 6 (2006)
13. Biggs, J.: Formulating and clarifying curriculum objectives. In: Teaching for Quality Learning at University, 2nd edn., pp. 34–55. Open University Press, Buckingham (2003)
14. Lopez, B.M.: Gameplay Design Fundamentals: Gameplay Progression. Gamasutra (2014), http://ubm.io/1mdLykE (accessed: March 28, 2014)
15. Ramsey, D.S.L., Efford, M.G.: Management of bovine tuberculosis in brushtail possums in New Zealand: Predictions from a spatially explicit, individual-based model. J. Appl. Ecol. 47(4), 911–919 (2010)
16. Holland, E.P., et al.: Thresholds in plant-herbivore interactions: Predicting plant mortality due to herbivore browse damage. Oecologia 172(3), 751–766 (2013)
17. Ball, S.J., et al.: A method for estimating wildlife detection probabilities in relation to home-range use: insights from a field study on the common brushtail possum (Trichosurus vulpecula). Wildl. Res. 32(3), 217 (2005)
18. Tompkins, D.M., Ramsey, D.: Optimising bait-station delivery of fertility control agents to brushtail possum populations. Wildl. Res. 34(1), 67 (2007)
19. Bradshaw, H.: Entertainment Education For The Computer Age: Investigating The Engaging Nature of Computer Games for Educational Application. In: ICERI 2010 Conference, pp. 3772–3781 (November 2010)
20. Fu, F.-L., Su, R.-C., Yu, S.-C.: EGameFlow: A scale to measure learners' enjoyment of e-learning games. Comput. Educ. 52(1), 101–112 (2009)

Designing Digital Climbing Experiences through Understanding Rock Climbing Motivation

Richard Byrne and Florian 'Floyd' Mueller

Exertion Games Lab, RMIT University, Melbourne, Australia
{rich,floyd}@exertiongameslab.org
http://exertiongameslab.org

Abstract. Interactive systems have been used successfully in sports to assist people in achieving their performance goals, however, we believe that some aspects are often overlooked. In this paper we focus on rock climbing and we examine existing work on climbing from varying fields, including sports science, psychology, and climbing literary works, in order to identify recurring motivational themes. In total we identify and describe five key themes from these works: "risk as a measure of progress", "maintaining challenge", "social engagement", "experiencing beauty and nature", and "documenting and reliving the experience". We then examine how existing digital climbing experiences address these themes and suggest ways in which these interactive climbing designs could embrace the themes they do not yet address. We believe this work will be important not only when designing digital climbing experiences, but also digital experiences for other extreme sports.

1 Introduction

Using technology to assist with or to encourage improvement in sporting performance is an emerging field of research and development. In recent years jogging, for example, has seen numerous devices or applications aimed at improving the performance of professionals and beginners alike (for example: Nike Plus [19] and Run Keeper [21]). These systems often aim at improving and monitoring an individual's performance by recording their activity and reporting how well they achieved the task. Other sports have also been investigated, such as: cycling [26], swimming [2], rowing [1], and rock climbing [11]. Recent research in rock climbing has focused on interactive climbing designs that provide new ways of interacting with the rock climbing wall. One caveat, we believe, when designing climbing experiences currently is that the technology often takes the focus, with designers asking first 'what can we do with the technology?'. However, we believe that what is overlooked is obtaining an understanding into *why* rock climbers choose to climb before developing the design. We believe this is an important consideration and something of a missed opportunity since it will allow for the development of digital climbing experiences that cater to climbers' needs and motivations, i.e. supporting the core of the extreme sport experience.

Y. Pisan et al. (Eds.): ICEC 2014, LNCS 8770, pp. 92–99, 2014.

To address this we survey existing literature related to climbing in order to identify a set of motivational themes we believe could be valuable to consider when designing to support climbing experience. To see how well these themes have been considered we reexamine existing digital climbing experiences and offer our suggestions for design opportunities which could allow these systems to address themes not yet supported.

2   Identifying Motivational Themes from Climbing Literature

We know as interaction designers that requirements of the desired user group should be kept in mind throughout the design [20, p.352-388]. However in climbing (and any extreme sport) it is important to consider more than the system requirements since for these groups the experience is just as important (if not more so):

> *"The whole experience of climbing is important, not one particular part or moment" - Scott Backes* [23, p.162]

In this section we investigate existing literature on climbing motivation, including climbing literary works and work from the fields of sport science, psychology and sociology in order to gain an understanding of *why* climbers climb. By identifying recurring observations and themes present in this work we were able to establish five key motivational themes (which are illustrated in figure 1).

2.1   Maintaining Challenge

Levenhagen [15] develops a stage model of climbing purposes describing two primary motivations for climbers: to experience achievement and flow, and to build character. Both these motivations require that challenge is maintained throughout the experience to ensure that a sense of progression is also experienced. This marriage of challenge and flow is also discussed by Csikszentmihalyi et al. [4] who state that an optimal experience of flow can be maintained by "setting ourselves challenges" [5]. Louková and Vomáčko [17] and Vomáčko and Gável [25] also found that "Challenge" was among one of the highest motivations reported by climbers. Therefore we can identify that maintaining challenge is a key theme as it helps to maintain flow and achievement, and to also allow the climber to build character through a sense of achievement.

2.2   Risk as a Measure of Progress

Interestingly we initially assumed that extreme sports attract thrill seekers who pursue the sport primarily for the risk involved. However, it appears that risk plays a larger role in climbing as discussed by Ewert [8] who states that climbing simply because of the risk is actually a low motivational factor. This highlights

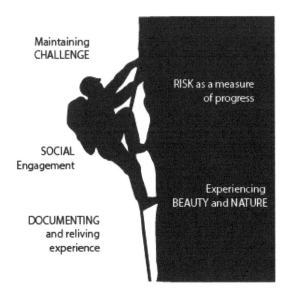

Fig. 1. Motivational themes identified from climbing literature

that risk can be a way to measure progress and performance improvement since a climber can evaluate how well they have progressed by climbing a route they previously considered too risky for their skill level. Fave et al. [10] also support this notion as they too explain how risk alone is not a primary motivation factor, but in actuality that it is useful in helping climbers to monitor and track their performance and progression.

2.3   Social Engagement

Climbers can be said to experience goals in one of two ways: through extrinsic and intrinsic motivations [17]. Intrinsic goals are those such as completing a new route to prove to climbers that they have progressed (as in the case of *risk as a measure of progress*), whereas extrinsic goals represent aspects such as social acknowledgement and competition [25]. De Leseleuc et al. [7] even discuss how climbers can be united in a community of belonging. The social aspects of climbing can therefore be said to be split into two categories: on the wall and off the wall. On the wall *social engagement* can include competition (completing a route a friend does not, doing the route faster, etc.) whereas off the wall can include friendly interactions and climbing discussions. For these reasons we believe that *social engagement* should be a key theme in climbing motivation.

2.4 Documenting and Reliving Experience

Levenhagen [15] comments that due to a sense of flow that exists in climbing it is apparent that climbers can also experience a sense of loss after the climb is completed. Simpson expresses how after his own climbing experience there is a *"post-coital depression, [a] fleeting saddening loss when it is over"* [22, p.116-117]. An extreme example of reliving previous experience was undertaken by Conrad Anker [18] who, using equipment relevant to the period, attempted to see if George Mallory (a pioneering climber whose body was found on Mount Everest) would have actually made it to the summit before he died. It is therefore apparent that the desire to relive the experience or document one's climb is another key motivation.

2.5 Experiencing Beauty and Nature

Vomáčko and Gável [25] discuss how beauty of mountains is a strong motivational factor which reinforces earlier work detailing how wilderness plays a key factor in adventure pursuits [8, 9]. Additional work has also discussed how mountains are naturally attractive to climbers [24] further enforcing that experiencing beauty and nature is a high motivational factor to climbers.

3 Motivational Themes Present in Existing Digital Climbing Experiences

In this section we look at several existing digital climbing experiences which we have grouped according to their shared design properties, i.e. interactive climbing walls, augmented and projection based systems and wearable systems. We identify the themes that are supported by these existing experiences and present design opportunities which theorise how each experience could incorporate the themes they do not currently support. We picked these systems by querying search terms such as "interactive climbing walls" and "climbing experience" on both the ACM Digital Library and Google, and choosing a selection that matched the above groupings.

3.1 Interactive Climbing Walls

There has been an interest in creating digital climbing walls solely for the purpose of providing new experiences for climbers. The *Digiwall* [16], for example, is an interactive climbing wall complete with custom hand and foot holds and an interactive sound system. The holds detect when they are touched and also have the ability to light up and illuminate different routes. Additionally the *Digiwall* has several games built into it based around these interactive holds such as encouraging the climber to touch the correct hold when it is illuminated. Similarly the *Wall-O-Tron* [3] makes use of a lighting system to suggest routes or holds that climbers need to interact with.

Themes Addressed. These systems encourage a sense of *challenge*: allowing for different routes to be created, objectives to be achieved and difficulty to be altered depending on climbing ability. They also encourage a sense of rivalry and specifically alter the core climbing experience by turning the wall into a social game experience and thus encouraging *social engagement*.

Design Opportunities. Though these systems address the themes of *maintaining challenge* and *social engagement* there exists the opportunity to embrace the additional themes that we have outlined. For example, *reliving the experience* could be embraced by recording the pattern of the climb and allowing the climber to "race" their previous attempt by playing it out on the wall in real-time. *Risk* is removed by the gaming element for more experienced climbers; perhaps the systems could alter routes in real-time based on how well the climber is ascending the wall in order to automatically adapt to their ability. The theme of *beauty and nature* is absent in this instance as the walls are situated indoors, however, theming the walls or creating a "realistic" rock face could help to create the illusion of being outdoors. Making use of a sound system to create an outdoor ambiance is also a potential approach to help facilitate the outdoor experience and hence *beauty and nature*.

3.2   Augmented and Projection-Based Systems

Daiber et al. [6] present the *BouldAR* system, which uses augmented reality to support collaborative boulder training. The system allows climbers to use their phones to make a virtual bouldering route by overlaying a computer-rendered image of the bouldering wall on the phone screen when the climbers hold their phones in front of the wall. This allows the climbers to click on the screen to outline their chosen route. Furthermore, users are able to track their progress and log successful and unsuccessful bouldering attempts by using a built-in diary. Study results found that participants preferred the smart phone to the paper solution when describing existing routes. This is an interesting finding as the results imply that a digital experience can be adopted by climbing enthusiasts in a positive way. Kajastila et. al. [13] also investigated augmented climbing by tracking the position of a climber and altering projected images on a wall based on their position. For example, climbers are able to move around the wall whilst being chased by a projected chainsaw, with the goal of not getting "hit" and surviving for the maximum amount of time. Additionally suggested climbing routes can be illuminated on the wall as a person climbs - suggesting different paths to take. Those not climbing were also able to participate by suggesting routes on the wall that the current climber should take. This is interesting as it is a system aimed at climbers of differing skills and abilities, which allows the experience to be altered accordingly based on climbers' needs.

Themes Addressed. These systems address the themes of *social engagement, maintaining challenge,* and *documenting and reliving the experience*. Since it is possible to alter routes and make new ones for the climbers on the fly the theme of *Risk as a measure of progress* is also addressed.

Design Opportunities. Currently these systems work indoors, if they could be extended to work outdoors then this would help embrace the theme of *experiencing beauty and nature* by making use of a natural, real world environment. Routes could perhaps be created by one climber for another that would take what is judged by the route creator as the most scenic. Projection systems could also be configured to simulate outdoor conditions indoors, such as simulating weather conditions, overlaying images of real mountain trails or displaying different scenery for different climbing attempts.

3.3   Wearable Systems

The *ClimbAX* [14] system was designed with climbers that wish to improve their performance in mind. Accelerometers are worn on the climber's wrists which record the climber's movements as they ascend the wall. An automatic assessment is then made on the recorded data in order to report to the climber post-climb information regarding their power, control, stability and speed during the climb. The purpose of the system is to automate and replicate the input climbers would receive from a real life coach. Results from a trial of the system found that the devices were accurate in predicting the score a climber may achieve at competition level. This is interesting since it illustrates how climbing experiences could be utilised by serious climbers who compete at competition level.

Themes Addressed There are several themes addressed by this system, the first is *maintaining challenge*, which is accomplished since the system reports on the progress of the climber allowing them to ensure they tackle more difficult routes or use new climbing techniques. *Documenting and reliving experience* is apparent since the progress is recorded and plotted on graphs that can be used in the future to gauge performance. Finally the theme of *experiencing beauty and nature* could be supported if the system is used outdoors.

Design Opportunities. *Risk as a measure of progress* is affected by such systems since the system is informing the climber that they are improving through data sets and graphs and not through their own judgement. Perhaps a better way to represent progress is to allow the climber to judge their own performance with the system offering suggestions of different routes the climber may want to climb next, e.g. "you did well, why not try something more difficult next time?". The theme of *social engagement* is limited in this system since a computer is informing the climber of the progress in a bid to replace a human coach. Perhaps such wearable systems could feed information regarding climbers' physiological status to a coach or fellow climbers so that they can help to guide the climber as they ascend a route. Maybe employing additional wearable tools could be a way to do this, for example, using a system like *Google Glass* [12] to relay audio transmissions to and from the climber. Motivational messages or information from the coach and other climbers could also be shown on the *Google Glass* display to offer support or suggestions through the climb in an attempt to address the theme of *social engagement*.

4 Conclusion

In this paper we have highlighted how understanding the motivation of climbers can be used when designing digital climbing experiences. We investigated this in order to address what we believed was a missed opportunity in designing these experiences without first understanding the motivation of climbers. We have presented five motivational themes derived from a review of existing literature including the fields of sports science, psychology, and climbing literary works. Additionally we have examined how these themes have been addressed by climbing experiences and offered design opportunities that can be considered in creating future digital climbing experiences.

This paper represents the initial stages of our investigation into designing digital climbing experiences through understanding climbing motivation and our future work will commence by implementing these themes into prototype systems. Through testing these systems with climbers we hope to examine our themes in order to produce guidelines that can be potentially considered not only when designing digital climbing experiences, but also digital experiences for other extreme sports.

References

[1] Anderson, R., Harrison, A., Lyons, G.M.: Rowing: Accelerometry-based feedback-can it improve movement consistency and performance in rowing? Sports Biomechanics 4(2), 179–195 (2005)

[2] Bächlin, M., Förster, K., Tröster, G.: Swimmaster: a wearable assistant for swimmer. In: Proceedings of the 11th International Conference on Ubiquitous Computing, pp. 215–224. ACM (2009)

[3] Bencho, B.: Brian Bencho: Hack A Day Blog - Wall-O-Tron, the inter-active rock climbing wall (2013), http://hackaday.com/2013/06/26/wall-o-tron-the-interactive-rock-climbing-wall/ (accessed: April 07, 2014)

[4] Csikszentmihalyi, M.: Flow: The psychology of optimal experience, vol. 41. Harper Perennial, New York (1991)

[5] Csikszentmihalyi, M., Csikszentmihalyi, I.S.: Optimal experience: Psychological studies of ow in consciousness. Cambridge University Press (1992)

[6] Daiber, F., Kosmalla, F., Krüger, A.: BouldAR – Using Augmented Reality to Support Collaborative Boulder Training, pp. 1–6 (February 2013)

[7] De Leseleuc, E., Gleyse, J., Marcellini, A.: The practice of sport as political expression? rock climbing at claret, france. International Sociology 17(1), 73–90 (2002)

[8] Ewert, A.W.: Playing the edge motivation and risk taking in a high-altitude wilderness like environment. Environment and Behavior 26(1), 3–24 (1994)

[9] Ewert, A.W., Hollenhorst, S.J.: Adventure recreation and its implications for wilderness. International Journal of Wilderness 3(2), 21–26 (1997)

[10] Fave, A.D., Bassi, M., Massimini, F.: Quality of experience and risk perception in high-altitude rock climbing. Journal of Applied Sport Psychology 15(1), 82–98 (2003)

[11] Fuss, F.K., Niegl, G.: Instrumented climbing holds and performance analysis in sport climbing. Sports Technology 1(6), 301–313 (2008)

[12] Google Glass (2014), http://www.google.com/glass/start/ (accessed April 04, 2014)

[13] Kajastila, R., Hämäläinen, P.: Augmented climbing: Interacting with projected graphics on a climbing wall. In: Proceedings of the Extended Abstracts of the 32nd Annual ACM Conference on Human Factors in Computing Systems, CHI EA 2014, pp. 1279–1284. ACM, New York (2014)

[14] Ladha, C., Hammerla, N.Y., Olivier, P., Plötz, T.: ClimbAX. In: The 2013 ACM International Joint Conference, p. 235. ACM Press, New York (2013)

[15] Levenhagen, M.: A stage model of why climbers climb and how it frames the discussions of recent climbing controversies. Journal of Mountaineering, 16–33 (2010)

[16] Liljedahl, M., Lindbergand, S., Berg, J.: Digiwall: an interactive climbing wall. Advances in Computer Entertainment Technology, 225–228 (2005)

[17] Louková, T., Vomáčko, L.: Motivation for climbing and mountaineering. In: 4th International Mountain and Outdoor Sports Conference. Outdoor Activities in Educational and Recreational Programmes, pp. 135–139 (2008)

[18] MacKenzie, M. In the Footsteps of Mallory and Irvine: The Wildest Dream. John Murray (2009)

[19] Nike Plus (2014), https://secure-nikeplus.nike.com/plus/ (accessed April 04, 2014)

[20] Rogers, Y., Sharp, H., Preece, J.: Interaction design: beyond human computer interaction. John Wiley & Sons (2011)

[21] Run Keeper (2014), http://runkeeper.com/ (accessed April 04, 2014)

[22] Simpson, J.: The Beckoning Silence. Mountain Books (2003)

[23] Twight, M.: Kiss Or Kill: Confessions of a Serial Climber. The Mountaineers Books (2001)

[24] Vause, M.: Mountaineering: The heroic expression of our age. In: Personal, Societal, and Ecological Values of Wilderness: Sixth World Wilderness Congress, vol. 2, pp. 83–86 (2000)

[25] Vomáčko, L., Gável, L.: Motivation to mountaineering. In: 5th International Mountain and Outdoor Sports Conference. Outdoor Activities in Educational and Recreational Programmes, pp. 122–142 (2010)

[26] Walmink, W., Chatham, A., Mueller, F.: Interaction opportunities around helmet design. In: CHI 2014 Extended Abstracts on Human Factors in Computing Systems, CHI EA 2014, pp. 367–370. ACM, New York (2014)

Assessing the Kinect's Capabilities
to Perform a Time-Based Clinical Test
for Fall Risk Assessment in Older People

Jaime A. Garcia[1], Yusuf Pisan[2], Chek Tien Tan[2], and Karla Felix Navarro[1]

[1] mHealth Lab – iNEXT Reasearch Group, University of Technology Sydney, Sydney, Austalia
[2] Games Studio, University of Technology Sydney, Sydney, Australia
Jaime.A.GarciaMarin@student.uts.edu.au,
{Yusuf.Pisan,ChekTien.Tan,Karla.FelixNavarro}@uts.edu.au

Abstract. The Choice Stepping Reaction Time (CSRT) task is time-based clinical test that has shown to reliably predict falls in older adults. Its current mode of delivery involves the use of a custom-made dance mat device. This mat is a measurement tool that can reliably obtain step data to discriminate between fallers and non-fallers. One of the pitfalls of this test is that the technology in use still imposes an obstacle on the degree of freedom to be able to perform adaptive exercises suitable for the elderly. In this paper, we describe a Kinect-based system that measures stepping performance through the use of a hybrid version of the CSRT task. This study focuses on assessing this system's capabilities to reliably measure a time-based clinical test of fall risk. Results showed a favorable correspondence and agreement between the two systems, suggesting that this platform could be potentially useful in the clinical practice.

Keywords: Kinect, Elderly, Fall Risk Assessment, Reaction Time Test, Stepping Performance.

1 Introduction

Since the release of the Microsoft Kinect, both research communities and industry have been actively investigating its potential use in the area of aged care and rehabilitation. This is mainly due to its capability to track real-time full body movements in 3D, a characteristic that was not available in early consumer game technologies such as the Nintendo Wii or the PS3. In the area of fall prevention and safety for the elderly, the Kinect has also gained much interest. Kinect-based applications range from health and home monitoring systems [1], through unobtrusive fall detection platforms [2]; coaching, rehabilitation and therapeutic tools[3], fall prevention training systems [4], to fall risk assessment tools [5]. Kinect-based serious games, being one of the most popular approaches, have shown a positive acceptance among seniors [6]. The fun factor inherent in such games and their ability to promote physical movements are ideal to encourage the elderly to exercise [7]. An example can be seen in the work done by Kim et al. [8], where the use of a commercial Kinect

Y. Pisan et al. (Eds.): ICEC 2014, LNCS 8770, pp. 100–107, 2014.

game showed to improve hip muscle strength and balance control in older adults after completing an 8-weeks intervention.

From a clinical perspective, the capabilities of the Kinect have also the potential to implement low-cost methods to assess fall risk in older adults. This is achieved through the collection of measurement that fulfill the requirements of certain clinical tests such as posture control [9], gait [10], dual tasking ability [11], and mobility [12], among others. Overall, these methods rely on the Kinect to obtain information of the human body positions in real-time, which are shown to be fairly accurate. For instance in the work done by Dutta et al [13], the Kinect demonstrated the ability to validly assess kinematic strategies of postural control. This suggests that the Kinect could be considered an effective tool when it comes to collection position-based measurements. However, for time-based measurements the Kinect introduces an additional challenge as it is a camera-based device restricted to process up to 30 skeleton frames per second.

The work presented in this paper focuses on evaluating the capabilities of the Kinect to reliably collect timing variables to fulfill the requirements of the Choice Stepping Reaction Time (CSRT) task, a time-based clinical test that has shown to reliably predict falls in order adults [14]. This study hence evaluates the validity of a Kinect-based system developed by the authors with a validated choice reaction time device. The latter has shown to effectively discriminate between groups of recurrent fallers and non-fallers [15]. The rest of the paper is structured as follows. Section 2 presents brief summary of related work in the field of fall risk assessment and describes the Choice Stepping Reaction time. Section 3 sets out the methodology used for this evaluation. Results and Discussion can be found in Section 4 and 5. Finally, conclusions and future work are presented in Section 5.

2   Related Work

The Choice Stepping Reaction Time (CSRT) task is a composite measure of sensorimotor functions, such as balance and strength, and cognitive functions such as attention and central processing speed [14]. The test is able to combine several dimensions of fall risk based on these composite metrics. For the CSRT Task, the person stands on the two central step panels of a wooden board (see Figure 1). One of four surrounding panels (front left *or LF*, front right *or RF*, left *or LL*, right *or RR*) illuminates randomly and the person is required to step on this panel as quickly as possible and then return to the center. The sequence is presented randomly as well as the time between trials so that the user is unable to anticipate the time and location of the next stimulus. The mean reaction time of 20 trials is then measured and analyzed for clinical diagnosis.

In the work done by Schone et al. [15], a Dance Mat Choice Step Reaction Time device was introduced and validated against the original CSRT Test. In this system, the CSRT Test is achieved through the use of a custom-made dance mat (or MAT) that contains 12 step panels. The mechanics of the test are the same as the original version of the CSRT, however, visual stimuli are presented on the LCD monitor and the user is expected to step accordingly on respective positions on the MAT (see Figure 4). In this work, the MAT showed high correlations with the laboratory-based measure of the CSRT test. Also, the ability to reliably differentiate between fallers and non-fallers was also confirmed. However, one of the pitfalls of this work is that the use of the Dance Mat still imposes an obstacle on the degree of freedom and does not allow for the collection of spatial parameters.

In [16], the authors introduced StepKinnection™, a system that uses the Microsoft Kinect's depth and motion capture technology to measure stepping performance through the use of a hybrid version of the Choice Stepping Reaction Time (CSRT) task. In this system, the person stands in front of a computer screen or TV connected to a Kinect PC. The representation of the player in the system is pair of shoes mirroring the person's feet movements (see Figure 2). Six symmetrically distributed square-shaped virtual panels are drawn on the screen representing the step panels surrounding the person. The mechanics of the test are the same as the original version of the CSRT with the exception that the person steps in space (see Figure 3).

User's actions such as a 'step' or a 'foot liftoff' are recognized by translating the user's lower limb movements obtained by the Kinect's depth sensor into the game-like platform. The system continuously retrieves spatial data (or skeleton frames) to determine whether a foot is intersecting one of the virtual panels. When the intersection of a foot and one panel is detected, the system records this action along with a timestamp. These actions are subsequently used for the calculation of the following time-based variables which are essential in the completion of the CSRT test: (1) Decision Time (DT): time elapsed between the instance where the sector turns green and the player lifts his/her foot off the central panel, (2) Movement Time (MT): time it takes for the user to step on a coloured sector once leg movement is initiated; (3) Response time (RT): Decision Time (DT) + Movement Time (MT). In addition to this, complementary spatial parameters are also captured for a more descriptive assessment of fall risk. These are: (1) Active Foot Positioning (AFP): (x,y,z) coordinates of the user's foot when stepping on a panel; (2) Observed Step Length (SL): distance between left and right foot while stepping on a panel; (3) Stepping Accuracy Coefficient (SAC): Difference between expected step length and observed step length.

The ability to collect these measures simultaneously makes this system potentially useful in a clinical setting as it can evaluate several dimensions involved in the assessment of fall risk in older people. However, since the Kinect is a camera-based device restricted to process 30 skeleton frames per second, the accuracy of the mentioned time-based measurements needs further evaluation.

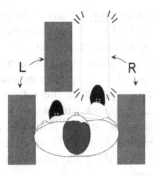

Fig. 1. Original version of the Choice Stepping Reaction Time (CSRT) test [14]

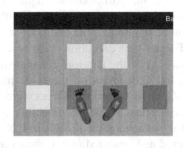

Fig. 3. Mechanics of Kinect-based CSRT Test [16]

Fig. 2. Interaction with the Kinect-based CSRT test [16]

Fig. 4. MAT version of the CSRT Test [15]

Furthermore, the work presented in this paper focuses on the assessment of Kinect's capabilities for perform the CSRT test. This study aims to find out whether the limitation imposed by the frame rate is determinant when collecting time-based measurements associated to human movements. The following section sets out the methodology used for this evaluation.

3   Methodology

A convenient sample of 10 individuals was recruited. Participants consisted of research students and lecturers from the University Technology Sydney. The eligibility criteria are described as follows: (1) Not contributed to the design of these instruments. (2) Able to walk independently without assistance, and (3) Fluent in the English language.

Participants were asked to perform the CSRT test on both systems. The order was randomized to counterbalance order effects. Prior to testing on the Kinect, each participant went through a calibration process in order to determine the proper floor plane[1] and the participant's height[2]. For both systems, participants were given a practice trial in order to familiarize with the mechanics of the test and to confirm the fully understanding of the instructions. Later, they were instructed to complete a full CSRT task where execution of the test was recorded by the corresponding controlling software. Once the test was completed, they were asked to complete a practice trial and a full CSRT task on the other platform. In this experiment, the software that controls the MAT and the Kinect were run in the same computer to minimize bias in the measurements due to variability in computational power. As instructed in the original version of the CSRT test, the mean Reaction Time (RT) of 20 trials is measured and analyzed. Also, the mean Decision Time (DT) and Movement Time (MT) were examined for a more descriptive assessment.

In order to determine the validity of the Kinect-based CSRT, this evaluation was conducted in two steps. Firstly, the consistency and association of the three parameters (DT, MT and RT) per participant per panel was assessed. Shapiro-Wilk test was utilized to assess the distribution of the time-based variables. The consistency and association of the three parameters (DT, MT and RT) were assessed by calculating the Pearson Correlation Coefficient and the Intraclass Correlation Coefficient model 3,1. Secondly, the RT values were used to compute the CSRT test for both the Kinect and MAT and a similar analysis was then conducted.

4   Results

Regarding to the consistency of the Reaction Times (RTs), the Shapiro-Wilk test showed normality across the log transformed time-based measures of the CSRT (Sig. > 0.05). The Pearson Correlation Coefficient showed high association between the values collected by Kinect and the MAT (Pearson r = .746) (Refer to Table 1). Likewise, the ICC model 3,1 confirmed the consistency and agreement of the RT values across the samples (ICC Single Measures = .657, Average Measures= .793, Sig = .000).

Regarding the consistency of the Decision Times (DT) and Movement Times (MT), complementary parameters computed on the MAT version of the CSRT test; the Pearson r analysis determined that the DT values were highly correlated; however, the MT values reported a poor association. (Refer to Table 1). Finally, the Choice Stepping Reaction Time (CSRT) test was calculated for both the Kinect and MAT as instructed in its original version. The Pearson r analysis showed high association between the CSRT values obtained by the Kinect and the MAT (Refer to Table 2). Similarly, the ICC model 3,1 confirmed the consistency and agreement between the CSRT measures computed with the Kinect and the MAT. (ICC Single Measures = .645, Average Measures= .784, Sig .016).

---

[1] To minimize bias in data collection due uneven surfaces or placing the Kinect on a slightly tilted table, a short calibration sequence was incorporated to determine the orientation of the actual floor plane (or ground).

[2] The participants' height is also measures and used to determine the distance of the panels (in this paper known as Expected Step Length). This makes the test equally challenging for audiences as panels are dynamically located based on the user's height which also takes away the limitation of the original test where the step panels are fixed.

Table 1. Correlation of Timing Variables (per Panel)

System	Panel	Outcome	Pearson r
Kinect-Mat	LF	DT	.6110
		MT	.2100
		RT	**.7320**
	LL	DT	.4350
		MT	.1230
		RT	**.7550**
	RF	DT	.7930
		MT	.7060
		RT	**.7980**
	RR	DT	.7030
		MT	.1570
		RT	**.7680**

Table 2. Correlation of CSRT, MT and DT

System	Outcome	Pearson r
Kinect-Mat	**CSRT**	**.7875**
	MT	.3329
	DT	.6430

5   Discussion

This study shows that our Kinect-based system is able to compute the Choice Stepping Reaction Time (CSRT) task. Timing variables such as Decision Time (DT), Movement Time (MT) and Reaction Time (RT) were analised to assess the capabilities of the Kinect to reliably perform a time-based clinical test. The variability of the reaction times was assessed and reported to be equivalently distributed in the Kinect and the MAT. Correlations between the Kinect and the MAT were high for RT suggesting that the Kinect could fulfill the requirements of the CSRT Test. In regards to the DT and MT values, the former showed high correspondence between the two systems whereas the latter reported a poor correlation. It is likely that the MT value did not agree completely due to the lack of precision in detecting the initiation of the user's leg movement. In the Mat this is determined by absence of pressure on the step panels whereas in the Kinect is determined by the location of the foot in relation to the virtual panels. The latter could have been affected by delays in the Kinect output data or the limitation imposed by the frame rate at what the Kinect operates at. In spite of this, the RT values were utilized to compute measure of the CSRT task. Statistical analysis and correlation demonstrated that Kinect measure of the CSRT confidently agreed with the CSRT values computed by the MAT. In addition to this, the data presented show that RT for the Kinect was overall shorter than for the MAT as shown in Figure 5, suggesting that this test might be slightly less cognitively demanding. It is likely that the immersive nature of this system and the appropriate provision of real-time feedback remove the extra processing time required to operate with the MAT (where stimuli are presented on the screen and the execution is expected to happen on the dance mat). Alternatively, participants may have felt more confident to step faster in space due to the absence of wearable sensors or a physical apparatus.

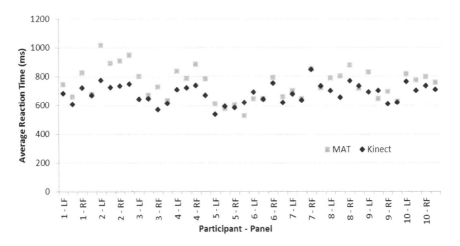

Fig. 5. Comparison between Average Reaction Times obtained with the Kinect and the MAT per Participant per Panel

6   Conclusion and Future Work

This paper describes an evaluation where we assessed the ability of a Kinect-based system to reliably perform the Choice Stepping Reaction Time (CSRT) task. This study involves a technical assessment where the Kinect time-based measurements were compared with a validated reaction time device that has proved to reliably discriminate between fallers and non-fallers. The results showed high association between the Reaction Times (RT) and Decision Times (DT) values obtained in both systems. Movement Time (MT) however did not show agreement most likely for the limitations in determining the initiation of the user's leg movement. Finally, RT values were utilized to compute the CSRT test in order to assess the responsiveness of the system. Statistical analysis showed that both systems correlate favorably, suggesting that the Kinect system might be valid and reliable. More importantly, this evaluation suggests that this Kinect-based system has the potential to be used in a clinical setting as it can consistently measure both spatial and time based parameters required for the fulfillment of a validated clinical test. Yet, the system's capability to reliably discriminate between fallers and non-fallers still requires further evaluation. The next stage of this study will involve the clinical validation of the step parameters, followed by the conduction of controlled trials to determine the ability of the system to discriminate between groups of fallers and non-fallers.

References

1. Chen, S.-T., Huang, Y.-G., Chiang, I.-T.: Using somatosensory video games to promote quality of life for the elderly with disabilities. In: 2012 IEEE Fourth International Conference on Digital Game and Intelligent Toy Enhanced Learning (DIGITEL), pp. 258–262. IEEE (2012)

2. Dutta, A., Banerjee, A., Dutta, A.: Low-cost visual postural feedback with Wii Balance Board and Microsoft Kinect-a feasibility study. In: 2013 IEEE Point-of-Care Healthcare Technologies (PHT), pp. 291–294. IEEE (2013)

3. Dutta, T.: Evaluation of the Kinect^{TM} sensor for 3-D kinematic measurement in the workplace. Applied Ergonomics 43(4), 645–649 (2012)

4. Ganesan, S., Anthony, L.: Using the kinect to encourage older adults to exercise: A prototype. In: Proceedings of the 2012 ACM Annual Conference Extended Abstracts on Human Factors in Computing Systems Extended Abstracts, pp. 2297–2302. ACM (2012)

5. Garcia, J.A., Pisan, Y., Tan, C.T., et al.: Step kinnection: A hybrid clinical test for fall risk assessment in older adults. In: CHI 2014 Extended Abstracts on Human Factors in Computing Systems, pp. 471–474. ACM, Toronto (2014)

6. Gerling, K., Livingston, I., Nacke, L., et al.: Full-body motion-based game interaction for older adults. In: Proceedings of the 2012 ACM Annual Conference on Human Factors in Computing Systems, pp. 1873–1882. ACM (2012)

7. John, M., et al.: SmartSenior's interactive trainer - development of an interactive system for a home-based fall-prevention training for elderly people. In: Wichert, R., Eberhardt, B. (eds.) Ambient Assisted Living. ATSC, vol. 2, pp. 305–316. Springer, Heidelberg (2012)

8. Kayama, H., Okamoto, K., Nishiguchi, S., et al.: Concept Software Based on Kinect for Assessing Dual-Task Ability of Elderly People. GAMES FOR HEALTH: Research, Development, and Clinical Applications 1(5), 348–352 (2012)

9. Kepski, M., Kwolek, B.: Fall detection on embedded platform using kinect and wireless accelerometer. In: Miesenberger, K., Karshmer, A., Penaz, P., Zagler, W. (eds.) ICCHP 2012, Part II. LNCS, vol. 7383, pp. 407–414. Springer, Heidelberg (2012)

10. Kim, J., Son, J., Ko, N., et al.: Unsupervised Virtual Reality-Based Exercise Program Improves Hip Muscles Strength and Balance Control in the Elderly: A Pilot Study. Archives of Physical Medicine and Rehabilitation (2012)

11. Lohmann, O., Luhmann, T., Hein, A.: Skeleton Timed Up and Go. In: 2012 IEEE International Conference on Bioinformatics and Biomedicine (BIBM), pp. 1–5. IEEE (2012)

12. Lord, S.R., Fitzpatrick, R.C.: Choice Stepping Reaction Time: A Composite Measure of Falls Risk in Older People. Journals of Gerontology Series A: Biological Sciences & Medical Sciences 56A(10), M627 (2001)

13. Parajuli, M., Dat, T., Wanli, M., et al.: Senior health monitoring using Kinect. In: 2012 Fourth International Conference on Communications and Electronics, ICCE (2012)

14. Schoene, D., Lord, S.R., Verhoef, P., et al.: A novel video game–based device for measuring stepping performance and fall risk in older people. Archives of Physical Medicine and Rehabilitation 92(6), 947–953 (2011)

15. Stone, E.E., Skubic, M.: Evaluation of an inexpensive depth camera for in-home gait assessment. Journal of Ambient Intelligence and Smart Environments 3(4), 349–361 (2011)

16. Stone, E.E., Skubic, M.: Evaluation of an inexpensive depth camera for passive in-home fall risk assessment. In: 2011 5th International Conference on Pervasive Computing Technologies for Healthcare (PervasiveHealth), pp. 71–77. IEEE (2011)

Code Your Own Game: The Case of Children with Hearing Impairments

Michail N. Giannakos and Letizia Jaccheri

Department of Computer and Information Science, Norwegian University of Science and Technology (NTNU), Trondheim, Norway
mgiannakos@acm.org, letizia@idi.ntnu.no

Abstract. It is well known in the computer science community that is important to encourage children to acquire coding skills and become creators of their own experiences and not only mere game consumers. Different children have different needs when approaching coding and making activities. Specifically, Deaf and Hard of Hearing (DHH) children, even when provided with accessible visual translations through sign language interpreters or real-time captions, need customized support. In our approach we have designed, implemented, and evaluated a workshop program of 12 children total, with the final goal of exploring and improving the design of appropriate workshops using the current learning environments. This paper presents an initial exploratory evaluation of a coding experience for children with hearing impairments and the development of a set of guidelines for improving the teaching of coding to children with DHH difficulties. An initial set of best practices was first developed through a focus group with experts; and afterwards, by employing content analysis, a revised set of guidelines was obtained. The results should be useful for special education teachers, curriculum designers and developers for K-12 education environments for DHH.

Keywords: Accessibility, Coding, Design Guidelines, Deaf, Hearing Impairments, Empirical Evaluation, Focus Groups, Games, Programming, Workshops.

1 Introduction

Currently, several efforts to broaden participation in programming and introduce computational literacy to young students [2], [9] are in progress. Children interact with visual programming tools like Scratch [14] to learn how to code by creating interactive stories, games, animations, and simulations. Sesame workshop [15] has given new insights into how programming for children needs to be approached; in order to be both educational and entertaining. The process for achieving this mix relies on a development model that integrates expertise in media production, educational content (or curriculum), and research with children. Sesame Workshop philosophy [15] identify some of the challenges and solutions in designing interactive educational activities that can be used by children. Buechley et al. [2] argue that there

Y. Pisan et al. (Eds.): ICEC 2014, LNCS 8770, pp. 108–116, 2014.

is a need to make children programming a far more informal, approachable, and natural activity.

Although, programming activities for children have drawn great interest in the last years, little information is available on how to introduce computational literacy to young students taking into account children with special needs and impairments. Children with disabilities face certain difficulties with the current approaches and methods to learn programming [3], [4], [10]. In particular, children with Deaf and Hard of Hearing (DHH) encounter challenges when learning how to code. Teachers and curriculum designers need to be aware and pay particular attention in these challenges.

In this paper, we present our experience from a game coding workshop focusing on children with DHH. With the knowledge extracted from this experience we aim to explore how design and technology can contribute to improve current learning practices for the benefit of children with DHH. This paper focuses on our efforts to develop a coding workshop that will allow DHH children to overcome their difficulties and explore their potential interest in game development and coding. Hence, we provide some first insights on: *How to design environments for facilitating coding for children with hearing impairments?*

In our efforts to investigate how game coding workshops could be designed to allow DHH children to overcome their difficulties, we designed, implemented, and evaluated a workshop program of 12 children with DHH. After the workshop, we organized a focus group with experts in DHH in order to capture their ideas and experiences with regard to the game coding workshop. Next, we employed a content analysis technique [11] in order to organize the data. As the final step of the process we used the structured data and derived guidelines for improving the design of the game coding workshop that address DHH difficulties.

2   Background

DHH is an impairment that can result from many reasons at different ages. DHH Children are a challenging target group for designers [8] [10]. Not only because it is harder to design environments for children rather than adults [9], but the fact that these children have DHH creates even more designing particularities. Most children today have hearing aid or a cochlear implant, but they do have special communication needs. In fact they can communicate orally, but only to a certain extent [12]. Often they miss a fluent mother tongue, which results in a lack of written and spoken language skills [12]. The primary form of communication within the deaf children is the sign language [1]. Sign language is not a visual form of the respective language (in our case Norwegian) but it is a different language with its own unique grammatical and syntactical structure.

Therefore, the lack of written and spoken language skills, which is common in children with DHH, has an impact on how they can be involved in different learning contexts [10] and therefore how these contexts can be designed.

This design of learning (in our case programming) environments to support children with special needs (in our case DHH) comes with additional challenges. For example, there are diverse stakeholders (e.g., special educators, designers, DHH experts) that need to be involved in the design of these environments and technologies, and from the children themselves and their families. Likewise, educators, researchers and practitioners with a variety of expertise need to work together to develop practical solutions with a chance of succeeding in realistic contexts.

3   Game Coding Experience

Twelve 12-year old children with DHH from the Deaf school of Trondheim in Norway participated in the game coding workshop. The workshop took part in the Norwegian Deaf Museum (see figure 1, for the context of the workshop). The schedule, the infrastructures and the main goal of the workshop were based from knowledge we obtained from prior similar experience [5] [6].

Fig. 1. The context of the game coding workshop

In particular, the children attended the workshops were instructed and assisted by a programming artist with an interpreter and during the workshop children worked with the Scratch programming environment. In order to better organize the workshop we closely collaborate with six experts (see table 1), which, after observing the workshop, responded to a survey and formed up a focus group. In selecting the experts, we focused on people's professional expertise in the domains of DHH, children and education.

Table 1. Participants and their expertise

Participants and their expertise	
Norwegian Deaf Museum Curator	Norwegian Deaf Museum Director of Education
Trondheim Deaf School teacher	Trondheim Deaf School teacher
Artist-Instructor Programmer	HCI researcher

Throughout the workshop, children worked in dyads and developed in total six interactive projects. Children worked collaboratively with the assistance of the visual programming language (see figure 2); record of children's activities was kept through photographs, videos, observation-reports and surveys from the experts; this information was used to evaluate the workshop and as an input experience for the next phase of the study.

Fig. 2. Children worked collaboratively and communicate with the assistance of the visual programming language

One of the goals of our study is to perform an exploratory evaluation of the game coding workshop and justify the special attention needed for children with DHH difficulties. As such, we used a quantitative survey-based approach. The survey was handed out to the six experts after the workshop and included the measures (factors) of children's: a) Enjoyment, b) Control and c) Easiness with respect to the programming workshop. In particular, the six experts were asked to rate, on a 7-point scale survey: a) how children seemed to enjoy the workshop, b) how much control of the workshop children had, and c) how easy was the workshop for children. Each one of the three factors was measured based on the literature with 2 or 3 questions (see Figure 3).

- The child seemed to enjoy programming during the workshop (Enj1)
- The child seemed interested in actively exploring programming in the workshop (Enj2)
- The child seemed entertained by the workshop in general (Enj3)
- The child was able to follow the tasks of the workshop (Cont1)
- The child has the skills and the ability to follow the tasks of the workshop (Cont2)
- The workshop was easy for the child (Easy1)
- The workshop was flexible for the child (Easy2)
- The concept of the workshop was clear and understandable from the child (Easy3)

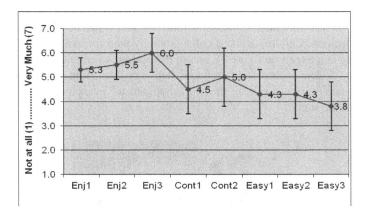

Fig. 3. Experts' responses to 7-point Likert-scale

With the quantitative approach we attempt to investigate DHH children difficulties during a game coding workshop. Based on experts' observations and survey responses (figure 3) we can agree that children enjoyed the workshop, however, their control towards the workshop was low. In addition, experts indicated that children found many concepts of the workshop hard to follow and unclear. Although this game coding workshop has been validated and improved through many user studies (e.g. [5] [6]), there is a lot of work need to be done in order to address DHH needs and justify them through design patterns into the current programming practices and environments.

The findings from the exploratory evaluation clearly demonstrate the need for improving DHH children programming experiences. To do so we need to design more accessible and closer to their needs environments by addressing a variety of visual child-programming environment interactions (e.g. Figure 4). Taking this into account, in the next section we analyze qualitative data in order to give some first insights.

Fig. 4. Child-Programming Environment Interaction with the assistance of the camera

4   Extracted Guidelines via Focus Group and Content Analysis Processes

Building on the experience from the game coding workshop, a focus group consisted of the six experts (see table 1 above) brainstormed and organized ideas and best practices for improving programming activities design. Using a focus group enables a wide variety of collective views and often leads to results based on a consensus among participants [11].

Content analysis is a technique used to categorize data (e.g., interviews, ideas) through a protocol. Content analysis enables the researchers to sift through large volumes of data and systematically identify properties, attributes and patterns embedded. The technique is considered useful for identifying and analyzing issues in gathered data [11]. In order to investigate how the experts' advices and best practices could be specifically relevant for children, the content analysis connected those, with three central "design" components for children [7]: *approach*, *settings* and *means*.

In particular, based on [7] 1) approach category was defined as all the attitudes and acts that professionals should aim to perform in order to contribute to a successful workshop; 2) settings category includes all the preconditions that help children enroll with the workshop more willingly and 3) means category includes the best practices referring to the concrete needs methods and materials.

The best practices and ideas of the experts could be relevant for several purposes, as such it was considered useful to sort them in a more generic way under the aforementioned three categories (see table 2).

Table 2. The extracted guidelines under the three main categories and the justification-example

Categories	Guidelines	Justification-Example
Approach	Follow children learning	Instructor should wait the interpreter to finish, give enough time to children to read information and repeat when children do not follow the instructions (as many times as needed).
	Use personal approach	The instructor should treat every child uniquely, and consider his/her individual difficulties. The instructor should keep eye contact with all the children to ensure that they are following him.
	Provide practical information	Reduce the amount of the provided information, by focusing to the practical information. Support the recall of communication patterns rather than building new ones and provide few but distinct choices to the child.
Settings	Different sessions with clear goals	The workshop should be well-structured with different and clear (IT-programming) competencies on each session and many breaks between the sessions.
	Very well prepared interpreters	Interpreters and instructors need to work together in advance, in order to reduce potential difficulties in communication and the vocabulary (sign language vocabulary is limited). Interpreters need to have some knowledge in the field (e.g., programming).
Means	Many, clear and big visual aids	Big screens, projectors and other visual aids are essential on assisting children communication (e.g., on figure 1 the big screen behind the instructor). Text should have clear large headings, and different notions should be distinguished with different colors and shapes.
	Support children-computer interaction via visual tools	Children-computer (program) interaction should be supported with various visual means. For instance children-program interaction through the web-camera (figure 4) motivates them to optimize their code.

5   Conclusions and the Way Ahead

In this paper we presented the results from the design, deployment and evaluation of a game coding workshop for children with DHH. Our results provide an initial attempt to exploit knowledge from experts in DHH and model this knowledge into useful guidelines for designers and developers who aim to address children with DHH as participants of programming learning workshop. Our research is characterized by a close collaboration between special educators, HCI researchers, and DHH experts. The study described in this paper has led to a set of guidelines for designing programming learning activities for children with DHH. The guidelines were backed by addressed experts' ideas and best practices and has been exposed to several stages of validation and organization (focus group, content analysis), which should provide some assurance of their validity. Based on this, seven design guidelines under three main categories have been proposed.

We want to emphasize that our findings are clearly preliminary with inevitably limitations. One important limitation is the absence of children's voices in this work. However, capturing, crossing and analyzing the experiences of the six experts allow us to portray design issues derived from hundreds of workshop sessions and teaching hours. Our future research will concentrate on further refinement of the proposed guidelines by applying and evaluating them on real conditions. Furthermore, educators, practitioners and researchers in the areas of 1) technology-enhanced STEM learning and 2) children with DHH should evaluate the proposed guidelines in order to ensure their understanding and seek suggestions and extensions. In the next step of this ongoing project we will continue our research with evaluating these guidelines with a mixed methods approach, and aim to improve and optimize them.

Acknowledgements. The authors would like to express their gratitude to all of the students for volunteering their time. Our very special thanks go to A. Eriksen, H. Mellemsether and L. Nordsveen.

References

1. Borgna, G., et al.: Enhancing deaf students' learning from sign language and text: Metacognition, modality, and the effectiveness of content scaffolding. Journal of Deaf Studies and Deaf Education 16(1), 79–100 (2011)
2. Buechley, L., Eisenberg, M., Catchen, J., Crockett, A.: The LilyPadArduino: Using computational textiles to investigate engagement, aesthetics, and diversity in computer science education. In: CHI 2008, pp. 423–432. ACM (2008)
3. Deibel, K.: Studying our inclusive practices: Course experiences of students with disabilities. In: ITiCSE 2007, pp. 266–270. ACM Press (2007)
4. Gellenbeck, E.: Integrating accessibility into the computer science curriculum. Journal of Computing Sciences in Colleges 21(1), 267–273 (2005)
5. Giannakos, M.N., Jaccheri, L.: An Enriched Artifacts Activity for Supporting Creative Learning: Perspectives for Children with Impairments. In: Anacleto, J.C., Clua, E.W.G., da Silva, F.S.C., Fels, S., Yang, H.S. (eds.) ICEC 2013. LNCS, vol. 8215, pp. 160–163. Springer, Heidelberg (2013)
6. Giannakos, M.N., Jaccheri, L.: Designing creative activities for children: The importance of collaboration and the threat of losing control. In: IDC 2013, pp. 336–339. ACM (2013)
7. Høiseth, M., Giannakos, M.N., Jaccheri, L.: Research-derived guidelines for designing toddlers' healthcare games. In: EA CHI 2013, pp. 451–456. ACM (2008)
8. Brashear, H., Henderson, V., Park, K., Hamilton, H., Lee, S., Starner, T.: American sign language recognition in game development for deaf children. In: ACM SIGACSEE 2006, pp. 79–86. ACM Press (2006)

9. Jacobs, J., Buechley, L.: Codeable objects: Computational design and digital fabrication for novice programmers. In: CHI 2013, pp. 1589–1598. ACM Press (2013)

10. Liffick, B.W.: An adaptive technologies course in a CS curriculum. In: ACM SIGACCESS 2005, pp. 192–193. ACM Press (2005)

11. Maguire, M., Bevan, N.: User requirements analysis: A review of supporting methods. In: Hammond, J., Gross, T., Wesson, J. (eds.) IFIP WCC 2002. IFIP, vol. 99, pp. 133–148. Springer, Boston (2002)

12. Moeller, M.P.: Early intervention and language development in children who are deaf and hard of hearing. Pediatrics 106(3) (2000)

13. Nakatsu, R., Rauterberg, M., Vorderer, P.: A new framework for entertainment computing: From passive to active experience. In: Kishino, F., Kitamura, Y., Kato, H., Nagata, N. (eds.) ICEC 2005. LNCS, vol. 3711, pp. 1–12. Springer, Heidelberg (2005)

14. Resnick, M., Maloney, J., et al.: Scratch: Programming for all. Communications of the ACM 52(11), 60–67 (2009)

15. Revelle, G.L.: Educating via entertainment media: The Sesame Workshop approach. Comput. Entertain. 1(1), Art. 7 (2003)

Developing Emergent Play in Collaborative Online Experiences

Damian Hills

UTS Games Studio, University of Technology, Sydney, Australia
damski@assimilate.net

Abstract. This paper will discuss common features of emergent play in the context of developing an online collaborative practice-based research project, *assimilate*. Emergent play features, such as development of fictional worlds will be identified, followed by a discussion of player experience of emergent play. The paper proposes an system framework that invites narrative emergent play facilitated by a set of clearly defined and simplified affordances that provide recognisable metaphors for collaboration.

Keywords: Interaction Design, Creativity Support Tool, Interactive Digital Storytelling, Narrative Intelligence, Conversational Information System, Cybernetics.

1 Introduction

Recent developments [1] in web application technology have developed appropriate research areas for experimentation in emergent play. The technology has allowed for server architectures to asynchronously support rich interface to develop new and interesting entertainment platforms. This is of special interest to developers and researchers interested in novel experiments for emergent play and collaboration.

This paper will discuss common features of emergent play in the context of developing an online collaborative practice-based research project, assimilate [2]. (Figure 1).

Fig. 1. Assimilate interface

The project is a software design for collaborative narrative construction adapted from previous designs for online collaboration. Emergent play features, such as

Y. Pisan et al. (Eds.): ICEC 2014, LNCS 8770, pp. 117–124, 2014.

development of fictional worlds will be discussed, followed by a discussion of player experience of emergent play. Finally, an outline of the project with appropriate analysis of how these features are applicable.

2   Interface

Emergence in games is considered a fundamental game feature where collections of simple rules gives rise to new variations on behavior or outcomes. [3] In the context of play within games and other interactive media including playable games [4], emergence is considered the most appealing of designs. As it allows for such narrative possibilities as re-playability and player generated creativity with full agency and immersive qualities.

Given the established problems with narrative and player agency [5] researchers are identifying common design features that generate emergent play. These can be considered applicable to both games and play, as the notable differences in how a narrative coherence is generated, either directed by top down processes, such as a drama management [6] or a bottom-up driven experience with the latter as the design goal of most desirability.

Two notable features will be discussed here, firstly the identification of boundaries that develop narrative coherence including fictional worlds, story worlds or contextual frames that place limits on emergence. Following this, the player experience of narrative emergence and possible solutions to maintaining collaborative engagement through an improvisational play.

2.1   Fictional World Coherence

Researchers of emergent narrative and play for digital experiences identify the development of the fictional world as basis for developing player or character based generated narratives. The experience of narrative differs greatly to the perception of narrative within films. For example, temporal events in games connects the play time, or discourse of the narrative (the sequence of events) directly with fictional time, or how the events are told [7]. Game narrative becomes problematic when presenting fictional time in any achronological order commonly seen in films or fiction. Narrative is rather a direct consequence of player action and not perceived as the action evolves. This paradox of narrative comprehension in games has shifted research into understanding how narrative emergence may develop directly in fictional worlds.

Games excel at the development of fictional worlds providing player agency and emergent play [8] with rich story-building features constructed by player activities. They contain spatial metaphors that develop narrative possibilities suggesting interfaces may play a prominent role in player developed narratives. Fictional world metaphors are linked with aspects of the real world that exhibit recognisable, familiar activities and also places boundaries on context. Defining contextual boundaries [9] contains the possibility space for emergence and maintains coherence through limitation. For a consistent and coherent world this is necessity as the link between emergent play, story and social world is deeply intertwined [10]. A play boundary in this case may just be an implicit or innate agreement on how to act, such as a 'magic circle' [11] or player attitude [12] or by placing specific design limitations on behavior to contain emergence [13].

Fictional worlds that aim for coherence should be designed to develop implicit events [14] rather than explicitly authoring sequences that will potentially exhaust the system of interesting outcomes. A good example of this can be seen in Minecraft [15], a successful player driven fictional world where activities mirror aspects of real world construction. However the true success of the Minecraft experience is largely dependant on social aspects of co-creativity and community engagement. For this reason, emergent fictional worlds need the drivers of collaboration and community to develop creative potential.

2.2   Player Experience and Participation

The narrative paradox as outlined by [16] and others suggests emergent play and narrative would benefit from a character based model where specific behaviors may be interpreted by the player and a narrative induced from these collective environmental cues. This presents further issues in maintaining narrative comprehension as it requires the active involvement of the player in the experience.

Players of emergent experiences are heavily dependant on the act of co-creation and collaboration for emergent narrative to be recognised at a macro level. Such an experience would require the player to act in similar ways to an improvisational actor with some understanding of narrative consequences based on actions of themselves and others. This has been discussed [17] [18] [19] and further evaluated as a possible scenario [20] of emergent development of interactive digital narrative. The findings conclude that actors develop shared mental models and cognitive converge over specific dramatic performances that drive narrative forward.

Cognitive patterns such as these could be useful for understanding design for emergent play with actors who have the appropriate concern for the mutual progression of the narrative scenario. However the issue is that players are generally not trained as improvisational actors nor are they necessarily open to cues for collaboration. For design of emergent play, providing these cues can equip players with the tools they need to perform more like actors sensitive to the narrative context at hand. As such, developing interface metaphors that describe or explain the simple actions possible in the fictional environment in contrast with the familiar actions in the real world, can demonstrate how to act accordingly. This type of metaphor can also be described as an affordance [21] and provides an innate understanding of how to perform within the environment.

Players perceive affordances they see in the fictional world and understand them through the affordances they commonly associate with the real world [22]. In other words, they import the knowledge from their interaction of the real environment to understand how to act in the fictional world. This is akin to a conversation where embodiment, or innate knowledge of how the body acts within the world, can be transferred or hybridised with the game world. This notion of an innate affordance stems from the theory of situated and embodied cognition [23] [24], that states our bodies share in part responsibility for the way we comprehend the environment. This theory has already had some impact in the fields of human-computer interface (HCI) [25] and is further discussed for its applicability to game play and player experience [22] [26] [27]. Situated cognition also has interesting implications for emergent game design and especially relates to aspects of interaction design and online player experiences. Researchers are evaluating the possibility of developing appropriate interface mechanics to enhance emergent play and narrative [28] [29]. Designing appropriate affordances will encourage players to perform more like actors and develop a level of collaborative engagement that produces more variations of behavior and novel outcomes. Further studies into motivations and aspects of play-style with emergent games [30] would also further techniques on how to develop such affordances.

3   Emergent Model – Assimilate

The following section presents the application of emergent play features for the assimilate system. The description includes an understanding of boundaries in narrative context and fictional world construction, followed by a holistic view of player experience with emergence and how interface mechanics support this collaboration for online deployment.

3.1   Developing Coherence with Simple Rules

The model [31] is based on Conversation Theory (CT) [32], a cybernetic theory of learning and social interaction, that self-organises a set thematic relationships based on group conversation with eventual agreement on the context and meanings. As is applicable to an emergent system, relationships are arranged from simple rules or formalisms that scale into larger networks of meaning and may be combined or pruned through player participation. These networks, known as entailment meshes [33] (Fig 2.), are based on a simple formalism such that each concept is interdependent on at least two others.

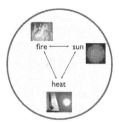

Fig. 2. Cyclic entailment relationship

The most fundamental mesh would consists of three concepts, with every concept drawing its meaning based on its relationship to the other two. With all three exhibiting this relationship, this is said to achieve coherence within the CT theory. Coherence in this case meaning a participant can begin with any concept in the mesh and shift procedurally through the relationships in any arbitrary direction while developing an understanding of the assembled themes. This freedom to shift within an assembled concept network provides numerous entry points or cyclicity, such that there are no 'dead ends' in the entailment structure. When entailment networks are scaled or merged through collaborative action this provides the flexibility in the narrative structure and allows each participant to formulate their own point of view while developing a mental model that others may share based on their own actions within the network.

3.2   Interface Metaphors for Emergent Conversation

Emergent play experiences can directly benefit from collaborative experiences and the development of schemes for co-creation of artifacts within the fictional world that build community and social development.

For online play experiences the boundaries of context in the fictional space are embedded in the metaphors of the interface. This extends the conversational process and shows aspects of intention surrounding the collective narrative construction [34].

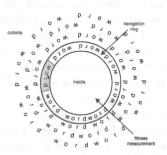

Fig. 3. Fitness measurement

Interface metaphors can support narrative comprehension and fictional world coherence through reflecting actions that are recognisable by other players and through revealing features of the system's inner processes.

Each player begins the experience by opening a 'ring' space and inputting a keyword that performs an internet search request. Retrieved video content circles the ring along with an associated annotated word tag. Salient or 'fit' tags (Fig 3.) are placed inside the ring and associated video content plays out within the ringed space in a sequence.

Tags that are outside the ring may be selected and dragged inside forming new sequences. The ring exhibits a physics model that responds to gestural movement, that may be expanded or reduced to narrow the amount of sequenced content.

Furthermore, each player's ring may be merged with others to form new combined sequences.

These interface mechanics are considered metaphors for narrative construction and maintain common recognizable aspects of conversation associated with storytelling, as such scope, exchanging views and merging ideas. (Fig. 4) These are either performed intentionally or inadvertently through the mechanics or player actions to produce dramatic or unexpected outcomes, a common feature of narrative emergence.

Fig. 4. Narrative Metaphors

The player rings are considered as agents in the experience that attempt to incorporate participants' creative actions and also show the self-organising conversational process. This is an attempt to visualise the system process, a form of expressive processing [35] that develops the relationship between system processes and the surface level interaction of the players. This relationship is central to idea of developing emergent play as it provides affordances to the player for enacting a conversation. In similar ways to enabling a group of improvisational actors, it exhibits clues on how actions are taking place in the fictional world and invites collaboration. This allows the player to enact a conversation with the fictional world and assume a dynamic role of narrator, player or observer.

The general approach to the interface and its incorporation with the system processes, looks to holistic paradigm for how mental models and cognitive convergence can take place. While he system formalises some narrative structure through self-organisation, the interface metaphors allow for creative possibilites. The combination of the fictional world, the interface affordances and the understanding of the player's mental model in relationship to the other players creates the possibility for an emergence to take place.

4   Discussion

This paper has presented a view of emergent play that considers players experience of real world knowledge to develop appropriate fictional world affordances. Our comprehension of the real world is a continual sense-making process that accumulates knowledge from the world based on our bodily relationship to the world. This takes into account a holistic view of how emergence occurs in the real world and its possible application in game worlds to drive narrative coherence.

A study of situated and embodied cognition can provide design clues for how players may perceive certain affordances. One such view explains how our tendency to side with simple narrative explanations for complex emergent behavior. However there is an inherent disconnect between the causal relationships at the emergent level, and the eventual narrative that is extracted [36]. From this view the possibility is that layering top down approaches, such as drama management over the emergent behavioral layer (agent behaviors) only serves to replace or simplify a chaotic system of possible micro-stories rendering the system sparse of creative possibilities.

One possible solution suggested in the paper is an interface that invites play as an improvisational actor with shared goals that are developed by visible and real embodied action of the players. This is facilitated by a set of clearly defined and simplified affordances that provide recognisable metaphors for collaboration.

In terms of narrative generation, this system model is clearly hit and miss and may not be applicable for a game market that requires player expectations to be met in most, if not all circumstances. However with online web applications this is perhaps not such a great requirement as players attitudes to gaming may very well shift with respect to browser based and casual games. For this reason emergence in online web applications may provide an interesting area for further research.

References

1. Marrin, C.: Webgl specification. Khronos WebGL Working Group (2011)
2. Hills, D., Van, T., Edmonds, E., Knight, A.: Collaborative Systems for Narrative Construction (2011)
3. Juul, J.: The Open and the Closed: Games of Emergence and Games of Progression (2006)
4. Ryan, M.-L.: From Narrative Games to Playable Stories: Toward a Poetics of Interactive Narrative. StoryWorlds: A Journal of Narrative Studies 1, 43–59 (2009)
5. Louchart, S., Aylett, R.: Emergent narrative, requirements and high-level architecture. In: Proceedings of the 3rd Hellenic Conference (2004)
6. Swartjes, I., Theune, M.: A Fabula Model for Emergent Narrative. In: Göbel, S., Malkewitz, R., Iurgel, I. (eds.) TIDSE 2006. LNCS, vol. 4326, pp. 49–60. Springer, Heidelberg (2006)
7. Juul, J.: Half-Real: Video Games Between Real Rules and Fictional Worlds. MIT Press (2011)
8. Jenkins, H.: Game design as narrative architecture. Computer (2004)
9. Suttie, N., Louchart, S., Aylett, R., Lim, T.: Theoretical Considerations towards Authoring Emergent Narrative. In: Koenitz, H., Sezen, T.I., Ferri, G., Haahr, M., Sezen, D., Çatak, G. (eds.) ICIDS 2013. LNCS, vol. 8230, pp. 205–216. Springer, Heidelberg (2013)
10. Pearce, C.: A study of emergent behaviour in online games and virtual worlds (2007)
11. Salen, K., Zimmerman, E.: Rules of Play: Game Design Fundamentals. MIT Press (2004)
12. Suits, B., Hurka, T.: The grasshopper: Games, life and utopia (2005)
13. Eladhari, M.P.: AI-Based Game Design: Enabling New Playable Experiences (2011)
14. Spierling, U.: Adding Aspects of "Implicit Creation" to the Authoring Process in Interactive Storytelling. In: Cavazza, M., Donikian, S. (eds.) ICVS 2007. LNCS, vol. 4871, pp. 13–25. Springer, Heidelberg (2007)
15. Persson, M.: Minecraft (2009)

16. Louchart, S., Aylett, R., Kriegel, M., Dias, J.: Authoring emergent narrative-based games. Journal of Game. (2008)
17. Louchart, S., Aylett, R.: Narrative theory and emergent interactive narrative. International Journal of Continuing Engineering Education and Lifelong Learning 14 (2004)
18. Swartjes, I., Theune, M.: An Experiment in Improvised Interactive Drama. In: Nijholt, A., Reidsma, D., Hondorp, H. (eds.) INTETAIN 2009. LNICST, vol. 9, pp. 234–239. Springer, Heidelberg (2009)
19. Fuller, D., Magerko, B.: Shared mental models in improvisational performance. In: Proceedings of the Intelligent Narrative Technologies III Workshop, p. 15. ACM (2010)
20. Magerko, B., Manzoul, W., Riedl, M., Baumer, A., Fuller, D., Luther, K., Pearce, C.: An empirical study of cognition and theatrical improvisation. In: Proceedings of the Seventh ACM Conference on Creativity and Cognition, pp. 117–126. ACM (2009)
21. Gibson, J.: The concept of affordances. Perceiving, acting, and knowing (1977)
22. Gee, J.P.: Video Games and Embodiment. Games and Culture 3, 253–263 (2008)
23. Hutchins, E.: Cognition in the Wild. MIT Press, Cambridge (1995)
24. Clark, A., Chalmers, D.: The Extended Mind. Analysis 58, 7–19 (1998)
25. Dourish, P.: Where the action is: The foundations of embodied interaction (2004)
26. Arjoranta, J.: Understanding Player Interpretation: An Embodied Approach (2013)
27. Rambusch, J.: The embodied and situated nature of computer game play (2006)
28. Freeman, D., La Pierre, N., Chevalier, F., Reilly, D.: Tweetris: A Study of Whole-body Interaction During a Public Art Event. In: Proceedings of the 9th ACM Conference on Creativity & Cognition, pp. 224–233. ACM, New York (2013)
29. Alofs, T., Theune, M., Swartjes, I.: A Tabletop Board Game Interface for Multi- User Interaction with a Storytelling System. In: Camurri, A., Costa, C. (eds.) INTETAIN 2011. LNICST, vol. 78, pp. 123–128. Springer, Heidelberg (2012)
30. Canossa, A.: Give me a Reason to Dig: Qualitative Associations Between Player Behavior in Minecraft and Life Motives (2012)
31. Hills, D.: A Conversational Framework for Emergent Collaborative Storytelling. In: Proceedings of the Intelligent Narrative Technologies III Workshop, pp. 1:1–1:4. ACM, New York (2010)
32. Pask, G.: Conversation, cognition and learning: A cybernetic theory and methodology. Elsevier, Amsterdam (1975)
33. Pask, G.: Conversation theory: Applications in education and epistemology. Elsevier, Amsterdam (1976)
34. Hills, D.: Collaborative Systems for Narrative Construction. In: Edmonds, E., Candy, L. (eds.) Interacting: Art, Research and the Creative Practitioner (2011), http://dora.dmu.ac.uk
35. Wardrip-Fruin, N.: Expressive Processing: On Process-Intensive Literature and Digital Media (2006)
36. Walsh, R.: Emergent Narrative in Interactive Media. Narrative 19, 72–85 (2011)

Race By Hearts

Using Technology to Facilitate Enjoyable and Social Workouts

Tobias Sonne and Mads Møller Jensen

Department of Computer Science, Aarhus University, Denmark
{tsonne,mmjensen}@cs.au.dk

Abstract. In this paper, we explore the qualities of sharing biometric data in real-time between athletes, in order to increase two motivational factors for gym-goers: Enjoyment and social interaction. We present a novel smartphone application, called Race By Hearts, which enables competition based on heart rate data sharing between users in real-time. Through an empirical study conducted in the gym, we show that sharing biometric data in real-time can strengthen social relations between participants, increase motivation, and improve the enjoyment of the fitness activity. Nevertheless, we found that introducing competition based on real-time sharing of biometric data can cause exasperation and discouragement for some athletes. Based on our findings from the study, we discuss how technology can facilitate and modify competition in fitness exercises in general.

Keywords: Exertion interfaces, interactive sport-training systems, biometric feedback, heart rate, wearable computing.

1 Introduction

Convincing oneself to go to the gym can be a hard task. Often people join the gym as a result of a sudden realization that the state of their physical condition was not in alignment with their self-image [2]. However, in the U.S. 67 % of people with a gym membership never use it [11], as they fail to make workouts part of their everyday life due to motivation deficiency. According to Crossley [2], regular gym-goers have a vocabulary of motives that continuously drives them to the gym, including enjoyment and social interaction. This paper seeks to utilize these two motivational factors, as a way to make regular indoor cycling classes more appealing, by enabling indoor cyclists to share biometric data with other cyclists in real-time.

The emergence of smartphone devices and compatible heart rate belts has enabled sports practitioners to measure and share biometric data via sharing networks, such as Runkeeper or Endomondo. The effects of real-time broadcasting of biometric data to social networks have shown to create a stronger tie between practitioners and their friends on social networks as well as to motivate practitioners during sports activities [3]. However, the social and competitive effects of gym-goers interacting through biometric data in real-time have not previously been investigated.

Y. Pisan et al. (Eds.): ICEC 2014, LNCS 8770, pp. 125–132, 2014.
© IFIP International Federation for Information Processing 2014

In this paper, we investigate the effects of introducing technology that facilitates a social interaction through real-time sharing of biometric data in an indoor gym context, thereby enabling competition in an otherwise non-competitive sport setting. We report on a study with 20 indoor cyclists, who were equipped with a smartphone running an application, called Race By Hearts (RBH), that enables interaction between cyclists by dynamically displaying and sharing heart rate (HR) data in real-time.

The results from our studies showed that sharing biometric data facilitates a social relation, motivates indoor cyclists to increase their effort, and improves the enjoyment of the fitness activity. Furthermore, we identified important challenges in terms of exasperation and discouragement, which can occur when introducing a competitive element in an exercise situation. Finally, we discuss how technology can facilitate different kinds of competition in non-competitive sports and change the original opponent format.

1.1 Indoor Cycling

Indoor cycling, also often referred to as spinning, is a high-intensity exercise where indoor cyclists use stationary bikes with adjustable resistance to follow the music and verbal instruction given by an indoor cycling instructor. The instructor instructs the indoor cyclists to adjust the resistance, the riding style (sitting / standing), and the cadence during class. Often the stationary bikes are placed in a half-moon cycle so that the cyclists face the indoor cycling instructor and vice versa. Because the bikes are stationary, heart rate belts and bike-mounted watt displays are the only measures the indoor cyclists can use to monitor their effort level.

The intensity of an indoor cycling class is very dependent on the chosen music, the elements in the particular program planned by the instructor, and instructor's ability to motivate the athletes during the class, which is why no two indoor classes are the same.

2   Related Work

Below we present related research in the area of using technology to improve or enhance enjoyment and social interaction within fitness and exertion games.

The HeartLink project by Curmi et al. is an example of a study investigating the effects of sharing biometric data within the field of sports. Curmi et al. found that sharing real-time biometric data on Facebook strengthened the social tie between athlete and her Facebook friends [3]. Moreover, the study found that athletes were more motivated during the sport event.

Fish'n'Steps is a social computer game, where each participant has a "personal fish" in a virtual aquarium together with other participants' fish [5]. The size of the fish is linked to the amount of steps taken, making it possible for the participants to see how they (their fish) compare to each of the other participants (fish). Being able to see the other participants fish created a stimulating challenge and provided a benchmarking mechanism, which made the participants aware of their comparative performance [5].

Numerous projects within the field of exertion games use HR as an interaction method for controlling games [8,9]. However, most exertion games focus on creating new fitness activities instead of using technology to augment existing fitness activities. Furthermore, common for many exertion games is that the biometric data is not directly shared between players, but instead used as a mechanism to control or balance the games [6].

In [7], Mueller et al. facilitated that spatially distributed joggers could jog together. The work investigates, among other things, how HR from the participants can be used to facilitate a social experience between joggers. Moreover, Walmink et al. have created a bike helmet with a HR display, which resulted in social interplay and increased engagement in the exertion activity [10].

Compared to the presented related work, our focus is on the motivational effects and challenges of using biometric data for interaction in existing fitness activities.

3   The Race By Hearts Smartphone App

To measure and share the individual HR of each participant in an interactive way, we developed an iPhone application called Race By Hearts (RBH). RBH displays HR, intensity level (based on percentage of MAX HR), and current intensity zone for all users in one list, which is shared between all users as seen on Figure 1. The users' positions in the list are dynamic and based on intensity level, where the user with the highest intensity is positioned on top. This enables the users to control their position within the list by adjusting their effort throughout a session. The use of intensity level, instead of HR, provides a natural balancing of the users' efforts. Each user's HR is captured via a Polar H7 heart rate belt, which is parried to RBH through a Bluetooth 4.0 connection.

Fig. 1. Left, RBH interface. *Right*, test setup where an iPhone 5 running RBH is mounted on an indoor bike.

RBH is strongly inspired by the design requirements for technologies that encourage physical activity presented by Consolvo et al. [1]: 'Give users proper credit for their activities', 'Provide personal awareness of activity level', 'Support social influence' and 'Consider the practical constraints of users' lifestyle'. In RBH, users are given credit according to their HR intensity and are awarded with an earned placement on the participants' list. Hence, the list facilitates social influence between the participants as their placements are determined by their relative performances. As the interactions are based on HR facts, RBH provides personal awareness of the activity level in real-time, and additionally enables users to view a history of past results.

4   User Studies

20 participants (13 female, 7 male) between 20 and 40 years old were recruited to evaluate the experience of sharing biometric data in real-time between indoor cyclists. 17 participants were recruited while they waited for an indoor cycling class to start and the remaining three participants were recruited by word of mouth. A total of seven experiments were conducted over five days, where the number of participants in each experiment varied from two to four athletes. The duration of each indoor cycling class was 55 minutes and five of the 20 participants knew each other on beforehand.

All participants participated once, except three women who insisted to try RBH twice. One participant had never tried indoor cycling before, four had little experience, and 15 were experienced indoor cyclist. The experienced cyclists regularly attended indoor cycling classes between two and six times a week. All participants said they attended indoor cycling classes because they believed it was an effective way to burn calories.

As described in the previous section, RBH uses the percentages of the athletes' MAX HR to calculate and display each athlete's position in the view. If the athletes knew their MAX HR this value was plotted into RBH, otherwise an estimate of the athletes MAX HR was calculated by subtracting their age from 220.

Directly after each of the seven indoor cycling classes ended, we conducted a group interview with the participants about their experience with RBH. The interviews mainly contained open-ended questions about the athletes' experiences with the RBH app. The group interviews were audio recorded and extensive notes were taken during the interviews to allow for further analysis and reflection. We chose a qualitative approach to investigate and understand how sharing real time biometric data between indoor cyclists affected the experience of the indoor cycling class. As we conducted the experiments 'in the wild', it was not possible to quantitatively evaluate and compare the participants' effort to regular indoor cycling classes, as no two classes are the same, as described in Section 1.1.

5   Discussion of User Studies

In this section, we present insights from the user studies and discuss the presence of competition facilitated by technology. We analyzed the data from the conducted interviews, and through extensive brainstorm sessions, using notes and sketching, we derived at two qualities that are enhanced by RBH: Relations and motivation. RBH gives practitioners the opportunity to interact and compete through biometric data in a setting and situation, where direct interaction has not been possible previously, and the two proposed qualities aim to capture the outcome of this new opportunity. However, by introducing competition in a non-competitive physical setting, we also encountered two challenges: Exasperation and Discouragement. These challenges should be addressed in future creations of competitive training systems based on biometric feedback. Lastly, as introducing RBH at indoor cycling classes showed substantial qualities and important challenges, we discuss how technology can be used to facilitate and modify competition and how this affects the exercise.

5.1   Qualities: Relation and Motivation

We discovered that in regular indoor cycling classes the majority of the participants tried to relate to other indoor cyclists, which is difficult to do. They look at facial expression, sweat, and cadence of the other practitioners, as ways to relate. However, the participants also pointed out that this only provided them with vague hints of how the other practitioners where doing, since they had no means to objectively compare their efforts. With the introduction of RBH, the participants were given an instrument for creating a closer relation to each other, which ultimately affected their performance. For instance, one participant said: "It gives an insight on whether you are falling behind, because you can see that others are struggling as well", and another said: "If you can see the others relaxing, you can do it yourself as well", supported by a third participant: "If the others are relaxing, you think 'I can give it more', and then you beat them".

The statements indicate that participants utilize the opportunity, provided by RBH, to relate to each other during indoor cycling sessions. The participants were constantly using the biometric data; as a frame of reference for physiological empathy, an excuse for relaxing, or as a reason to increase the effort. Thus, RBH possibly strengthen social relations between users, which is remarked upon as a strong motivational factor for gym-goers [2].

All participants indicated that they were influenced by the other participants' biometric data with statements such as: "At some point I was in the bottom of the list and 10% after the nearest [participant], and when I realized it, I instantly pushed myself harder to get to the same intensity level". The simple dynamical ranking of users in RBH, seemed to work as a game mechanism, where being in the top was the most desirable and being in the bottom was undesirable, exemplified by remarks such as, "He [the instructor] said to ride in single pace, but I could see that you both were going faster, so I refused to be down there [the bottom of the list]", and, "You give a little extra to keep it [the position in the list] when you are finally op there [the top of the list]".

The comments indicate that the simple biometric interaction between participants mediated by RBH, introduced an element of competition to the class that is not possible during normal indoor cycling classes. This element of competition motivated the participants to increase their intensity in order to compete with the other participants, resulting in a more efficient workout.

The two qualities, relation and motivation, indicate that sharing biometric data in real-time can help facilitate social relations and enable competition between athletes in a fitness activity, where neither is possible in regular classes. Hence, all participants except one agreed that RBH made the indoor cycling class more enjoyable.

5.2   Challenges: Exasperation and Discouragement

As described in the previous section, RBH motivated participants to increase effort in order to climb the dynamic list of shared biometric data. However, for one participant the pressure from the others became too significant and transformed into a felling of exasperation, which ultimately caused her to cover the iPhone with a towel. This occurred two-thirds into the indoor cycling class and afterwards the participant stated that, "you look at it all the time, and you think, 'well, I can give a little extra', but in the end it was too much, and I thought 'well, I should just ride in my own pace'". This example illustrates how real-time sharing of biometric data can be a powerful motivational tool as it infers competition. Thus, developers and users should be aware that the consequences of the motivational effects of a competition could lead to exasperation.

In another test, one participant had an exhausting workout the day before, making her legs sore on the test day. As a result, she struggled throughout the session trying to match the intensity of the other participants, which she quickly realized was impossible for her, due to the condition of her legs. During the retrospective interview, she revealed that she was discouraged by the fact that she was not able to compete. The chance of experiencing discouragement is mostly likely to happen if the physical fitness level between users is too significant. Thus, users should aspire to compete against other users in similar physical condition. However, future research should also address how to improve fitness-level balancing in biometric-based competitions, beyond the use of intensity.

The two cases presented in this section point to challenges that can be induced by sharing biometric data between athletes in real-time during exercises. Even though remarks from two participants highlighted negative consequences of sharing biometric data, they both stated that they would rather ride with RBH than without in future indoor cycling classes.

5.3   Facilitating Competition Using Biometric Data

Since the findings of our user studies exhibit how influential and powerful the competitive element is in terms of motivation, achieved effort and enjoyment, we wish to discuss the presence of competition, and how competition can be facilitated and modified by technology. In this discussion, we use indoor cycling as our case, however, the argumentation should be valid to other non-competitive sports as well.

Indoor cycling, like many other indoor fitness exercises, does not naturally provide means for practitioners to compare their effort to their peers. Nevertheless, our study revealed that some indoor cyclists use various visual cues to estimate the efforts of others. However, as no concrete data can be inferred about the level of intensity of other indoor cyclists, these sparse visual cues only work as a vague competitive element.

The use of devices such as HR watches and bike-mounted watt displays facilitates an impartial competition, where indoor cyclists can compete with themselves by comparing their performance to previous achievements. However, several participants from our study commented that they had stopped using these devices after a while, as they ended up always competing against their all time best performance, which often caused a demotivating feeling. We argue that this kind of competition can be described as a subsequent competition in the game-mechanics framework presented by Jensen et al. in [4]. A subsequent competition is defined by having a predefined static goal for the competitor to beat, which compares to indoor cyclists trying to beat their MAX HR or maintain the highest average intensity through a class. According to Jensen et al., this form of competition suffers from an inopportune pressure, which tends to make participants give up early if mistakes are made during the performance or the goal seems impossible to beat. This was exemplified in our study by a participant remarking that, "For a period I used the bikes with mounted watt displays, but I went sick of it after a while, because I kept trying to get higher, but I couldn't".

The introduction of sharing biometric data between participants facilitated a platform for competition, which in our study influenced the relation between the indoor cyclists and improved their motivation. We argue that sharing biometric data in an interactive way, as mediated by RBH, facilitates what Jensen et al. frames as a concurrent competition. A concurrent competition is defined by practitioners trying to beat a dynamic goal, which constantly change in relation to the performance of their opponents. In these competitions, the competitors feel a substantially stronger and more constant pressure, due to ongoing indication of their opponents' progress [4]. This observation was exemplified in our study as well, emphasized by the statements on motivation and in the case of exasperation, presented in the section above.

6   Conclusion

In this paper, we have presented a smartphone application, called Race By Hearts, which enables real-time sharing of biometric data between athletes, thereby facilitating a competition in a non-competitive setting. Through an empirical study, we have shown that sharing biometric data in real-time strengthens social relations between participants, increases their motivation, and improves the enjoyment of the fitness activity. However, we also found that introducing competition based on real-time sharing of biometric data can cause exasperation and discouragement for some athletes if not handled carefully. To put our findings in perspective, we discussed the presence of competition within indoor cycling, and how competition can be facilitated and modified by technology. However, in order generalize the presented qualities and challenges, more extensive studies are needed, both within indoor cycling and other non-competitive sport settings.

Acknowledgement. We thank all participants, as well as Fitness World for granting us permission to engage with their costumers and attending the indoor cycling sessions. We also thank Morten Boye Mortensen for his work with the Race By Hearts app.

References

1. Consolvo, S., Everitt, K., Smith, I., Landay, J.A.: Design Requirements for Technologies That Encourage Physical Activity. In: Proceedings of the SIGCHI Conference on Human Factors in Computing Systems, pp. 457–466. ACM (2006)
2. Crossley, N.: In the Gym: Motives, Meaning and Moral Careers. Body & Society 12(3), 23–50 (2006)
3. Curmi, F., Ferrario, M.A., Southern, J., Whittle, J.: HeartLink: Open broadcast of live biometric data to social networks. In: Proceedings of the SIGCHI Conference on Human Factors in Computing Systems, pp. 1749–1758. ACM (2013)
4. Jensen, M.M., Rasmussen, M.K., Grønbæk, K.: Exploring Opponent Formats. In: Anacleto, J.C., Clua, E.W.G., da Silva, F.S.C., Fels, S., Yang, H.S. (eds.) ICEC 2013. LNCS, vol. 8215, pp. 48–60. Springer, Heidelberg (2013)
5. Lin, J.J., Mamykina, L., Lindtner, S., Delajoux, G., Strub, H.B.: Fish'n'Steps: Encouraging Physical Activity with an Interactive Computer Game. In: Dourish, P., Friday, A. (eds.) UbiComp 2006. LNCS, vol. 4206, pp. 261–278. Springer, Heidelberg (2006)
6. Mueller, F., Vetere, F., Gibbs, M., et al.: Balancing exertion experiences. In: Proceedings of the SIGCHI Conference on Human Factors in Computing Systems, pp. 1853–1862. ACM (2012)
7. Mueller, F., Vetere, F., Gibbs, M.R., Edge, D., Agamanolis, S., Sheridan, J.G.: Jogging over a distance between Europe and Australia. In: Proceedings of the 23nd Annual ACM Symposium on User Interface Software and Technology, pp. 189–198. ACM (2010)
8. Nenonen, V., Lindblad, A., Häkkinen, V., Laitinen, T., Jouhtio, M., Hämäläinen, P.: Using heart rate to control an interactive game. In: Proceedings of the SIGCHI Conference on Human Factors in Computing Systems, pp. 853–856. ACM (2007)
9. Stach, T., Graham, T.C.N., Yim, J., Rhodes, R.E.: Heart Rate Control of Exercise Video Games. In: Proceedings of Graphics Interface 2009, pp. 125–132. Canadian Information Processing Society (2009)
10. Walmink, W., Wilde, D., Mueller, F.: "Floyd." Displaying Heart Rate Data on a Bicycle Helmet to Support Social Exertion Experiences. In: Proceedings of the 8th International Conference on Tangible, Embedded and Embodied Interaction, pp. 97–104. ACM (2013)
11. Gym Membership Statistics | Statistic Brain, http://www.statisticbrain.com/gym-membership-statistics/

The Effect of Familiar and Fantasy Aesthetics on Learning and Experience of Serious Games

Erik D. van der Spek[1], Tatiana Sidorenkova[1], Paul Porskamp[2],
and Matthias Rauterberg[1]

[1] Eindhoven University of Technology, PO Box 513 5600MB Eindhoven, The Netherlands
[2] T-Xchange, PO Box 217 7522NB Enschede, The Netherlands
{e.d.vanderspek,g.w.m.rauterberg}@tue.nl,
tatyana.sidorenkova@gmail.com, paul.porskamp@txchange.nl

Abstract. Serious games have shown potential as learning material, but are not very engaging. One reason why games are considered to be fun is their ability to provide us with an interesting fantasy world to explore and play in, but this seems at odds with the more serious nature of formal training. In this study, a two by two (familiar versus unfamiliar visual setting and familiar versus unfamiliar story setting) single-blind experiment (N=60) was performed, testing the effect of the familiarity of aesthetics on game experience and learning. Significant effects of story condition on learning and game experience was found, with a familiar story setting leading to better learning, but subdued game experience. Other effects were not significant.

1 Introduction

Games are learning systems, and what makes a game fun is in part the pleasure derived from learning new patterns and being able to apply this new knowledge in solving problems [1]. It is therefore unsurprising that games are now also applied to learning and instruction of more serious materials (i.e. 'serious games'). After three decades of development and research, serious games have been found to be on average efficacious and in most cases even more so than traditional instruction [2, 3]. However, as [3] notes, much is still unknown on how serious games should be designed to be efficacious learning tools, and evidence for serious games to be more engaging is even wholly lacking.

2 Fantasy and Familiarity

Games are fun, among others, because they provide a fantasy setting, and invoke curiosity by showing virtual worlds that are alien or incongruous with everyday settings [4]. This however can be at odds with the more grounded demands of serious games, where it is the everyday setting or real world application that is regularly the object of study. It is often argued that the better games mimic the real world, the

Y. Pisan et al. (Eds.): ICEC 2014, LNCS 8770, pp. 133–138, 2014.
© IFIP International Federation for Information Processing 2014

higher the transfer of learning [5]. Furthermore, learning is contingent on being able to link new information to existing prior knowledge in the long term memory [6] and while encountering an alien environment may foster curiosity, it may consequently be inefficient for learning, as the player is unable to integrate newly obtained game knowledge with prior knowledge obtained in the real world. From this one could argue that it is cognitively sound to have games with familiar, real world settings, though perhaps at the expense of engagement.

Conversely, the fantasy and curiosity that a game's fantasy setting affords, is also important for learning. It leads to more engagement with the learning material [4, 7], as well as more cognitive effort [8]. In previous research on serious games design, it was found that the inclusion of unexpected surprises in the narrative improved cognitive effort and subsequently deep comprehension of the instructional material, though not motivation [9]. Conversely, in other research the introduction of a curiosity inducing intervention led to more engagement, but not learning [10]. However, neither was focused on stimulating fantasy. Perhaps most critically, a game without fantasy is "simply an abstract context—a simulation of reality" [11]. Play occurs when someone steps into 'the magic circle', a place where disbelief is suspended and the player becomes immersed in an imaginary world [12]. Without some kind of fantasy that engages a player's imagination, play may not arise, and the serious game is less a game, and more training.

According to Schell, every game rests on four pillars: aesthetics, mechanics, technology and narrative [13]. For this research we tried to answer the question whether the aesthetics of a serious game should be familiar (i.e. corresponding with the real world), or a fantasy setting, in order to optimally stimulate learning and engagement. For this, we created four versions of an existing strategic decision-making (SDM) game, a picture of which can be seen in Figure 1.

The game was designed to train experts to make decisions based on incomplete or conflicting data and subsequently provide insight into their own decision-making process [14]. In the game, the player was confronted with a scenario about an important person that went missing. As the head of a crisis team, the player is tasked to make decisions based on advice that is provided by a number of experts in his or her team. In a 2x2 design, both the visual aesthetics and the story setting were either familiar or fantasy. The mechanics, technology and plot were kept the same.

Fig. 1. Strategic Decision-Making game. Image and game courtesy of T-Xchange.

3   Method

3.1   Participants

The strategic decision-making game was designed for experts (in this case operational analysts in a military setting). However, at the time of the experiment not enough experts in the field with a similar level of prior knowledge could be found for a large(r) scale study. Therefore, we opted for research with university students (55% undergraduate, 45% graduate level). In total 60 participants, 33 males and 27 females within the age range of 18 to 41 years old (M = 25.1, SD = 4.69) were recruited for the study. The majority of participants, 63.3% (N = 38), played computer or/and video games. The participants were randomly assigned to one of the four conditions. As a reward for the participation, the participants received a coupon worth €5.00.

3.2   Materials

As the game was designed to train decision-making in dilemmas that did not have clear right or wrong answers, the learning goals were rather diffuse. Consequently as a measure for learning we used the Structural Knowledge Assessment (SKA) [15], which elicits a participant's knowledge structure about the game. This knowledge structure can then be compared to that of an expert, which results in a similarity score. For more explanation see [15], for the referent knowledge structure used to compare participant's knowledge structures against, see Figure 2.

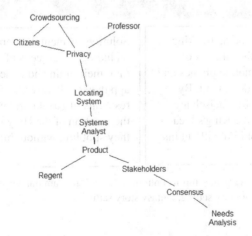

Fig. 2. Referent knowledge structure

In order to measure how involved the player was in the game, and to some extent how much of a game they felt the instructional material was, we used the Game Experience Questionnaire (GEQ) [16]. Lastly, a small knowledge test with 5 three item multiple choice questions was administered, that tested whether the participant remembered a few events in the game. This was mostly done as an extra check to determine the validity of the SKA.

3.3   Design

The experiment was a 2x2 pretest posttest design, where the game's visual aesthetic was either familiar or fantasy, which was contrasted with the story being either contextualized in a familiar setting or a fantasy setting. See Figure 3.

| Solution: A social media tracking system including the citizens of Monacisch, their mobile phones and an app they could download. By law, the people of Monacisch are required to call in the King's location once they spot him without his security detail. | Solution: A mental computing system including the citizens of the planet Arraki, their brain and a mental computing app they could download. By law, the residents of Arraki are required to call in the location of the Holy Emperor once they spot him without his Holy Guards. |

Fig. 3. Conditions of the game, top to bottom, left to right: familiar visual aesthetic, fantasy visual aesthetic, familiar story setting, fantasy story setting

4   Results

4.1   Learning

One outlier with IQR > 1.5 was removed from the familiar story condition, leading to valid N=59. A 2x2 full factorial ANCOVA with post-intervention SKA as dependent variable, pre-intervention SKA as covariate and Story and Visual conditions as fixed factors, shows a significant main effect of Story on learning, ($F(1,54) = 5.25$, $p < 0.05$, $\eta_p^2 = .089$), with the familiar story setting leading to better learning than the fantasy story ($M = 0.097$ versus $M = 0.57$ respectively). There was no significant main effect of Visual condition ($F(1,54) < 1$) and no significant interaction effect ($F(1,54) < 1$). If the outlier was not removed, the main effect of Story would have shown a trend: ($F(1,55) = 2.84$, $p = 0.098$, $\eta_p^2 = .049$).

4.2   Game Experience

A 2x2 MANOVA with the fourteen factors of the Game Experience Questionnaire (see section 3.2) as dependent variables and the conditions Story and Visuals as fixed factors, shows a significant main effect of Story on Game Experience Questionnaire (Wilk's $\lambda = 0.52$, $F(3,43) = 2.84$, $p < 0.005$, multivariate $\eta^2 = 0.48$). Separate ANOVAs reveal that this is due to significant effects of condition on Negative Feelings ($F(1,56) = 6.67$, $p < 0.05$), Positive Experience ($F(1,56) = 8.18$, $p < 0.01$), Tiredness ($F(1,56) = 9.10$, $p < 0.005$) and Returning to Reality ($F(1,56) = 5.28$, $p < 0.05$). In all cases, ratings were higher in the fantasy story condition than in the familiar story condition. No significant main effect was found for the visual conditions, nor a significant interaction effect.

5   Discussion and Future Work

The results of the experiment indicate a catch 22 between learning and game experience in serious games, at least when it comes to the aesthetics of the game. Games with a fantasy environment offer a stronger game experience, but this is achieved at the cost of lower learning gains. If the learning goals of a serious game are the most important aspect, a more familiar setting should be used, but at the cost of a subdued game experience. This could give some explanation why serious games are efficacious though not very engaging [3]. Research on ways to circumvent this problem is therefore paramount.

It is also possible that fantasy aesthetics have an interaction effect with game mechanics, where a higher engagement could lead to a stronger will to engage with the game mechanics, i.e. gaming the system, but less to learning the information. This relationship should be scrutinized.

There are a number of other limitations to the research, which should also be clarified in future work. The learning in this game is very verbally focused, and less procedural. This could have an effect on the visual aesthetics conditions and pertaining results, where learning (and knowledge assessment) in our experiment was mostly on verbal knowledge, and subsequently the participants could have paid less attention to the visuals, leading to non-significant effects in the visual condition.

Furthermore, it could be argued that the setting and difficult task in the game were simply too alien for the players, that they needed some recognizable elements in order to engage with the game. Research by Kintsch and Mandler among others has highlighted that topics that are completely new for the learner will not lead to more cognitive interest [8]. This however seems at odds with the totally new fantasy offered by games. Future research will need to determine whether and where there is a middle ground of offering the right amount of fantasy, while tapping into the prior knowledge of the learner.

Lastly, our experiment used novice participants. An expertise reversal effect is very much possible, where novices still struggle to generate schemata and therefore prefer familiar contexts to integrate new knowledge with prior knowledge, whereas experts already have relevant schemata and could prefer fantasy settings that challenge them in applying these. Therefore, research with experts is still very much needed.

References

1. Koster, R.: Theory of Fun for Game Design. O'Reilly Media, Inc. (2013)
2. Sitzmann, T.: A Meta-Analytic Examination of the Instructional Effectiveness of Computer-based Simulation Games. Pers. Psychol., 489–528 (2011)
3. Wouters, P., van Nimwegen, C., van Oostendorp, H., van der Spek, E.D.: A Meta-Analysis of the Cognitive and Motivational Effects of Serious Games. J. Educ. Psychol. 105, 249–265 (2013)
4. Malone, T.W.: Toward a theory of intrinsically motivating instruction. Cogn. Sci. 5, 333–369 (1981)
5. Alexander, A., Brunyé, T.: From gaming to training: A review of studies on fidelity, immersion, presence, and buy-in and their effects on transfer in pc-based simulations and games. In: I/ITSEC, pp. 1–14 (2005)
6. Mayer, R.E.: Designing Instruction for Constructivist Learning. In: Reigeluth, C.M. (ed.) Instructional-design Theories and Models, vol. 2, pp. 141–159. Erlbaum, Mahwah (1999)
7. Dickey, M.D.: Murder on Grimm Isle: The impact of game narrative design in an educational game-based learning environment. Br. J. Educ. Technol. 42, 456–469 (2011)
8. Campion, N., Martins, D., Wilhelm, A.: Contradictions and Predictions: Two Sources of Uncertainty That Raise the Cognitive Interest of Readers. Discourse Process. 46, 341–368 (2009)
9. van der Spek, E.D., van Oostendorp, H., Ch. Meyer, J.-J.: Introducing surprising events can stimulate deep learning in a serious game. Br. J. Educ. Technol. 44, 156–169 (2013)
10. Wouters, P., Van Oostendorp, H., Boonekamp, R., Van Der Spek, E.: The role of Game Discourse Analysis and curiosity in creating engaging and effective serious games by implementing a back story and foreshadowing. Interact. Comput. 23, 329–336 (2011)
11. Gunter, G.A., Kenny, R.F., Vick, E.H.: Taking educational games seriously: Using the RETAIN model to design endogenous fantasy into standalone educational games. Educ. Technol. Res. Dev. 56, 511–537 (2007)
12. Paras, B., Bizzocchi, J.: Game, motivation, and effective learning: An integrated model for educational game design. In: Proceedings of DiGRA 2005 (2005)
13. Schell, J.: The Art of Game Design: A book of lenses. CRC Press (2008)
14. http://www.txchange.nl/portfolio-item/mayors-game/
15. Wouters, P., Van der Spek, E.D., Van Oostendorp, H.: Measuring learning in serious games: a case study with structural assessment. Educ. Technol. Res. Dev. 59, 741–763 (2011)
16. Poels, K., de Kort, Y., IJsselsteijn, W.: It is always a lot of fun!: exploring dimensions of digital game experience using focus group methodology. In: Proceedings of the 2007 Conference on Future Play, pp. 83–89 (2007)

Designing a Digital Experience for Young Children with Developmental Disabilities

Peta Wyeth, Joshua Hall, and Daniel Johnson

Faculty of Science and Engineering, Queensland University of Technology, Australia
{peta.wyeth,joshua.hall,dm.johnson}@qut.edu.au

Abstract. This paper reports on the development of a playful digital experience, Anim-action, designed for young children with developmental disabilities. This experience was built using the Stomp platform, a technology designed specifically to meet the needs of people with intellectual disability through facilitating whole body interaction. We provide detail on how knowledge gained from key stakeholders informed the design of the application and describe the design guidelines used in the development process. A study involving 13 young children with developmental disabilities was conducted to evaluate the extent to which Anim-action facilitates cognitive, social and physical activity. Results demonstrated that Anim-action effectively supports cognitive and physical activity. In particular, it promoted autonomy and encouraged problem solving and motor planning. Conversely, there were limitations in the system's ability to support social interaction, in particular, cooperation. Results have been analyzed to determine how design guidelines might be refined to address these limitations.

Keywords: Young children, developmental disability, interactive experience, design guidelines, evaluation, play and games.

1 Introduction

Increasingly, innovative technology is being utilized in early childhood settings and there is clear evidence that well designed systems have the potential to engage young children, respond to their developmental needs and stimulate learning through play [3]. However there is limited research focused on the design of new technology for children with developmental disabilities, especially within the early childhood years. Effective integration of playful technology into settings that include children with developmental disabilities is an ongoing challenge and our research is focused on addressing this issue. The research was guided by two research aims. Firstly, our objective is to identify the design requirements necessary to create playful interactive experiences that are meaningful and appropriate for young children with developmental disabilities. Our second aim involves understanding the extent to which the experience developed supports cognitive, social and physical play.

Y. Pisan et al. (Eds.): ICEC 2014, LNCS 8770, pp. 139–146, 2014.

2   Background

Developmental disabilities can be defined as "a set of abilities and characteristics that vary from the norm in the limitations they impose on independent participation and acceptance in society" [4].There are a number of studies that specifically examine the use of educational games for children within developmental disabilities [1, 2, 6]. Research has demonstrated the effectiveness of computer games in supporting engagement [5], facilitating social skills [1] and providing opportunities to role play behaviors that are challenging in real social contexts [2]. However, a majority of the research in the field is focused on children aged between 7 and 14.

Our own previous research focused on the development of game-based interactions for adults with intellectual disability resulted in the development of the Stomp platform [8]. The floor-based system allows users to interact with digital environments by triggering pressure sensors embedded within a 2 × 3 meter floor mat. Interactive applications are projected onto the mat using a short throw projector. The platform effectively turns the floor into a large pressure sensitive computer screen. The system is designed so that actions such as stomping, stepping and sliding in Stomp are like stomping, stepping and sliding in the real world [8]. We use Stomp in our research as a means through which young children may engage in inclusive digital learning experiences.

3   Designing a Stomp Application for Children with Developmental Disabilities

In order to understand the requirements of an interactive experience for young children with developmental disabilities we involved teachers and support staff from an early childhood center that caters specifically for children with developmental disabilities. Initially, four informal meetings were undertaken to gain information on the types and nature of disabilities of the children who attended the school and to explore attitudes to technology designed to support children with developmental disabilities. From the initial meetings we established that the teachers felt it was appropriate to use the Stomp platform to create a playful experience for children aged between four and six years. Two individual semi-structured interviews and one focus group involving three teaching staff followed these initial meetings. These discussions lasted between 45 minutes and one hour and were designed to illicit specific information with respect to the design of an interactive experience for the children attending the centre. These discussions resulted in the development of the interactivity design goals that were used to guide the design of the new application.

General Interaction Goals: Interviews with teachers established that the interactive experience must not rely too heavily on a child's social skills, as this is often one of the most impaired abilities of children attending the school. As concepts such as teamwork are relatively new to this age group, any collaboration must be simple. For the most part, interaction is between the teacher and student. Therefore methods that enable greater communication between these two parties are just as important as improving student-to-student social skills. Four specific design guidelines were developed as a result:

- G1: Interaction should be clearly defined and simple.
- G2: The experience should facilitate supervisor / teacher interaction with the student.
- G3: The experience should facilitate interactions between students.
- G4: Interaction should not rely on successful collaboration or teamwork from students.

Input: Motor skills of the children vary, and the range encompasses those mildly impaired to children who are heavily impaired. System input requiring gross motor skills must take into consideration the physical build of a child. Actions need to be constrained to the reach, jump and step distance of a five-six year old child. Often developmentally delayed children's hand eye co-ordination is limited, therefore input actions requiring reflexes or accuracy will need ample room and time. Reaction time and spatial awareness is often impaired and events requiring actions must allow for this and occur at a slower speed. Object motion should be slow and relatively predictable. We developed three design guidelines based on this information:

- I1: System input should only rely on simple fine and gross motor skills.
- I2: Design actions that allow ample room and time for participants to react.
- I3: Input rules and boundaries should be clear and intuitive.

Feedback: Directions need to be clear, discreet and repetitive to ensure the message is conveyed. Once an action or task is complete audio/visual feedback should be provided to ensure children comprehend that a goal has been achieved. When conveying messages or events visually, content must be modest in color and intensity. Over stimulation and confusion may result from an excessive range and intensity of colors, shapes and objects being visible on the screen space. Excessive noise or loud sudden sounds can disturb some children. Three specific design guidelines stem from this information:

- F1: Feedback should be clear and discreet.
- F2: All forms of feedback should not be excessive or loud.
- F3: Feedback should occur immediately after input from a child.

4   The Anim-Action Experience

Anim-action is a collaborative art experience playable on the Stomp interactive surface to maximize the advantages of using a system that allows for whole body interaction. Participants can work together or individually to create, color and draw animal characters that come to life. Three stages were included in the experience; these were designed to progress the participant from simple to more complex learning goals (see Fig. 1).

Fig. 1. Anim-Action Interactions – (from left to right) draw mode, color mode and detail mode

Each mode has been designed to incorporate the interactivity and goals identified in section 3. Stage one, draw mode, requires participants to start drawing the outline shape of their created animal character. The participant walks along the dashed outline of the shape, activating solid line pieces until the shape is a continuous solid outline. In color mode the participant may choose colors from a selection available from the side bar. Colors may be selected by simply stepping or jumping on them. Painting will occur when the child stands inside the animal outline area. Detail mode keeps the color bar on the side of the mat, but also introduces additional animal details as objects on the opposite side of the mat. Details, such as body parts and facial features, can be added by jumping or stepping on an object (e.g. eye) and then placing the body part on the animal. Correct positioning is indicated by a highlighted outline. Selecting from the color pallet either before or after object selection changes the color of these body parts. The Anim-action experience was designed to meet the interactivity design guidelines and educational goals in the following ways.

General Interaction: The space for social interaction is clearly defined and children are able to step anywhere on the mat without penalty (G1). Teachers are readily able to observe interactions and guide/instruct children as required (e.g., guiding a task, suggesting some cooperative activity) (G2). Stage 2 and 3 provide opportunities for children to engage in simple social interactions (e.g., in stage 2 one participant might select a color and the other paints, or both children might be involved in painting different areas of the shape (G3). While there are varied levels of social interaction from observing, through to advising and interacting (G3), interaction does not rely on any collaboration or teamwork (G4).

Input: The space for interaction takes up a large portion of the 3m x 2m floor mat and each interactive piece (e.g., line in draw mode, paint blob in color mode) provides a generous activation zone that is larger than a child's foot (I1, I2). The main objectives of the activities be can achieved through simple stepping motions (I1). The visual properties of the application ensure that input rules are simplified. For example, the dashed outline, as the only element on the mat initially, invites the participant step on that line to see what happens (I3). There is continuity from Stage 1 to Stage 2 as the outline shape remains the same. This allows the participant to work within the same area of the floor and follow similar rules of interaction (I3). A color in the color palette is already active when color mode starts. Consequently, a child can start painting without actively selecting a color (I3). Similarly, a body part choice is activated when detail mode becomes available (I3). No time constraints are enforced by the system (I2) and primary interactions occur within the boundary of the animal (I3).

Feedback: When in draw mode, the system responds to a child stepping on the outline of the shape by changing the dashed line to a solid line section and emitting a "click" sound effect (F1). During paint and detail mode, only one selection can be chosen at a time (e.g., a color blob from the paint palette, or a body part from the details menu) (F1). Upon selection of the color or body part in the system responds with visual and aural feedback and the chosen object remains highlighted when active (F3). A subtle glow effect is used to indicate the selection that is currently active (F2). During color mode, one foot step on the mat is represented as one individual paint splat (F1). Once a participant steps on any area within the shape outline, a paint splat effect is created (F3). To guide children towards shape selection in detail mode, an initial shape outline (e.g. eye) is highlighted on the animal's body (F1). When a shape piece has been correctly placed, feedback is given via a visual and audio cue (F3). Once this has occurred a new missing shape piece will be highlighted (F1). All visual and aural effects are designed to clearly depict an outcome, while at the same time being subtle in color and format so as not to over stimulate or distract children (F2). All system feedback is immediate (F3).

5   Anim-action Evaluation

Thirteen children, aged 5 and 6, participated in the evaluation of the Anim-action. Twelve boys and one girl from four different classes were involved. The study took place on six days during a two week period and study findings are based on observations of participants' engagement in the Anim-action experience. Each session lasted approximately 45 minutes and the observation method was based on existing teacher assessment schemes. The use of teachers to make assessments has been found to be highly effective in assessing the behavior of children with developmental disabilities [7].

Teaching staff observed each child and recorded the child's displayed behaviors on an observational checklist sheet. Observation items were divided into four categories: cognitive (five items); social divided into two sub-categories: communication (four items) and social interaction (four items); and gross motor physical skills (three items). Observed behaviors were scored based on the level of assistance required during interaction for each checklist item. For a particular skill, such as color matching (cognitive), a child would be given a score between zero and five. The scoring system is as follows: 0 – no behavior exhibited; 1 – child did not initiate activity and at least two types of prompts were provided (e.g., verbal and physical); 2 – child did not initiate activity and one type of prompt was provided; 3 – child initiated activity and at least two types of prompts were provided; 4 – child initiated activity and one type of prompt was provided; 5 – child completed activity independent of support.

6   Findings

Analysis of data was performed to determine what kinds of interactions children were engaged in while playing Anim-action. We examined independent behavior, as defined as a child receiving a score of 5 (independent) or 4 (limited prompting) for a particular item. Similarly, dependent behavior is defined as a child receiving a score of 1 (dependent) or 2 (partially dependent). Results indicate that most children were able to engage independently in the cognitive activities of color matching (85%), shape matching (85%), problem solving (77%), task focus (85%) and body awareness (85%). Fig. 2 details the results for cognitive engagement across the five items measured. Similarly, most children were able to independently engage in physical activities while playing Anim-action (Fig. 3). They independently exhibited concentration on movement (85%), balance (100%) and motor planning (92%).

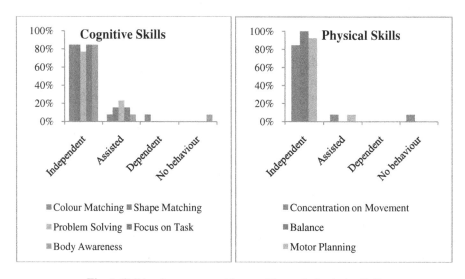

Fig. 2. Children's engagement in cognitive and physical activity

Scores for independent activity were considerably lower in the communication and social interaction categories. In both areas a more bi-modal distribution is evident, such that children were either relatively independent in their behavior, or no behavior was exhibited at all (see Fig. 3). Investigation of communication skills engaged in while playing Anim-action shows that requests for help were limited, with 11 of the 13 children never requesting help. There was slightly more evidence of independent labeling of objects (54%), turn-taking communication (62%) and general communication (46%). While results show that cooperation was limited, with 10 of the 13 children exhibiting no cooperative behavior, children were observed engaging in other independent social activity: 62% were able to independently regulate their behavior and 62% were able to independently wait for a turn and all children listened for direction (either independently or with assistance).

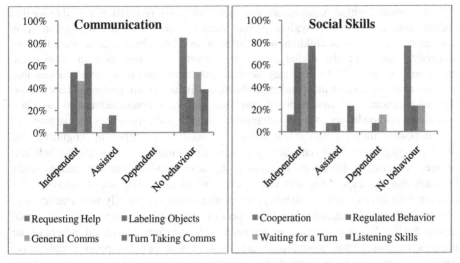

Fig. 3. Children's engagement in social activity

7   Discussion and Conclusion

Results indicate that Anim-action was effective in promoting physical and cognitive engagement for young children with developmental disabilities. Of particular note was the evidence of independent problem solving and motor planning that occurs during the Anim-action experience. The staged approach to introducing complexity in both physical and cognitive activity through a carefully considered design may explain this result. Children were introduced to simple, structured gross motor activity (i.e. line following), before being required to move from one part of the play space to another in order to achieve their goals. The experience implicitly enforced simple interaction rules and while there was no negative feedback, a lack of responsiveness for incorrect activity may have encouraged children to focus on moving their bodies to achieve the desired outcome. Similarly, problem solving was introduced gradually and visual cues (e.g. the outline of a body part) provided scaffolding for the problem solving process. Immediate visual feedback allowed children to assess the effectiveness of their actions. Children are immersed in planning and problem solving activity.

These results suggest that children were less engaged in social interaction. The system was designed so that children could work effectively autonomously and independently. There was no explicit requirement for social interaction, with G4 explicitly aimed at ensuring that interactions did not rely on collaboration. In light of the findings it may be necessary to rethink criterion G4 and how such a requirement is implemented. For example, while cooperation might not be necessary, more encouragement of, and reward for, engagement in shared experiences could be included. These findings also demonstrate that design decisions related to criteria G2 and G3 need to be reconsidered. It is perhaps necessary to consider an implementation that includes more systematic and overt mechanisms for teacher-student and student-student interactions.

The automated within Anim-Action experience may also be partly responsible for this finding, with the system providing prompt cues to guide a child's interaction. This automation may result in children not needing to ask for help. It also appears that the immersive nature of the digital experience results in a reduction in cooperative interaction. At the same time, it may be these automated and immersive qualities that have led to an increase in independent problem solving and motor planning. This tension between autonomy and immersion, on one hand, and social connectedness on the other, needs to be acknowledged in the development of new digital experiences for learning.

The results indicate that Anim-action is effective in supporting cognitive and physical engagement. Children's ability to work autonomously and not ask for help can be seen as positive. However, it needs to be acknowledged that the current study indicates that the experience was not as effective in facilitating social behavior. For children with developmental disability, where interaction is primarily with teachers and support staff, social interaction is a key aspect of early intervention programs. It would appear that the design of a digital system needs to be carefully considered in light of our findings to ensure that mechanisms are built in that better support collaborative behavior. It may also be that such digital experiences are most effective when they focus on one aspect of children's development and not another with experiences that attempt to simultaneously achieve all possible development goals ultimately being less successful. Future research will also explore the extent to which this pattern of results extends to other Stomp experiences and comparable non-digital activities.

Acknowledgements. We would like to thank all of the staff and children at Nursery Road State Special School, Queensland who participated in this study.

References

1. Battocchi, A., Ben-Sasson, A., Esposito, G., Gal, E., Pianesi, F., Tomasini, D., Venuti, P., Weiss, P., Zancanaro, M.: Collaborative puzzle game: A tabletop interface for fostering collaborative skills in children with autism spectrum disorders. Journal of Assistive Technologies 4(1), 4–13 (2010)
2. Durkin, K.: Videogames and young people with developmental disorders. Review of General Psychology 14(2), 122–140 (2010)
3. Edwards, S.F. A Research Paper to Inform the Development of an Early Years Learning Framework for Australia. Dept. of Education and Early Childhood Development (2008)
4. Odom, S.L., Horner, R.H., Snell, M.E., Blacher, J.: Handbook of developmental disabilities. The Guilford Press (2007)
5. Pares, N., Masri, P., van Wolferen, G., Creed, C.: Achieving Dialogue with Children with Severe Autism in an Adaptive Multisensory Interaction: The "MEDIATE" Project. IEEE T. Vis. and Comp. Graphics 11(6), 734–743 (2005)
6. Piper, A.M., O'Brien, E., Morris, M.R., Winograd, T.: SIDES: A Cooperative Tabletop Computer Game for Social Skills Development. In: Proc. CSCW 2006. ACM Press (2006)
7. National Joint Committee on Learning Disabilities. Comprehensive Assessment and Evaluation of Students with Learning Disabilities (2010)
8. Wyeth, P., Summerville, J., Adkins, B.: Stomp: An Interactive Platform for People with Intellectual Disabilities. In: Proc. ACE 2011, p. 8. ACM Press (2011)

Computational Methodologies
for Entertainment

ARENA - Dynamic Run-Time Map Generation for Multiplayer Shooters

Anand Bhojan and Hong Wei Wong

School of Computing, National University of Singapore
{banand,wei}@comp.nus.edu.sg

Abstract. In this paper, we present simple and novel method to procedurally generate the game maps for multiplayer shooter games faster (in order of seconds) without compromising the expected features of a good multiplayer shooter environment.

Keywords: games, procedural content generation, game map generation.

1 Introduction

1.1 Procedural Content Generation

Procedural Content Generation (PCG) is the use of algorithmic means to create content [17] [19] dynamically during run-time. Instead of trekking the same grounds which gets stale with time, PCG promises a more novel experience every playthrough. PCG was utilised in games as early as 1978. A notable example is *Rogue* [12] [1] which spawns a new genre known as Roguelikes. Core features include randomly generated levels, item locations and so on. PCG's influence extends to racing games like *Gran Turismo 5*, which procedurally generates its tracks [13]. First Person Shooter (FPS) *Borderlands* series procedurally generates weapons [5].

1.2 Multiplayer Shooter

We believe that an exception to PCG lies with environments/maps for multiplayer shooters such as Battlefield [4], which remains one of the most popular genres to date [18].

The reader should note the difference between a multiplayer and a standard shooter, which often follows an approximately linear path. The competitive nature of multiplayer shooters brings additional challenge of ensuring fairness through the positioning of strategic points. Moreover, players typically have more freedom to move around the map. It is for these reasons the designers often take a different approach to craft multiplayer maps.

We limit our scope to the game mode **Capture and Hold**, popularised in games like Killzone [6] . Every player belongs to one of 2 teams. Littered around the map are *flags* that are captured by placing players in close proximity. A captured flag (can be recaptured) lowers the *team points* for the opposing team continuously. A team point of

Y. Pisan et al. (Eds.): ICEC 2014, LNCS 8770, pp. 149–158, 2014.

0 signals the victory of the opposing team. To win, teams have to actively defend and pursue flags.

In this paper, we present a novel method that can generate dynamic maps almost as soon as the player press the 'Play' button, while ensuring the quality. The method is simple, practically feasible and we have implemented and evaluated it with a test game. In the rest of the paper, we first discuss the motivations for this work in Section 2 and then related works in Section 3. In Section 4 we describe the design goals of map generation method. Section 5 explains the design of the map generator. Implementation and evaluations are described in Section 6. Finally we conclude the paper with the summary at Section 7.

2   Motivation

In this work, we are attempting to automatically create playable, balanced (fairness) and interesting maps for multiplayer shooters, with a novel approach built using Search-based PCG [17]. While PCG is used by some multiplayer shooter game designers, who would procedurally generate maps and then manually tweak them to ship with the final product, our goal is to remove the human intervention for manual tweaking completely. This means that the generation should be completed within a span of seconds, or else the patience of the player could wear thin. If we are successful, the development time and cost needed to create maps for similar games could be drastically reduced. The result would be increased longevity that stems from the near limitless amount of maps for players to play in.

3   Related Work

Güttler et al. [7] identified some basic spatial properties of multiplayer FPS games and proposes several heuristics for better level design. In addition, the insights provided by several industry leaders of leading game companies on design of a good multiplayer game ([14], [9] and [8]) are incorporated in formulating our design goals. Search-based PCG (SBPCG), an approach to PCG, was introduced by *Togelius et al.* [17]. We will be employing a similar approach in our solution. *Togelius et al.* also managed to procedurally generate tracks for a racing game [15] and maps for strategy game Starcraft [16]. In both cases, SBPCG was used with a simulation based fitness function. *Kerssemakers et al.* [11] introduced a procedural PCG generator to generalise the creation of PCG to games again with the use of a simulation-based fitness function. However, the use of simulation-based fitness function is not suitable for our goals, due to the time it takes to create a map is long and it is not suitable for practical implementations due to the strict real time requirements imposed by the games and game players. Work done by *Cardamone et al.* [3] to evolve interesting maps for a FPS leveraging on SBPCG is a great starting point for our research. However, a great amount of work have to be done to ensure that the map can be generated in a span of seconds. Moreover, the maps that are generated are seemingly low on navigability and aesthetics, which are basic features of any good multiplayer game. In contrast, navigability and aesthetics are part of our design goals.

4   Map Design Goals

We describe what we want to achieve by identifying elements of interesting maps (of multiplayer shooters) so that they can be incorporated into our design. **1) Fast Generation** - We wish to generate the maps in real-time. In other words, the final map has to be generated within a span of seconds to minimise player frustration. **2) Collision Points** - *Güttler et al.* [7] defines collision points as areas that see the most clashes and where most tactical choices are made. Tactical choices begin with preparations (route to take and so on), and ends with a confrontation. The designer should be aware of them to give more opportunity for tactical choices [8]. In contrast, a map with no clear or too many such points are likely to see players stumping onto opponents unexpectedly. **3) Flow** - The designers in [9] emphasise on *flow*, an "invisible flow (that is) continually impelling the player onwards". As this is too abstract, we deconstruct it into measurable components (Navigability and Pacing). Navigability - *players should be able to recognize where they are and where they should go*. Pacing - *confrontation should last enough duration to be fun. It should be accompanied by some respite, but not to the extent of inducing boredom [7]. Also, the map should not have disruptive dead ends.* Even though they may not fully encompass it, we have observed that they provide reasonably good flow and serve as good starting point for future research. **4) Fairness** - Each team should have same chance of victory [7], which is related to flags. A team with flags closer to its spawn point has a higher chance of capturing them. **5) Aesthetics** - The design must have the potential to meet aesthetics demand of players. There is a rich set of taxonomy that collectively define aesthetic [10]. For instance, a map cannot constitute entirely of blocks. Instead, it should contain trees, vehicles and so on to create more natural challenges. In addition, having diverse items improve navigability, as players can use them to get their bearings.

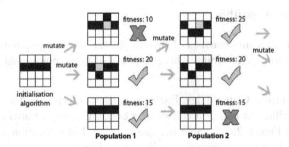

Fig. 1. Illustration of a SBPCG process. Only accepted maps are used in the next population.

5   Map Generator Design

In this section we describe our algorithm to generate interesting maps for multiplayer shooters, which makes use of the popular **Search-Based Procedural Content Generation** (SBPCG) [17] method. We employ *generate-and-test approach* as illustrated in Figure 1.

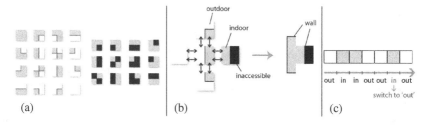

Fig. 2. a. Types of Game Tiles (not complete), b. Rule of Adjacent Game Tiles, c. Removing artifacts horizontally

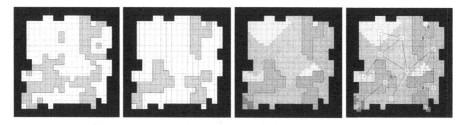

Fig. 3. Initialisation Algorithm Phase I-IV. Each colour represents a region, and the brown icon is a door.

We first present how a map ***blueprint*** is created by our initialisation algorithm in Section 5.1. Then, we detail how it evolves with a fitness function to produce the final map blueprint and how it is mapped to the actual game environment in Section 5.2.

5.1   Initialisation Algorithm

Our initialisation algorithm consists of several phases. We first populate the blueprint piece by piece before determining where to place strategic points and computing its fitness.

PHASE I: Populating Game Tiles. Each game tile comprises of four smaller **cells**, which belong to either an *indoor* area (inside a building), *outdoor* area or *inaccessible* area as shown in Figure 2a. A game tile can be placed in a location adjacent to another game tile only if the neighbouring cells match (Figure 2b). We call this adjacency requirement as *Rule of Adjacent Game Tiles*.

The map uses a grid layout, with each 'square' occupied by a game tile. The grid is first enclosed by a layer of fully inaccessible game tiles. This ensures players cannot move outside the map. Next, game tiles of random types are placed in unoccupied 'squares', constrained by the rule of adjacency (Figure 2b). This is repeated until it is fully filled. An example of the generated map can be seen in Figure 3.

PHASE II: Cleaning Up. We notice several artifacts like overly small buildings or protruding parts of buildings' remains. We scan the map blueprint both vertically and horizontally, removing single cells which are surrounded by cells of different types as

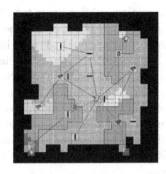

Fig. 4. Map blueprint after Phase V. The shields are the spawn points. The flag icons show the position of the flags. The shield and sword icon near the centre represents a collision point. The thicker lines are covers.

Fig. 5. Visual Appearance of the Game Environment

depicted in Figure 2c. This is necessary to give the map a 'cleaner' look with more regularly shaped buildings which would otherwise hurt its navigability.

PHASE III: Identifying Regions. To analyse the map, the algorithm requires an understanding of its layout. We first identify **regions** of the map, which are either *indoor* or *outdoor*. Region detection is done by applying a *Flood Fill* algorithm to the cells, stopping when it reaches its maximum size or when no cells are left. This is repeated until all accessible cells belong to a region. The maximum size is proportional to the map's size and can be tweaked. Note that cells of different types cannot share the same region; Indoor region contains only indoor cells and outdoor region contains only outdoor cells.

PHASE IV: Connecting Regions. By identifying regions, we can construct an undirected *graph* with each *node* located approximately at the region's centre. Nodes are connected by an *edge* if players can move directly from one to the other without passing through a third one. At this stage, no edges exist between indoor and outdoor regions. For every indoor region, edges are created to connect to an neighbouring outdoor region. This adds a *door* between them and improves the connectivity of the map. The same applies to *all* indoor regions of bigger buildings with multiple regions. It is therefore natural to have multiple doors at different points within it. Otherwise, moving deeper into a large building always result in a dead end. Most parts of the generated map is connected after this phase. However, there are exceptions where regions are fully surrounded by inaccessible cells.

PHASE V: Positioning of Strategic Points. Spawn Points, position of Flags, Collision Points and Covers are strategic elements which are depicted in Figure 4. Two **Spawn Points** are required for 'Capture and Hold' games, one for each team. They are positioned by identifying the two nodes of the graph that are the furthest away from each other geographically. Four **Flags** (*team flags*) are planned for the map. Each team is assigned a flag (captured) at the beginning of the play. They are positioned at the nodes closest to the teams' spawn points. The two remaining flags are neutral (not captured). A straight line is first 'drawn' between spawn points. Each side of the line will contain a neutral flag. They bound to a node with the minimum difference in travelling distance (using the *Dijkstra algorithm*) from both spawn points to preserve fairness. **Collision Points** are identified by the *degree* of the node. A high degree node most likely belongs to a region that players are prone to meet as many different routes will lead to it. We observed that a degree of *five* and above makes a good condition for a collision point. **Covers** are placed approximately at the meeting point of regions that have an edge to the collision points. This helps with promoting tactical choices as it provides more options to players who are more likely to meet at collision points. Covers are also placed at nodes which have not been assigned anything. Since these nodes are usually at region centres, the covers act as good places to hide if a firefight is to break out at that region. Without it, there may be too many open areas.

5.2   Evolution

Fitness Computation. A fitness is assigned for the evolutionary algorithm to tell how good the map is. There are 3 approaches [17]. *Interactive Fitness Function* grades it based on interaction with a player. As this is physically impossible, this approach is not considered. *Simulation-Based Fitness Function* uses AI (Artificial Intelligence) agents to play through a portion of the game for evaluation. Many research works ([15], [11] and [3]) used simulation-based fitness functions. However, its weakness lies in the time required to compute it.

Therefore, we will be employing *Direct Fitness Function*, where a content is judged by retrieving a list of features. In our solution, the fitness is computed by simply summing up the values for all of the following features which are derived based on the design goals presented at the beginning of this Section. 1) **Connectivity** - Returns 1 if the graph is connected (as detected in Phase IV). Otherwise, returns 0. All regions are reachable in a connected map. 2) **Forced Collision Points** - Returns 1 if there are one or two collision points. Returns 0 if there are zero or more than two collision points (no clear collision points). Ideal number of collision points depends on the map size. 3)**Flag Fairness** - Difference in the distance travelled to own team flag. This is measured by finding the travelling distance from the spawn points to the corresponding team flag. The returned value is normalised to 0 to 1, with 0 being maximum distance apart and 1 being approximately the same distance apart. 4) **Overall Flag Fairness** - Similar to Flag Fairness, but returns the difference in distance travelled to all flags from the spawn points instead.

Evolution and Mapping. The first population consists of three map blueprints generated with the initialisation algorithm. They are then mutated three times each, producing nine more blueprints. Each mutation removes part of the map and repopulate it with the initialisation algorithm. With that, the population is complete with twelve map blueprints. Three of the best maps (based on their fitness values) are picked and mutated three times to form the second population. This continues until enough populations are processed. The final map blueprint obtained after the evolution is then used to create the actual environment. Doing so is a direct mapping of each abstract game tile (in blueprint) to one of the many variations of concrete and matching game tiles seen by the player.

6   Evaluation

6.1   Evaluation Methodology

We developed a FPS game to implement our solution. Video demonstration of our algorithm and playable version of our game are available at our project homepage [2]. We evaluated the effectiveness of the evolutionary algorithm on producing good maps and its compliance with the design goals.

6.2   Effectiveness of Evolution

We created *3 different maps* using our solution. We run the evolution algorithm for 55 populations (approximately 10 seconds in a Intel Core i7 laptop) each time to generate the map. The maximum average summed fitness is 4.0, as the fitness for each of the 4 features is normalised from 0.0 to 1.0. The *average summed fitness* of the processed population against the *number of populations processed* so far is plotted in Figure 6. The positive gradient shows that the evolutionary methods does improve the quality of the map as more population are generated and mutated. It also shows that the fitness stabilises after 26 populations (which takes about 5 seconds).

The fitness for each feature (with unnormalised values) of generated maps are shown in Table 1. Based on the fitness function that we have defined, the maps are all connected (with *Connectivity* of value 1.0), meaning that no regions are blocked from the rest. The algorithm is also effective in constraining the number of collision points (with *Forced Collision Points* of value 1.0, indicating that there are either 1 or 2 collision points.). For both *Flag Fairness* and *Overall Flag Fairness*, we show the unnormalised values. These values indicates the absolute difference in moving from the spawn points to own team flags for Flag Fairness, and the difference in moving to all flags for Overall Flag Fairness. A value of 1.0 means their distance are exactly one cell apart. Given our result, the values are very low, with the highest being 1.03510, which is barely one cell apart. To give a clearer perspective, one cell will take only approximately a second to travel. Henceforth, we can conclude that the flags are placed in positions that are largely fair for both teams.

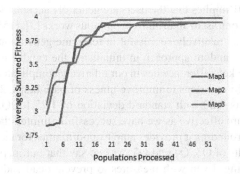

Fig. 6. Change in fitness when evolving

Table 1. Fitness values of generated maps (after 26 populations)

	Map 1	Map 2	Map 3
Connectivity	1.0	1.0	1.0
Forced Collision Points	1.0	1.0	1.0
Flag Fairness (unnormalised)	0.3246	1.0351	0.4806
Overall Flag Fairness (unnormalised)	0.0031	0.3103	0.5568

Table 2. User Study - Demography

Gender	Female (5), Male (48)
Proficiency Level in Games	Never Played (1), Novice (10), Average (26), Expert (16)
Frequency of Playing Games	Never Played (2), Few Times a Month (14), Few Times a Week (16), Almost Every Day (21)
Played any FPS game before	Not sure about the game type (2), No (5), Yes (46)

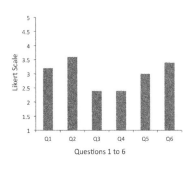

Fig. 7. User Study Results

6.3 Meeting Design Goals

A user study was conducted to test if the map generated using our method meets the design goals. The game was ported to run in a browser environment. The URL of the game with a starting page containing the introduction to the game, game rules and mechanics were sent to all participants. The users were allowed to play the game multiple times before taking the survey. A brand new map is generated with every playthrough. Table 2 shows the demography. The survey had 6 questions with Likert scale of 1 to 5 for each question. The questions: Q1) How fast is the loading process? [1 being unacceptably slow and 5 being very fast] Q2) Did the combats took place all over the map or in few key locations? [1 being only sparsely located and 5 being focused on a few areas] Q3) Was it easy to navigate your way to your opponents and flags? [1 indicating very easy and 5 being very hard] Q4) Did you run into many dead ends? [1 indicating none and 5 indicating many] Q5) Please rate the pacing of the game. [1 being too fast/slow paced and 5 being very well-paced] Q6) Did the placement of the flags give fair chances for both teams? [1 being very unfair and 5 being very fair]

The results shown in Figure 7 are discussed below. **1) Fast Generation** - As discussed above it took about 10 seconds (10.1s, 9.9s and 11.5s respectively for Map1,Map2 and Map3) to generate the maps with 55 populations while 26 are sufficient. We feel that this loading time is reasonable for a commercial game. The mean user score of 3.19 with a standard deviation of 1.08 for Q1 implies that the users are generally acceptable of the time taken to generate a map. In contrast to algorithms in previous works [3], [15], [16] which takes hours, our algorithm is relatively successful in real-time generation. Previous works typically take a highly random approach in initialising the candidate, and relies too heavily on evolution. The key difference lies in our relatively complicated initialisation process, which takes additional steps to improve fitness of base maps. **2) Collision Points** - The sample mean is 3.60 with standard deviation of 1.25 for Q2 implies the design of collision points are effective as we have successfully limited the points of confrontation. The covers surrounding it provides ample opportunities for tactical choices. **3) Flow** - From the results of Q3, Q4 and Q5, we can say that our maps have fairly good navigability and pacing. Even with measures to prevent dead ends, they remain in some areas that are hard to detect. The buildings on the left and right are large but do not have doors other than the ones that leads to the centre. Players may find themselves trying to find flags deeper into them only to discover a dead end. This can be improved by tweaking the maximum region size. Pacing is susceptible to many confounding factors, such as the speed of movement, rate of fire, speed of reloading and so on, and is therefore not exclusively dependent on the map design. **4) Fairness** - We measure the time to navigate from both spawn points to all four flags by playing through the map. It takes 58.88s to move from the blue base and 60:21s to move from the other base. The small difference between these values implies high fairness. The sample mean of 3.36, standard deviation of 0.98 for Q6 implies that the placement of flags are largely fair for our users. **5) Aesthetics** - The look of the game depends on the artist. In general, However, what we can observe from the map is that the buildings have decent shapes and the objects such as trees and wagons are placed naturally as shown in Figure 5.

7   Conclusion

We first presented our findings of what constitutes a good game environment for multiplayer shooters, before designing and implementing an algorithm for the procedural generation of a map that can satisfy all the criteria. We then evaluated the maps by measuring the effectiveness of the evolution to produce better maps and to check whether the result satisfies what we have set out to do. Our evaluations show that we can generate game map procedurally for multiplayer shooters in less than ten seconds without compromising the common design requirements (flow, positioning of collision points, fairness and aesthetics) of commercial multiplayer shooters. Hence, in contrast to previous works, our method is practically feasible for run-time dynamic map generation and can be immediately used by game industry.

References

1. Rogue 1984 - the dos game, the history, the science, `http://science-fiction.fch.ir/rogue/doc/Rogue_1984-The_DOS_Game-The_History-The_Science.html` (retrieved March 2014)
2. Anand, B., Wei, W.H.: Arena- procedural map and music generation for multiplayer shooters (project page), `http://www.comp.nus.edu.sg/~bhojan/arena`
3. Cardamone, L., Yannakakis, G.N., Togelius, J., Lanzi, P.L.: Evolving interesting maps for a first person shooter. In: Di Chio, C., et al. (eds.) EvoApplications 2011, Part I. LNCS, vol. 6624, pp. 63–72. Springer, Heidelberg (2011)
4. DICE: Battlefield 4 multiplayer, `http://www.battlefield.com/battlefield-4/gameplay/multiplayer` (retrieved January 2014)
5. Gearbox: Borderlands 2 information, `http://www.borderlands2.com/us/#info` (retrieved January 2014)
6. Guerrilla: Killzone home, `http://www.killzone.com/en_GB/killzone.html` (retrieved January 2014)
7. Güttler, C., Johansson, T.D.: Spatial principles of level-design in multi-player first-person shooters. In: Proceedings of the 2Nd Workshop on Network and System Support for Games, NetGames 2003, pp. 158–170. ACM, New York (2003)

8. Hill, S.: Game design theory: Multiplayer level design, http://www.alteredgamer.com/game-development/60255-game-design-theory-multiplayer-level-design/ (retrieved January 2014)
9. Holloway, J.: Deathmatch map design: The architecture of flow, http://www.gamasutra.com/view/feature/195069/deathmatch_map_design_the_.php (retrieved January 2014)
10. Hunicke, R., LeBlanc, M., Zubek, R.: MDA: A formal approach to game design and game research. In: Proceedings of the AAAI-2004 Workshop on Challenges in Game AI, pp. 1–5 (July 2004)
11. Kerssemakers, M., Tuxen, J., Togelius, J., Yannakakis, G.: A procedural procedural level generator generator. In: 2012 IEEE Conference on Computational Intelligence and Games (CIG), pp. 335–341 (2012)
12. Loguidice, B., Barton, M.: Vintage Games: An Insider Look at the History of Grand Theft Auto, Super Mario, and the Most Influential Games of All Time, 1st edn. Focal Press (February 2009)
13. PolyphonyDigital: Gran turismo 5 course maker, http://www.gran-turismo.com/us/products/gt5/coursemaker/ (retrieved January 2014)
14. Scimeca, D.: How to build the best multiplayer fps maps, http://www.g4tv.com/thefeed/blog/post/719216/how-to-build-the-best-multiplayer-fps-maps-part-one (retrieved January 2014)
15. Togelius, J., De Nardi, R., Lucas, S.: Towards automatic personalised content creation for racing games. In: IEEE Symposium on Computational Intelligence and Games, CIG 2007, pp. 252–259 (2007)
16. Togelius, J., Preuss, M., Beume, N., Wessing, S., Hagelback, J., Yannakakis, G.: Multiobjective exploration of the starcraft map space. In: 2010 IEEE Symposium on Computational Intelligence and Games (CIG), pp. 265–272 (2010)
17. Togelius, J., Yannakakis, G.N., Stanley, K.O., Browne, C.: Search-based procedural content generation. In: Di Chio, C., et al. (eds.) EvoApplicatons 2010, Part I. LNCS, vol. 6024, pp. 141–150. Springer, Heidelberg (2010)
18. VGChartz: Global yearly chart (2013), http://www.vgchartz.com/yearly/2013/Global/ (retrieved January 2014)
19. Watson, B., Muller, P., Wonka, P., Sexton, C., Veryovka, O., Fuller, A.: Procedural urban modeling in practice. IEEE Computer Graphics and Applications 28(3), 18–26 (2008)

Personas versus Clones for Player Decision Modeling

Christoffer Holmgård[1], Antonios Liapis[1],

Julian Togelius[1], and Georgios N.Yannakakis[1,2]

[1] Center for Computer Games Research, IT University of Copenhagen, Denmark
{holmgard,anli}@itu.dk, julian@togelius.com
[2] Institute for Digital Games, University of Malta, Malta
georgios.yannakakis@um.edu.mt

Abstract. The current paper investigates how to model human play styles. Building on decision and persona theory we evolve game playing agents representing human decision making styles. Two methods are developed, applied, and compared: procedural personas, based on utilities designed with expert knowledge, and clones, trained to reproduce play traces. Additionally, two metrics for comparing agent and human decision making styles are proposed and compared. Results indicate that personas evolved from designer intuitions can capture human decision making styles equally well as clones evolved from human play traces.

1 Introduction

The current paper investigates how to create generative models of human player behavior or playing style in games. This can be seen as a method for understanding game-playing behavior. Generative models of playing behavior are also potentially useful in procedural play testing for procedural content generation, for simulation based testing, and within mixed-initiative game design tools for instant feedback during the design process. In other words, agents that play like humans can help understand content as it is being created, by playing it. This paper assumes that game players exhibit bounded rationality, i.e. they play to optimize some objective or set of objectives, but that they might not be very good at it. Playing style could then be characterized by how the players' in-game decisions differ from those of an agent that played rationally (given some set of objectives). We investigate this by using AI methods to train agents that behave rationally, and see to what extent they can predict human players' behaviors.

In previous work we have designed a simple turn-based, tile-based rogue like game which features monsters, treasures and potions in mazes [6]. 38 players played 10 levels of this game, and we recorded their every action. Next, we analyzed the design of the game to extract a number of possible affordances which we translated into partially conflicting objectives that a player might seek to fulfill (e.g. kill all

Y. Pisan et al. (Eds.): ICEC 2014, LNCS 8770, pp. 159–166, 2014.

monsters, avoid danger or get to the exit quickly). Using these affordances we trained agents to play the game rationally for each objective. We call these agents procedural personas. Both Q-learning [6] and evolutionary algorithms [5] were used to train high-performing agents; the evolved agents have the benefit that they generalize to levels they were not trained on. The agents' behavior was compared to play traces of the human players through a metric we call the action agreement ratio (AAR) which compares agents and humans at the action level. But is this really the right level of analysis for comparing players to agents? It could be argued that the microscopic level of comparing actions gives a biased view of how well an agent's behavior reproduces player behavior, and that it is more interesting to look at behavior on the level of conscious decisions. Further, are we right to assume boundedly rational behavior given some set of objectives? It might be that with the same agent representation, we could train agents that reproduce player behavior better by using the actual playtraces as training data.

The current paper tries to answer these two questions. We propose a new playtrace comparison method (tactical agreement ratio) that instead of asking whether an agent would perform the same action as the player in a given state asks whether it would choose to pursue the same affordance in that state. We also train agents to behave as similarly as possible to human players using play- traces as objectives; we call such agents clones. Clones are compared to personas on both seen and unseen levels, using both action-level and affordance-level comparison. In the following we briefly outline the relations between persona theory, decision theory, player modeling, and the resulting concept of procedural per- sonas. We briefly describe our testbed game, MiniDungeons, and the methods we used to create game playing personas and clones, before we present the results from comparing the resulting agents to the human players.

2   Related Work

In this section we outline our concept of procedural personas, relating it to its roots in decision theory and the use of personas for game design.

Decision Theory and Games: The personas used for expressing designer notions of archetypical player behavior in MiniDungeons are structured around the central concepts of decision theory. Decision theory states that whenever a human makes a rational decision in a given situation, the decision is a result of an attempt to optimize the expected utility [7]. Utility describes any positive outcome for the decision maker and is fundamentally assumed to be idiosyncratic. This means that in principle no definite assumptions can be made about what can provide utility to the decision maker. The problem is further complicated by the fact that the effort a decision maker directs toward attaining maximum util- ity from a decision can be contingent on the expected utility itself. For problems that are expected to provide low utility even in the best case, humans are prone to rely more heavily on heuristics and biases for the decision making process [11, 4]. In practice, however, for structured, well-defined problems, insights from e.g. psychology or contextual information about the decision maker or the de- cision problem may provide us with opportunities for assuming which decisions are important and which outcomes may be of utility to the decision maker. As decision spaces, most games are special cases since the available decisions and their consequences are highly structured by the game's mechanics and evaluation mechanisms. Games, through their design, often provide specific affordances [3] to the player, and suggest utility for various outcomes. This perspective forms the basis for our understanding of player behavior in our testbed game, as we assume that players are interacting with the game in accordance with the rules, understanding and responding to the affordances of our game. This, in turn, mo- tivates our use of utility for attaining game rule based affordances as the defining characteristics of the personas we develop. Similar theoretical perspectives have been described by other authors, notably Dave Mark in [8].

When attempting to characterize player decision making styles in games using utilities, it is important to consider the level of decision making relevant for the game, as described in [1]. Here, we model players at both the individual action level as well as at the more tactical level of game affordances. Below we describe how we apply simple utility based agents by using linear combinations of utilities to define personas that represent archetypical decision making styles in our testbed game at two levels of abstraction.

Player Modeling: The concept of personas was first adapted to the domain of (digital) games under the headline of play-personas by Canossa and Drachen who define play-personas as "clusters of preferential interaction (what) and nav- igation (where) attitudes, temporally expressed (when), that coalesce around different kinds of inscribed affordances in the artefacts provided by game de- signers" [2]. Our long term research agenda is to operationalize the play-persona concept into actual game playing procedural personas, by building generative models of player behavior from designer metaphors, actual play data, or combi- nations of the two.

Generative models of player behavior can be learned using a number of dif- ferent methods. A key dichotomy in any player modeling approach lies in the influence of theory (vs. data) for the construction of the player model [15]. On one end, model-based approaches rely on a theoretical framework (in our case per- sona theory or expert domain knowledge) and on the other hand, computational models are built in a model-free, data-driven fashion. In this paper, personas represent the model-based approach while what we term clones represent the data-driven approach. Model-free player modeling can be done by imitating the player directly, using supervised learning methods on the playtraces, or indirectly using some form of reinforcement learning to train agents to behave in a way that agrees with high-level features extracted from the playtraces [12]. Evolutionary computation can be used to optimize an agent to behave similarly to a playtrace or optimize it to exhibit the same macro-properties as said playtrace [9, 12, 14]. Direct imitation is prone to a form of overfitting where the agent only learns to cope with situations which exist in the playtraces, and might behave erratically when faced with new situations. Indirect imitation to a large extent solves this problem by learning a more robust, general strategy, which could be termed a decision making style. In the following section we give a brief introduction to our test bed game.

3   MiniDungeons

The testbed game, MiniDungeons, implements the fundamental mechanics of a roguelike dungeon exploration game where the player navigates an avatar through a dungeon containing enemies, powerups, and rewards. The turnbased game puts the player in a top-down viewed tilebased 12 by 12 dungeon con- taining monsters, potions, and treasures. Impassable tiles constitute the walls of the dungeon, while passable tiles contain enemies or items for the player. All of the level is visible to the player who can move freely between passable tiles. When the player moves to a tile occupied by a monster or item, immediately the monster is fought or the item is collected and applied. The player has a 40 hit point (HP) health counter and dies if this drops to zero. Monsters randomly deal between 5 and 14 HP of damage while potions heal 10 HP up to the maximum value of 40 HP. Treasures have no game mechanical effect other than adding to a counter of collected treasure. The game contains one tutorial level and 10 "real" levels. For further details on the test-bed game and discussion of its properties, we refer to [6]. The necessary data for developing and evaluating the agents was collected from 38 anonymous users who played MiniDungeons online; this re- sulted in 380 individual playtraces on the 10 MiniDungeons levels provided. The data was subsequently used to evolve clones and baseline agents as described be- low. Fig. 1 shows a selected level from the game, along with human play traces from the level, exemplifying the diversity of human decision making styles ex- pressed in even a simple game like this.

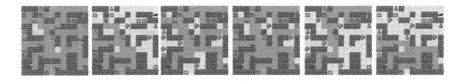

Fig. 1. Heatmaps of six selected human playtraces in Level 2 of MiniDungeons, showing a diversity of player decision making styles

4   Method

This section describes the two agreement ratio metrics used to evaluate persona and clone likeness to humans, the fitness functions for personas and clones, and the evolutionary approach used. The metrics address the problem of decision characterization at two different levels of abstraction.

Action Agreement Ratio: The first metric used to evaluate agent to human likeness is the action agreement ratio (AAR). AAR considers each step of a human playtrace a distinct decision. To produce the AAR between an agent and a human player, all distinct game states of the human playtraces are reconstructed. For each game state, the agent being tested is inserted into the game state and queried for the next preferred action, essentially asking: "What would you do?". If the action is the same as the actual next human action, the agent is awarded one point. Finally the AAR is computed by dividing the points with the number of decisions in the human playtrace.

Tactical Agreement Ratio: The second metric used for evaluating the likeness between agents and humans is the tactical agreement ratio (TAR). TAR only considers reaching each distinct affordance in the level a significant decision, ignoring the individual actions in between. For MiniDungeons the affordances considered relevant are: fighting a monster, drinking a potion, collecting a treasure, or exiting a level. For each affordance reached in the human play trace, the resulting game state is reconstructed and the agent being tested is inserted into the game state. The agent is then allowed as many actions as necessary to reach the next affordance, again asking the question "What would you do?", but at the tactical affordance level. If the next encountered affordance matches the actual next human one, the agent is awarded a point. Finally the TAR is computed by dividing the points with the number of affordances reached in the human playtrace.

Evolved Agent Controllers: The controllers of the game agents are represented as seven linear perceptrons. Each perceptron takes 8 inputs describing safe and risky path distances to the nearest affordances in the map. Further details of the controller representation is given in [5]. Controllers are evolved using a $(\mu + \alpha)$ evolutionary strategy without self-adaptation. For each generation the top 2% performing elite individuals remain unchanged, the lowest performing half of the remaining population is removed, and single-parent offspring from the remaining individuals are produced to maintain the population size. Finally all individuals not existent in the elite are mutated. Mutation is accomplished by changing each connection weight in the network with a random number drawn from a Gaussian distribution centered around zero with a standard variation of 0.3, a value recommended in [13] and confirmed as useful for this game by in- formal experimentation. All experiments are done using a population size of 100 individuals, trained for 100 generations. Controllers are initialized with random connection weights for all connections in the linear perceptrons.

Personas: For the purpose of the experiments 5 individual personas with different utility configurations were defined, based on designer interpretations of likely gameplay in MiniDungeons. The personas were intended to represent five hypothetical extreme decision making styles in interacting with the game: an Exit (E) persona who simply tries to escape the level, a Runner (R) persona who tries to escape the level in as few steps as possible, a Survivalist (S) persona who tries to avoid risk, a Monster Killer (MK) persona who tries to kill all monsters and escape the level, and a Treasure Collector (TC) persona who attempts to collect all treasures and escape the level. The decision making styles are defined by the utility weights presented in Table 1, and serve as a metaphor for the relative importance of the affordances to the archetypical player represented by the persona. When assigned to personas, utility points from a level are normalized by the maximally attainable utility for the same level. Personas are evolved by, for each generation, exposing them to 9 of the 10 levels of MiniDungeons, yielding 50 agents in total. For each generation, their fitness is computed as the average of the normalized utility scores from the seen levels. All subsequent evaluations presented in this paper are done using 10-fold cross validation, i.e., a persona is evaluated on the level which it was not exposed to during evolution.

Clones: Clones, like personas, are evolved by exposing them to 9 of the 10 levels of MiniDungeons. Their fitness value is computed as the average nor- malized AAR across all 9 seen levels. One clone per player per map is evolved, yielding 380 agents in total. All subsequent tests are done using 10-fold cross validation, evaluating the clones on unseen levels.

Baseline Agents: In order to evaluate the limits of the perceptron-based representation, a set of baseline agents is evolved, one agent for each human playtrace, 380 total. These are exposed to a single level of MiniDungeons. Their fitness scores are computed directly from AAR in an attempt to establish the closest fit to each human player that the representation can achieve.

5   Results

This section compares the two presented evaluation metrics, and compares the ability of personas, clones, and baseline agents to represent human decision making styles in MiniDungeons. Table 2 shows the mean of the agreement ratios for each kind of agent evolved, using both the AAR and TAR metrics. The ratios indicate that all agents achieve higher agreement with human playtraces when evaluated with the AAR metric than with the TAR metric. Additionally, they indicate that when using AAR clones perform only slightly better than personas ($t = -3.23$, $df = 753.00$, p < while when using TAR the clones perform substantially better than the personas ($t = -39.26$, $df = 721.51$, p < 0.001), as tested using Welch's t test. Using AAR, the baseline agents perform significantly better than both personas and clones ($df = 2$, $F = 62.59$, p < 0.001), but when using TAR they perform significantly worse than the clones ($df = 2$, $F = 59.1$, p < 0.001), as tested using ANOVA. Table 3 shows which personas exhibited the best ability to represent human playtraces, for each MiniDungeons level and in total. For each human playtrace, the personas with the highest AAR and TAR, respectively, are identified. Both metrics generally favor the Treasure Collector persona as the best match for most playtraces, although there is some discrepancy between the two measures in terms of which personas represent the human playtraces best.

Table 1: Utility weights for the five de- signed personas.

Affordance	E	R	S	MK	TC
Move	-0.01	-0.02	-0.01	-0.01	-0.01
Monster				1	
Treasure					1
Death			-1		
Exit	0.5	0.5	0.5	0.5	0.5

Table 2: Agreement ratios for per- sonas, clones, and baseline agents.

Agent	Metric	Mean	SD
Personas	AAR	0.75	0.08
Clones	AAR	0.77	0.08
Baseline Agents	AAR	0.81	0.09
Personas	TAR	0.62	0.11
Clones	TAR	0.66	0.13
Baseline Agents	TAR	0.61	0.13

Table 3. Best persona matches based on Action Agreement Ratio (AAR) and Tactical Agreement Ratio (TAR), respectively.

| | AAR | | | | | | | | | | | TAR | | | | | | | | | | |
	1	2	3	4	5	6	7	8	9	10	Total	1	2	3	4	5	6	7	8	9	10	Total
E	0	2	5	1	0	1	5	1	2	3	20	0	1	2	0	0	1	0	0	1	1	6
R	0	0	0	0	0	0	0	0	0	0	0	0	2	3	1	0	3	6	0	1	0	16
S	0	1	0	0	0	0	0	0	0	0	1	0	1	4	0	0	0	0	0	0	1	6
MK	8	8	0	2	3	1	7	2	2	0	33	5	3	1	4	0	1	2	3	4	0	23
TC	30	27	33	35	35	36	26	35	34	35	326	33	31	28	33	38	33	30	35	32	36	329
Total	38	38	38	38	38	38	38	38	38	38	380	38	38	38	38	38	38	38	38	38	38	380

6   Discussion

It seems that the AAR metric achieves higher agreement ratios than the TAR metric. The two metrics aren't directly comparable, however, as the level's specific layout has a higher influence on the AAR value than the TAR value. Additionally, clones and baseline agents were evolved toward AAR, rather than TAR, for these experiments. Evolving toward TAR might have yielded different results. Other external playtrace comparison metrics could advantageously be used for calibration such as aggregated statistics of in-game event occurrences or other action/edit-distance based methods such as the Gamalyzer metric [10]. The fact that personas and clones perform roughly equally well, when mea- sured by AAR, suggests that the persona method is a viable approach to mod- eling player decision making styles from expert knowledge. The method is less playtrace-dependent and computationally expensive than the cloning method, but needs an expert game designer. Still, some players may exhibit decision making styles that cannot be captured by the designer's intuition, and would be captured better by the cloning approach, as suggested by the higher agreement ratios obtained from the clones. In order to address this issue, we would propose using observed deviation from initial persona behavior to guide the evolution of new utility configurations for subsequently derived personas, combining the persona and cloning approaches.

7   Conclusion

This paper presented two methods of modeling player decision making styles. One was based on personas, evolved from designer expert knowledge, the other was based on clones, based on human playtraces. Two metrics were used to evaluate the agents' abilities to represent human decision making styles. The methods were shown to perform almost equally well when compared at the ac- tion level, while clones performed better than personas when compared at the affordance level.

Acknowledgments. We thank the players of the game. The research was supported, in part, by the FP7 ICT project C2Learn (project no: 318480) and by the FP7 Marie Curie CIG project AutoGameDesign (project no: 630665).

References

1. Canossa, A., Cheong, Y.G.: Between Intention and Improvisation: Limits of Game- play Metrics Analysis and Phenomenological Debugging. DiGRA Think, Design, Play (2011)
2. Canossa, A., Drachen, A.: Play-Personas: Behaviours and Belief Systems in User-Centred Game Design. In: Gross, T., Gulliksen, J., Kotzé, P., Oestreicher, L., Palanque, P., Prates, R.O., Winckler, M. (eds.) INTERACT 2009. Part II. LNCS, vol. 5727, pp. 510–523. Springer, Heidelberg (2009)
3. Gibson, J.: The Concept of Affordances. Perceiving, Acting, and Knowing, pp. 67–82 (1977)
4. Gigerenzer, G., Gaissmaier, W.: Heuristic Decision Making. Annual Review of Psychology 62, 451–482 (2011)
5. Holmgård, C., Liapis, A., Togelius, J., Yannakakis, G.N.: Evolving Personas for Player Decision Modeling. In: IEEE Conference on Computational Intelligence and Games (2014)
6. Holmgård, C., Liapis, A., Togelius, J., Yannakakis, G.N.: Generative Agents for Player Decision Modeling in Games. In: Foundations of Digital Games (2014)
7. Kahneman, D., Tversky, A.: Prospect theory: An Analysis of Decision under Risk. Econometrica: Journal of the Econometric Society, 263–291 (1979)
8. Mark, D.: Behavioral Mathematics for Game AI. Course Technology Cengage Learning (2009)
9. Ortega, J., Shaker, N., Togelius, J., Yannakakis, G.N.: Imitating Human Playing Styles in Super Mario Bros. Entertainment Computing 4(2), 93–104 (2013)
10. Osborn, J.C., Mateas, M.: A Game-Independent Play Trace Dissimilarity Metric. Foundations of Digital Games (2014)
11. Rubinstein, A.: Modeling Bounded Rationality, vol. 1. MIT Press (1998)
12. Togelius, J., De Nardi, R., Lucas, S.M.: Towards Automatic Personalised Content Creation for Racing Games. In: IEEE Symposium on Computational Intelligence and Games, CIG 2007, pp. 252–259. IEEE (2007)
13. Togelius, J., Lucas, S.M.: Evolving Controllers for Simulated Car Racing. In: The 2005 IEEE Congress on Evolutionary Computation, vol. 2, pp. 1906–1913. IEEE (2005)
14. Van Hoorn, N., Togelius, J., Wierstra, D., Schmidhuber, J.: Robust Player Imitation using Multiobjective Evolution. In: IEEE Congress on Evolutionary Computation, CEC 2009, pp. 652–659. IEEE (2009)
15. Yannakakis, G.N., Spronck, P., Loiacono, D., André, E.: Player Modeling. In: Artificial and Computational Intelligence in Games, pp. 45–55. Dagstuhl Publishing, Aarbrücken/Wadern (2013)

Fractal Complexity in Built and Game Environments

Daniel Della-Bosca, Dale Patterson, and Sean Costain

Griffith University, Gold Coast, Australia
{d.della-bosca,d.patterson,s.costain}@griffith.edu.au

Abstract. Fractal patterns provide an automated mathematical method to create rich and engaging visuals. These methods have been applied in the design of physical and game spaces to only a limited extent. The current physical and virtual game worlds are dominated by rectangles, squares and linear concepts. This research studied the nature of fractal patterns and in particular the use of differing levels of fractal complexity to design physical and virtual environments. The findings from the randomized trial identified differing levels of fractal complexity and their aesthetic appeal to participants. These levels of fractal complexity were then applied to spatial environments in games to create spaces that were more or less appealing to the participant. The principle of using fractal complexity as a design tool to make an environment more or less comfortable provided game and architectural designers an additional mechanism to enhance spaces and levels of participant engagement.

Keywords: fractal, surface, complexity, built environment, computer game.

1 Introduction

The world of computer games and their interactive environments is one filled with a mixture of differing spatial locations. Much like the real world, each virtual location features structural elements, both man made and natural. Every location and surface is created geometrically and carefully designed to provide players with a particular visual, ideally immersive, experience. The repetitive process, at heart of fractal mathematics, generates engaging, often uncannily natural patterns, images and objects [1,2,3]. The potential to use this fractal technique to enhance the surface textures and bump maps in game spaces was the key focus of this project.

In aesthetic terms, 'An object is said to be self-similar if it looks "roughly" the same at any scale' [1,2], an image is called fractal if it displays self-similarity, that is, it can be broken into parts, each of which is (approximately) a reduced size copy of the whole. The father of fractals, Benoit Mandelbrot, summarized his career as the 'ardent pursuit of the concept of roughness.' [1]. It is this "roughness" that creates the link to natural surfaces, spaces and objects, where fractal patterns are comparatively common [1], [3], [4], [5]. Analysis of architectural design also identifies fractal "cascade of details" in many iconic structures such as the Sydney Opera House, Taj Mahal and others, all applying fractal systems to positive impact [6,7,8].

Games design procedural techniques, including fractal systems have been used for content generation to good effect [3],[4],[9]. Aesthetics are less clearly understood.

Y. Pisan et al. (Eds.): ICEC 2014, LNCS 8770, pp. 167–172, 2014.

2   Fractal Dimension, Complexity and Design

The concept of a fractal pattern being self-similar does not inherently require it to be either complex or simple. There exists a range of possible levels of fractal complexity within this mathematical space. For example the 2D fractal dimension (D value) ranges anywhere between 1.0 and 2.0. A pattern that fills the plane in very simplistic terms (a low order of roughness/irregularity) has a D value close to 1, and a pattern that fills the plane with detailed and intricate structure will have a D value close to 2. From a designers perspective this allows the ability to consider the fractal dimension as a changeable variable to alter the visual and aesthetic nature of the fractal content being created. For 3D objects the dimension ranges from 2.0-3.0.

Fig. 1. Early experimental fractal forms from this project demonstrating natural features

Several research studies have measured the aesthetic preferences of participants with regard to images with varying levels of fractal complexity, indicating an average aesthetic preference for a fractal complexity level in the range of 1.3 to 1.5 [10,11].

3   Experimental Study of Fractal Complexity

Earlier studies of fractal dimension and complexity have dealt with mixed imagery from both nature and digital systems, including variations in shape, color and pattern. This research sought to reduce the amount of variables in the imagery studied and to more specifically explore the link between fractal dimension and its aesthetic appeal. The study included twenty-five participants from a range of cultures ranging in age from 18 to 52 years. Each participant was presented with a range of surface options, these surfaces included a range of digitally created fractal surfaces and objects, each with differing levels of fractal dimension. Fractal patterns can of course be extremely complex and involve variations in color, depth, shape and pattern. To keep the experiment to the simple focus of the fractal dimension, the surfaces produced were generated for their aesthetic neutrality (lack of association to natural or synthetic commonly recognised form). Each surface was presented in consistent simple neutral color and the base shape/function used to create the fractal pattern was consistent. The only varying element was the dimension of fractal complexity in the surface patterns (see Figure 2 for examples of some surfaces used (different levels of fractal dimension).

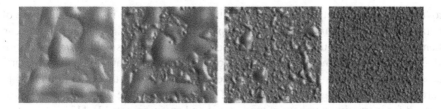

Fig. 2. Fractal surfaces used in experimental trial

The study entailed the observation and questioning of the participants regarding their interactions with these fractal surfaces. The participants were observed interacting with the visual and tactile fractal surfaces before being questioned regarding their preferences (surfaces featured 3D relief elements in physical and displacement/bump maps in visual, as result D values here are in the 2 to 3 range).

The participants visual preferences as recorded in the trial indicate that 18 of the 25 participants (72%) showed a visual preference for surfaces and objects within the fractal range of D=2.3 to D=2.5. This finding matches the results from earlier studies and highlights the fact that the fractal dimension, independent of other factors such as colour, is playing a key role in the aesthetic appeal of the surface and that the simple adjustment of the fractal complexity can alter the perception of the surface significantly [5], [10], [11]. The observational findings from the study also strongly demonstrated this altered perception of the surface, caused by change in its fractal dimension. Of specific note were the correlations between response time and the observation of emotive signal, for example, the observed facial cues associated with negative responses were very strong in relation to an unseen response (virtual tactile/touch) but almost imperceptible in relation to a negative visual response. These observations also found that the unseen tactile response is usually quick, under a three second response time, especially in regard to the objects which offer a greater level of manipulation. The visual response however was usually much slower and considered. Observation of the participants showed that visual preference was given only after careful comparison and categorisation. The key difference with this study was that the fractal surfaces presented were automatically created to meet fractal dimensional values and varied only in this factor. Thus the findings indicate that the fractal dimension itself played a key role in the aesthetic appeal, or otherwise, of a surface.

4   Applying Fractal Principles and Designs

The contemporary built environment, in both the real world and the virtual game worlds, is dominated by the Cartesian concept of space. The world of architecture, bricks, textures, UV, tiles, panels and pavement offer a familiar rectilinear package in which to place our identities, both virtual and real. The familiarity is based upon collective experience; a mechanistic experience built brick at a time. In contrast the natural world is filled with rough edges, asymmetries, complex interactions, profound depth of scale and above all, life. Fractals and other forms of recursive patterns can provide rich visuals, not only in the real natural world but also in the virtual space of interactive computer games [10], [12]. In particular these mathematical patterns can often provide more natural appearing shapes and three-dimensional structural forms [5]. The use of fractal/recursive methods to automatically create complete structural game environments has been explored in several projects and this offers potential to address some issues regarding the scale of modern interactive computer games and the need for increasing numbers of new spaces and environments [3], [13].

As the results from this study indicate, people find objects and surfaces that are too simple (D values < 2.25) or too complex (D values > 2.75) to be less appealing. By quantifying this through fractal dimension/complexity, this provided a mechanism through which spaces could be designed to be more or less appealing. The second phase of this research involved not simply understanding the nature of aesthetic response to fractal dimension, but actively adjusting the fractal dimension for effect.

4.1   Fractal Surface Designs and Complexity in Game Environments

Applying fractal techniques to surfaces that require a more natural feel, and hence the breakup of the simple linear nature of polygonal and flat textured surfaces, into richer "self-similar" patterns has been explored in various forms. The most common examples of this include the use of fractal methods to add noise and natural disturbance to fog, dust and water patterns [4], [14]. The key focus of these uses is in natural surfaces, although the principals have potential in other areas.

The second phase of this project addressed the application of fractal patterns in surfaces, but not those used in natural features like water and fog, but instead looked at the use of fractal surfacing in the built environment. Stepping into the very heart of the rectilinear world of bricks, tiles and pavers, this research applied the concepts and knowledge gained in the earlier trials, on fractal complexity, to these built environment features. The focus of this work was on the use of surfacing techniques in the form of texture and bump maps applied using a special shading mechanism based around creating different levels of fractal complexity in the surface.

4.2   Fractal Surface Design and Implementation

To apply the concept of fractal complexity to the design of surfaces a tiling technique was implemented. The fractal complexity was controlled through the use of tiled textures based on a simple equilateral triangle. These tiles were different to the normal rectangular tiles used in texture maps and were instead sphinx hexiamond based tiles (consisting of six equilateral triangles arranged as in Figure 3). These tiles can be added together to make larger versions and also recursively subdivided to differing levels of complexity in a classic fractal self-similar manner.

Fig. 3. Sphinx hexiamond tiles and laying patterns

The use of alpha channel based textures, with the sphinx hexiamond based tile pattern, and a shader that transformed and re-combined them based on fractal dimension provided the ability to utilize fractal tile patterns at varying levels of fractal complexity. This level of complexity can be varied by arranging tiles in differing patterns and also by subdividing the tiles into greater levels of detail (see Figure 4 for examples).

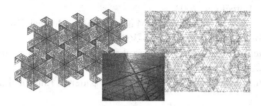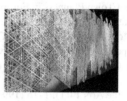

Fig. 4. Laying tiles using differing methods to achieve differing fractal complexity levels

This implementation provided a practical method, using simple tile based elements, to algorithmically create surfaces with differing levels of fractal complexity on demand. When combined with the knowledge of aesthetic preference of fractal complexity levels, this provides a means to create new surfaces of both aesthetically pleasing (D 2.3-2.5), and, perhaps for some game scenarios, aesthetically undesirable form (eg. 2.5+ for spaces to become more uncomfortable for players).

5   Conclusions and Discussion

Fractal patterns offer an automated mathematical mechanism to create rich patterns. These rich patterns can be applied in interactive game environments and in many cases can add a natural feel to the spaces in which they are used. The findings from this study have identified that differing levels of fractal dimension and complexity in a surface have a direct affect on the viewers comfort with that surface. Applied to games design, through the use of texture and bump maps, applied using non-standard shaders to construct the fractal complexity, this allows the designer to apply an automated mathematical approach to creating surfaces that can make the viewer more or less comfortable with the space.

References

1. Mandelbrot, B.B.: The fractal geometry of nature. Macmillan, New York (1983)
2. Mandelbrot, B.B.: Fractals: Form, change and dimension. WH Freemann and Company, San Francisco (1977)
3. Walsh, P., Prasad, G.: The use of an aesthetic measure for the evolution of fractal landscapes. In: 2011 IEEE Congress on Evolutionary Computation (CEC), pp. 1613–1619. IEEE Press, New York (2011)
4. Fan, N.: Realistic Rendering of Three-Dimensional Ocean Waves Based on Fractal. Advanced Science Letters 11(1), 469–472 (2012)

5. Pentland, A.: Fractal-based description of natural scenes. IEEE Transactions on Pattern Analysis and Machine Intelligence 6, 661–674 (1984)

6. Bovill, C.: Fractal Geometry in Architecture and Design. Birkhäuser, Boston (1996)

7. Salingaros, N.: A scientific basis for creating architectural forms. J. Arch. Plan. Res. 15, 283–293 (1998)

8. Salingeros, N.: Connecting the Fractal City. In: Keynote Speech, 5th Biennial of Towns and Town Planners in Europe, Barcelona (2003)

9. Patterson, D.: Using Interactive 3D Game Play to Make Complex Medical Knowledge More Accessible. Procedia Computer Science 29, 354–363 (2014)

10. Spehar, B., Clifford, C., Newell, B., Taylor, R.: Universal aesthetic of fractals. Computers & Graphics 27(5), 813–820 (2003)

11. Aks, D., Sprott, J.: Quantifying aesthetic preference for chaotic patterns. Empirical Studies of the Arts 14(1), 1–16 (1996)

12. Hendrikx, M., Meijer, S., Van Der Velden, J., Iosup, A.: Procedural content generation for games: A survey. ACM Transactions on Multimedia Computing, Communications, and Applications (TOMCCAP) 9(1) (2013)

13. Bourke, P., Shier, J.: Space Filling: A new algorithm for procedural creation of game assets. In: Proceedings of the 5th Annual International Conference on Computer Games Multimedia & Allied Technology (2013)

14. Haase, F., Klein, M., Tarnowsky, A., Wolter, F.: Interactive fractal compositions. In: Proceedings of the 11th ACM SIGGRAPH International Conference on Virtual-Reality Continuum and its Applications in Industry, pp. 181–188. ACM Press, New York (2012)

Artificial Intelligence Model
of an Smartphone-Based Virtual Companion

Elham Saadatian*, Thoriq Salafi, Hooman Samani,
Yu De Lim, and Ryohei Nakatsu

Keio-NUS CUTE Center, NUS
elham@nus.edu.sg

Abstract. This paper introduces an Artificial Intelligence (AI) model
of a virtual companion system on smartphone. The proposed AI model is
composed of two modules of Probabilistic Mood Estimation (PME) and
Behavior Network. The PME is designed for the purpose of automatic
estimation of the mood, under uncertain and dynamic smartphone context. The model combines Support Vector Machine (SVM) and Dynamic
Bayesian Networks (DBNs) to estimate the probabilistic mood state of
the user. The behavior network contorts the behavior of the interactive
and intelligent virtual companion, considering the detected mood and external factors. In order to make the virtual companion more believable,
the system consists of an internal mood state structure. The mood of the
agent, could also be inferred from another real human such as a remote
partner. The fitness of the artificial companion behavior in relation to
the users mood state was evaluated by user study and effectiveness of
the system was confirmed.

Keywords: Artificial Intelligence, Entertaining Virtual Companion, Affective Computing.

1 Introduction

The aim of this research is to employ various sensors integrated in the modern smartphones to observe the behavior of users and develop smart systems
to enrich communications and interactions. Emerging field of mediated affective
communication relates to the technologies that aim to mediate personal communication across distance. Contemporary lifestyle changes have led to design
and adoption of technologies in support of modern lifestyle. In our earlier work,
a comprehensive study of existing prototypical systems and related conceptual
studies was investigated [9].

Intelligent virtual agents are human-like embodied characters [5]. These autonomous artificial characters have applications in many fields, such as computer
game [11], conversational agents [1], and affective robotics systems [10] and many
more. In this study, we have proposed and AI system for intelligent affective virtual companion on smartphone. In this respect, a model is proposed to detect

---

* Keio-NUS CUTE Center, National University of Singapore, Singapore.

Y. Pisan et al. (Eds.): ICEC 2014, LNCS 8770, pp. 173–178, 2014.

the mood state of a user (based on the smartphones sensors' data), and generate corresponding reactions to the detected mood. The methodology is described in details by exploring mood recognition from smartphone sensory data, controlling the behavior of the virtual companion and visualization of the working process. The proposed model has been implemented and evaluated, which is described in this paper.

2   Methodology

The proposed methodology is anchored on the idea of combining uncertainty modeling with behavior networks, proposed in few previous works such as [3,4]. The improvement on the initial previously proposed ideas is made by considering the mood history of user using DBNs, using more sensors from the smartphone and fusion of inference techniques, as well as customized design of the behavior network for the specific purpose of the artificial affective companion. The system performs two functions of mood inference and behavior generation, which are detailed below.

2.1   User Mood Recognition from Smartphone Data

The mood estimation module of the system (PME) is composed of SVM and DBNs. SVM detects the physical activity level using accelerometer data and DBNs is designed to infer and map the valence and arousal result to the two-dimensional valence arousal model as illustrated in [8].

The DBNs is selected due to the uncertainties and dynamic environment of the smartphone [7]. DBNs is well suited to the problem of inferring high-level information such as the mood state by using the low-level data obtained from the smartphone. That is because the mood state of the user depends probabilistically on many different factors. For example, with the accelerometer, we can know whether he is moving or not, and if so, whether he is moving fast or slow, and with the GPS, we can estimate the user location, whether he is at home or at work or somewhere outdoors. This low-level data obtained from the smartphone sensors, can predict the conditional probability of the user status. By setting the logic based, conditional probabilities of the user mood in relation to the smartphone sensor data, the mood state could be estimated without the need of precise knowledge and training the system such as in the method proposed by [6]. Figure 1 shows the designed DBNs model. The model infers the valance and arousal level of the user, which could be mapped to the Valance-Arousal Model (VAM) and define the detected mood state.

2.2   Behavior Controller of the Virtual Companion

After detecting the users mood state, there is a need for an algorithm to control the respective artificial companion behavior. In this respect, a behavior network is designed. In the proposed behavior network, The environment and sensing part

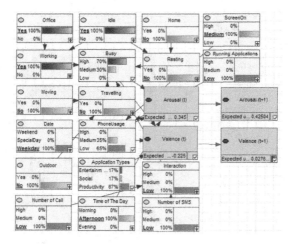

Fig. 1. Dynamic baysian network for mood estimation

of the behavior network comes from DBNs output, which consists of user and the agents internal (or a remote user) mood and local time. There are three goals in this behavior network, imitation, feedback and special time. The imitation goal triggers the character to emulate his or her partner's mood. The feedback goal intends to give feedback for the user's mood. The special time goal greets the user about the time change. The special time goal is triggered when there is a change in the time period, such as morning afternoon and evening. The feedback goal will be triggered only when there is a prominent user's mood that reaches a certain threshold, otherwise the imitation goal will be activated. In the feedback mode, the personality of the partner is considered and represented by the animation speed. The behavior network will determine the animation of the character behavior, and the animation speed of the character depend on the personality of the partner. The more extrovert the partner is, the faster the animation of the character will move. The designed behavior network is shown in 2.

2.3   Visualization of the Working Process of the System

In order to demonstrate the generated behaviors of artificial companion, an experiment with two partners is performed. The reason for choosing a second real user (partner) is to attribute the artificial agent's mood to a real user. Artificial agents with anthropomorphic features could be perceived more natural and realistic [2]. The first five sets of the mood data from the user, and its partner with the respective animated agent's behavior is shown in figure3. The proposed AI is applied in a smartphone Android app and the prototype screen shot is shown in Figure 3f.

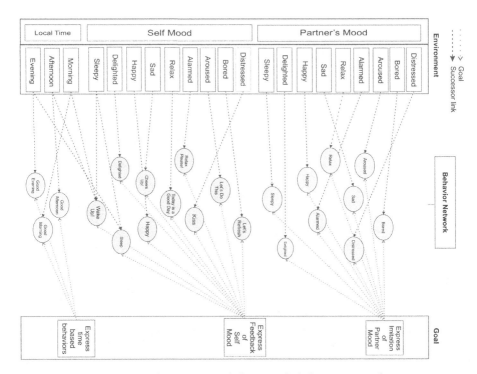

Fig. 2. Behavior network for agent's behavior control

(a)   (b)   (c)   (d)   (e)   (f)

Fig. 3. Visualization of the auto-generated animated agent behaviors for different scenarios.
(a) Special-time morning- User Mood 22.02% Relax- Partner Mood 20.84% Relax.
(b)Not an special-time- User Mood 44.39% Relax- Partner Mood 16.77% Happy.
(c)Not an special-time - User Mood 64.61% Sad - Partner Mood 22.37% Happy
(d)Not an special-time User Mood 46.71% Relax Partner Mood 46.40% delighted.
(e)Not an special-time- User Mood 54.99% Relax- Partner Mood 52.16% Sleepy.
(f) An screen shot of the app on Android phone

3   System Evaluation

In order to evaluate the system, $(n = 10)$ active smartphone users, including five females and five males, aged between 21 to 33, $(Mean = 25.8, SD = 3.82)$, were randomly selected from National University of Singapore's staff and students. None of the participants had previous experience of interacting with similar technologies such as empathetic virtual agents or emotional robots. The evaluation was performed in two stages using a simulator. The first stage the PME module was evaluated and in the second stage, the fitness of the virtual companion behaviors was tested.

The PME was tested by comparing 120 samples of mood data inferred from the proposed PME model against the self-reported user moods. Each user has logged the smartphone usage and context data such as time, location, running apps, call logs etc. in relation to their self-perceived mood. The self-perceived user mood state was compared against the result of the proposed model. The Mann-Whitney U test was used to evaluate whether or not there was any significance difference in the valence arousal space between self-perceived and the automatically inferred results. The p value for two tailed is 0.64 for the valence space, and 0.73 for the arousal space. Both p values are higher than 5%. Therefore, could be concluded that there is no significance difference in the proposed model and user self-perceived affective state. This suggests the success of PME model in the correct inference of the mood state of the user.

In the second experiment, the goal was to confirm that the interactive companion could produce corresponding behaviors, which relates to the mood. The fitness of the virtual companion behaviors points to the correspondence of the auto-generated agent's behavior from the point of view of the users. Since, the suitability of the behavior is a subjective issue and cannot be measured quantitatively we adopted the method proposed by [12] to assess the model. In this method, the participants were given 10 different combinations of the user mood (themselves), artificial companion's mood, and time of the day (special time or not). For each scenario of the mentioned combinations, they observed 5 randomly generated behavior by the animated agent followed by 5 behavior generated by the proposed behavior network. Afterward, they were asked to rate the appropriateness of the behavior from 1 (strongly inappropriate) to 5 (strongly appropriate). The mean fitness scores of each participant were calculated as shown in table 1. The result was analyzed by Wilcoxon signed-rank test with the fitness scores. As a result, the p value was obtained as $0.005 < 0.5\%$ which confirms the proposed model succeeded in generating suitable behavior compared to randomly generated behaviors.

Table 1. Mean fitness ranks

Participant	pa1	pa2	pa3	pa4	pa5	pa6	pa7	pa8	pa9	pa10
Random	2.75	2.25	1.87	2.5	3.125	2.25	2.75	1.62	2.5	2.12
Behavior Net.	4	4.25	3.37	3.25	3.25	3.87	3.62	3.62	4	3.12

4   Conclusion

The aim of this study was designing an (AI) model for smartphone to detect the user's mood state and generate adaptive behaviors via an animated artificial companion with internal mood state. The internal mood state of the agent could also come from another smartphone user. The AI model was developed based by fusion of a novel DBNs and Behavior network model. The system was tested by users, and the fitness of the generated behaviors were confirmed.

Acknowledgement. This research is supported by the Singapore National Research Foundation under its International Research Center Keio-NUS CUTE Center @ Singapore Funding Initiative and administered by the IDM Program Office.

References

1. Alfonsi, B.: "Sassy" Chatbot Wins with Wit. IEEE Intelligent Systems, 6–7 (2006)
2. Duffy, B.R.: Anthropomorphism and the social robot. Robotics and Autonomous Systems 42(3), 177–190 (2003)
3. Han, S.-J., Cho, S.-B.: A hybrid personal assistant based on bayesian networks and a rule-based system inside a smartphone. International Journal of Hybrid Intelligent Systems 2(3), 221–234 (2005)
4. Han, S.-J., Cho, S.-B.: Synthetic character with bayesian network and behavior network for intelligent smartphone. In: Khosla, R., Howlett, R.J., Jain, L.C. (eds.) KES 2005. LNCS (LNAI), vol. 3681, pp. 737–743. Springer, Heidelberg (2005)
5. Herrero, P., de Antonio, A.: Modelling intelligent virtual agent skills with human-like senses (2004)
6. LiKamWa, R., Liu, Y., Lane, N.D., Zhong, L.: Moodscope: building a mood sensor from smartphone usage patterns. In: Proceeding of the 11th Annual International Conference on Mobile Systems, Applications, and Services, pp. 389–402. ACM (2013)
7. Malm, E.J., Jani, M., Kela, J., et al.: Managing context information in mobile devices. IEEE Pervasive Computing 2(3), 42–51 (2003)
8. Ouwerkerk, M.: Unobtrusive emotions sensing in daily life. In: Sensing Emotions, pp. 21–39. Springer (2011)
9. Saadatian, E., Samani, H., Toudeshki, A., Nakatsu, R.: Technologically mediated intimate communication: An overview and future directions. In: Anacleto, J.C., Clua, E.W.G., da Silva, F.S.C., Fels, S., Yang, H.S. (eds.) ICEC 2013. LNCS, vol. 8215, pp. 93–104. Springer, Heidelberg (2013)
10. Samani, H.A., Saadatian, E.: A multidisciplinary artificial intelligence model of an affective robot. International Journal of Advanced Robotic Systems 9 (2012)
11. Welsh, S., Pisan, Y.: Enhancing information acquisition in game agents (2005)
12. Yoon, J.-W., Cho, S.-B.: An intelligent synthetic character for smartphone with bayesian networks and behavior selection networks. Expert Systems with Applications 39(12), 11284–11292 (2012)

Entertainment Devices, Platforms and Systems

SONAR: Communication System for Supporting Information Gathering and Social Interaction in a Niche Market

Junichi Hoshino, Takeru Umemura, Sachi Urano, and Daiki Satoi

University of Tsukuba, 1-1-1-#3M309 Tennodai Tsukuba, Ibaraki 305-8573, Japan
jhoshino@esys.tsukuba.ac.jp
http://www.entcomp.esys.tsukuba.ac.jp/

Abstract. We propose a new communication system by which niche people can obtain cross-cutting information and communicate with other people based on each personality. The system graphically displays the degree and direction of other people's hobbies who are interested in the keyword niche people input, and relation between the knowledge e.g. movies, music, animation, history, geography using nodes. So, we can search friends who have similar interest and direction in hobbies. From the demonstration experiments, we obtained good results that the system could help niche people to gain and exchange useful information.

Keywords: Niche, Communication System, Cross-Cutting Information.

1 Introduction

Hobbies, while they enrich our daily lives, also play a large role in the economy. Having a hobby is also an important activity from the health perspective, as having a hobby is one criterion used to measure health[1][2], and people with a hobby are found to be three times less likely than people without a hobby to contract liver-related diseases[3]. The recent trend - brought to us by technological advancements that allow us to spend our spare time in more ways than ever - is an increase in people with "niche" interests, especially among the younger population, that immerse in entertainment fields that resonate with their values[4]. Therefore, there is an increasing demand for a new system that allows for active information gathering by the users themselves; the uniformity of information provided by mass media has increasingly limited value.

Existing online services that offer information related to hobbies are not useless, with their efforts to make information in demand more accessible through implementation of search categories (movie, music, anime, etc.) as well as selective suggestions based on specific content accessed by the user. However, the users' needs for niche information, as well as communication and exchange of information with other users, has been given very little consideration.

On the other hand, there are services focused on supporting inter-user communication for acquisition of information. Social networking services, such as mixi and Quora, allow users to join communities based on interests and comment on topics created by other users. However, even within these communities, the direction and depth of the

Y. Pisan et al. (Eds.): ICEC 2014, LNCS 8770, pp. 181–188, 2014.
© IFIP International Federation for Information Processing 2014

users' interests vary greatly, hindering dialogue between commenting users, and making it difficult to gain information that matches the particular user's interests.

Online forums such as 2 Channel and 4chan do a better job of inducing communication with their interface, making it easy to access cross-boundary information based on the user's interests. Yet, the linear format of these threads makes it difficult to discern one conversation from another, obscures the topic itself, and deteriorates the utility and relativity of the information posted. As a result, niche users are forced to gather information through repeatedly searching with clever keywords or comparing multiple websites. Having both users superficially interested in trendy topics and users with in-depth knowledge on specific topics also causes miscommunication, misunderstandings, and sometimes arguments, wasting precious time that could be spent on the hobby itself to fruitless conversation.

As a means to visually support acquisition of information, visualization experts are researching query development using Boolean algebra and Venn diagrams[5], "VR-VIBE," a system that displays clusters of documents related to the user's interests[6], "Vizster," a service that graphically illustrates the connections between SNS users[7], "VISTORY," which balances public and private events on the same timeline[8], among others. There are also services that facilitate acquisition of information by clever display of information, such as Document Lens[9], Perspective Wall[10], Graphical Fisheye View[11], and TreeMap[12][13]. However, these research projects do not pay enough consideration to visualizing users' unique interests or supporting exchange of information based on user interests.

In this article, I will make a proposal of a communication system that allows users with niche interests to share information with each other, while also employing visualization to facilitate acquisition of knowledge across boundaries. This system will graphically display specific information about other users' interests, including direction and depth, and show how this information relates to the user's knowledge on the topic through nodes and timelines. By displaying the current interests of people with similar direction and depth of interest in a topic, as well as acquiring and sharing detailed information on that topic, this system aims to facilitate social interaction.

2   Discussion of System Design

Consideration to the requirements of a communication system that facilitates hobby-related activity brings us to two conclusions: the necessity of a means to help users acquire detailed information in multiple fields, as well as easily understandable representation of the relation of this information to the users themselves.

In this system, visual representation of individual users' specific interests will be achieved by colored beams radiating from circular user nodes (representing individual users), whose color and length will change according to niche, as well as visualizing time spent on the interest by variation in the size of the circle. A list of the top 10 interests of the user will also be displayed. By referencing this information during conversations, users will be able to better understand whether their counterpart is widely interested in trendy topics or is deeply interested in a niche, as well as know how much knowledge they have on the topic. Visualizing interests in this manner will reduce awkward conversation and facilitate meaningful exchange by allowing users to select to engage other users with interest characteristics especially meaningful to them.

The user nodes will display the ratio of interest within a topic by the length of up to 12 colored beams (representing subgenres) and the amount of knowledge of the topic by the size of the gray circle (Fig. 1). The colors of the beams are selected based on the PCCS (Practical Color Co-ordinate System), and the beams are placed clockwise around the node starting with red at 12 o'clock, with intervals between beams at 360/[no. subgenres] degrees. In the case of music, the ratio will be [no. plays within genre]/[total no. plays].

In addition to visualization of user interests, integrated presentation of information from Wikipedia, Amazon, YouTube, official sites, and more during conversation will help facilitate meaningful exchange. This system will offer two operation modes, "trace mode" and "timeline mode." Trace mode will allow users to find queries to search for information they feel they needed during conversation with other users, based on the visualized interest information of other users. Timeline mode displays information on the query clicked in chronological order. This function enables users to view videos of interest, encyclopedias, or shopping sites while remaining on the website, and to have other users recommend new content to them. Timeline visualization is proven to be useful for displaying integrated events with chronological information[14], but in this project it will be used to search for information on graphical content while communicating with multiple users.

3   Structure of Proposed System

3.1   System Structure

The proposed system consists of a data input section, a database section, and a data output section. The data input section will receive user input and RSS information from web services. The database section will structure data and export it in XML format. The data output section will analyze the XML and visualize the information (Fig. 2). The interface consists of: the main panel, which displays interest information(1); the information panel, which displays detailed interest information(2); the picture panel, which displays video sharing website YouTube(3); the icon panel, which displays the pages of encyclopedia website Wikipedia and shopping website Amazon(4); and the communication panel, used to communicate with other users(5) (Fig.3). The main panel will display information in either trace mode or timeline mode (Fig.4). The information panel gives the user detailed information such as top 10 favorite works or chronological tables. The communication panel allows the user to communicate with other users,

Fig. 1. Design of user node

Fig. 2. System overview of SONAR

based on information found on other panels. Topics are displayed for each query node, making it easy for a user to follow a specific conversation of interest.

3.2   Trace Mode

Trace mode allows users to find new queries from a sea of information by referencing the interests of multiple users starting from the user node described in chapter 2.

Structure of Query Nodes. Detailed information users want to know is often spread across various websites such as Wikipedia, YouTube, Amazon, or fan sites, and the necessity to switch pages and search for information obstructs smooth conversation. This system realizes smooth conversation and information acquisition by detecting queries entered during a conversation, making search requests to multiple information websites, and displaying information relevant to the topic integrally on the trace mode interface.

Other than user nodes, this system utilizes query nodes, icon nodes, and timeline nodes (Fig.5). When the user enters a search request into the text box at the top of the screen, a query node is placed in center-screen, with an icon node and timeline node nearby. The letters W, Y, and E on icon nodes represent Wikipedia, YouTube, and E-Commerce website (Amazon, within this article), and clicking on these letters will switch information displayed in the picture panel and icon panel to information related to the keyword. Icon nodes can be set to any website the user likes (e.g. official websites, 2 Channel), and a maximum of 5 can be displayed at any time. Clicking on the timeline node will switch the main panel from trace mode to timeline mode. Node locations are calculated by physical simulation using the spring model, and arranged optimally.

Executing Trace Mode. When the user enters a keyword related to their topic of interest, the database section exports data containing information on query nodes, and the data output section's layout algorithm rearranges these nodes on-screen (Fig.6). For example, if a user takes interest in The Beatles in a conversation and enters the band name into the text box, icon nodes W, Y, E, and timeline node T will appear around the query node, making reading Wikipedia articles, watching video clips of songs, or checking CD and DVD reviews on Amazon intuitive, meaning the user can easily share this information while continuing their conversation. Clicking on the query node will expand the information panel. If at any time the user feels the screen is cluttered with too many nodes, nodes may be dragged and dropped to other locations.

Fig. 3. Overview of user interface

Fig. 4. Left: Information panel that displays the top 10 of taste in music, Center: Information panel that displays the chronology of history, Right: Communication panel

3.3 Timeline Mode

Timeline Objects. Information is often presented in a timeline to make clear their chronological relationship[14]. By placing events in chronological order (Fig.7, right side), the order of these events can be clearly recognized, and by comparing this timeline with other timelines (Fig.7, center), relationships that are hardly noticeable when individually inspected can be discovered and understood. The length and width of timeline objects represent duration and number of events, respectively, with beginning times and dates at the bottom, ends at the top. Timeline mode uses data from Wikipedia.

Executing Timeline Mode. Clicking a query node in trace mode will display multiple events related to that query as a timeline object in chronological order. Clicking on captions in timeline objects will change the chronological table displayed in the information panel. Adding a new query will create a new query node, and an edge will extend to related events within the timeline object. Double-clicking captions in timeline objects will highlight the chronological chart related to the query node (Fig.8).

4 Evaluation Experiment

In order to investigate whether users with niche interests can gain and exchange more cross-boundary information by using our system, on June 28, 2012, we had 18 subjects - 13 male and 5 female, aged 22 to 26 - who like rock music search for information in any way they please for 30 minutes, then answer the questions on the survey provided on Table.1 from the choices "1: Strongly disagree, 2: Disagree, 3: Neutral, 4: Agree, 5: Strongly Agree." Later, we gave them access to our system for 30 minutes, and had them answer survey questions given on Table.2 to gain their insight. Fig.9 shows the results of the surveys noted in charts 3 and 4, with the green bars representing traditional measures of information acquisition, and the orange bars representing acquisition using the proposed system. The vertical axis shows the average score for each question,

Fig. 5. Definition of each nodes

Fig. 6. User interface of trace mode   **Fig. 7.** Timeline objects   **Fig. 8.** User interface of timeline mode

and the error bars atop each histogram shows standard deviation. Table.3 shows t-test results. There was a significant difference in the 5% range for questions 1 and 3, as well as that in the 0.1% range for question 2. In other words, the t-test revealed significant difference between information acquisition by traditional methods and our system for all questions. Because our system scores a higher average and lower standard deviation than traditional methods for questions "were you able to find cross-boundary information on your interest?", "did this service help in conversation and exchange of information with other users?", and "would you like to continue to use this service as a method of interest information acquisition?", we conclude that our system is useful in users gaining cross-boundary information on a topic, or exchanging such information.

Furthermore, the 84.2% rate of subjects choosing answers 4 or 5 for question 4 supports the validity of the method of data presentation by our system. With a spread of 3.78, answers to question 5 "did user nodes help you find points in common with other

Table 1. Survey questions on information acquisition through previous methods

| Q1. Were you able to find cross-boundary information on your interest? |
| Q2. Did this service help in conversation and exchange of information with other users? |
| Q3. Would you like to continue to use this service as a method of interest information acquisition? |

Table 2. Survey questions on information acquisition through our system (SONAR)

| Q1. Were you able to find cross-boundary information on your interest? |
| Q2. Did this service help in conversation and exchange of information with other users? |
| Q3. Would you like to continue to use this service as a method of interest information acquisition? |
| Q4. Did you easy to understand the presentation of data? |
| Q5. Did user nodes help you find points in common with other users? |
| Q6. Did query nodes help you understand the relation between objects? |

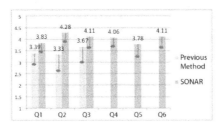

Fig. 9. Mean and standard deviation of the scores in evaluation experiment

Table 3. Result of t-test in evaluation experiment

	Q1	Q2	Q3
t-values	2.115	4.135	1.913
P-values (one-sided test)	0.0247499	0.000346	0.036372

users?" show that not every user benefited from the current user node system. As reasons, 2 subjects commented that they "could not find anyone with common interests," and 1 commented that they "used user nodes as a means to distinguish between oneself and others, not as a method to find common interests." However, some users were able to actively utilize user nodes for information acquisition, such as looking back on the music they listened to by viewing the length of colored beam for each genre, or by chatting up users with similar nodes.

The high average score of 4.11 for question 6 "did query nodes help you understand the relation between objects?" suggests the usefulness of nodes when gathering information within niche fields.

In the free comment section, subjects gave feedback such as "Users on the system were all interested in the same topic and thus reacted much more during conversation on the topic, whereas the majority of Twitter users will not," "while existing SNS connect individual users, I felt that the focus on having a common interest facilitated frank communication," "being able to know the interests of other users through user nodes, and learning more about the topic in question was very nice," "being recommended something in a conversation seemed to prompt me to investigate things I previously wouldn't have," and "the strategical connections between objects helped me gain information on cross-boundary connections." These comments are proof that the system achieves its goals of supporting cross-boundary information on interests and facilitation of information exchange between users. The efficacy of the node system, allowing users to discover new queries from a sea of information, is also apparent.

5   Conclusion

We have proposed to you a new communication system that helps users gain cross-boundary information as well as information between the users themselves. This system allows users to follow nodes to discover potential friends that have similar characteristics of interests, gain information across boundaries, and exchange information with other users. Furthermore, communication with others with similar interests will facilitate social interaction.

we conducted a system evaluation experiment, and the results suggested that our interest-based cross-boundary search and presentation of information is effective for niche fields. Observation of interaction revealed that users were utilizing the icon nodes placed around query nodes to reference YouTube, Wikipedia, Amazon, and other websites in the course of their conversation. Therefore, it can be inferred that our system is effective to a degree when it comes to interest visualization and supporting the acquisition of information based on user interest.

The evaluation experiment revealed that sometimes a user will not be able to find another user with similar interests, especially in cases when the user specifically listened to artists relatively unknown to the extent that nobody else within the subject group knew of them. However, this can be expected from the small size of the subject group, and the likeliness of similar cases will decrease when the system is launched to the public and sees users with a wide range of interests joining, increasing the range of cross-boundary information shared even further.

In the future, we would like to have many people use our system, so that we can improve the dynamic and specific properties of this service through analysis of compiled usage data.

References

1. Matsumoto, J.: A Study on Diagnostic Test of the Degree of Health. Journal of Health Science 9, 159–180 (1987) (in Japanese)
2. Tokunaga, M.: Development of Health and Life Habit Inventory (DIHAL. 2). Journal of Health Science 27, 57–70 (2005) (in Japanese)
3. Morimoto, K.: Lifestyle and Health. Journal of the Japan Society of Acupuncture and Moxibustion 53(2), 141–149 (2003) (in Japanese)
4. Suzuki, S., Shigeno, H., Matsumura, K., Kanatsugu, Y.: A Rule-base Contents Conversion Framework for TV Broadcasting Services. IPSJ SIG Technical Report. 2006-ITS-27 120, 185–192 (2006) (in Japanese)
5. Jones, S.: Graphical Query Specification and Dynamic Result Previews for a Digital Library. In: Proceedings of the 11th Annual ACM Symposium on User Interface Software and Technology (UIST 1998), pp. 143–151 (1998)
6. Benford, S., Snowdon, D., Greenhalgh, C., Ingram, R., Knox, I., Brown, C.: VR-VIBE: A Virtual Environment for Co-operative Information Retrieval. Computer Graphics Forum 14(3), 349–360 (1995)
7. Heer, J., Boyd, D.: Vizster: Visualizing Online Social Networks. In: IEEE Symposium on Information Visualization (InfoVis), pp. 32–39 (2005)
8. Nomata, Y., Hoshino, J.: VISTORY: Visualizing Relations of Multi-timelines. The Journal of the Society for Art and Science 7(2), 55–64 (2008) (in Japanese)
9. Robertson, G.G., Mackinlay, J.D.: The Document Lens. In: Proceedings of the 6th Annual ACM Symposium on User Interface Software and Technology (UIST 1993), pp. 101–108 (1993)
10. Mackinlay, J.D., Robertson, G.G., Card, S.K.: The Perspective Wall: Detail and Context Smoothly Integrated. In: Proceedings of the SIGCHI Conference on Human Factors in Computing Systems (CHI 1991), pp. 173–176 (1991)
11. Sarkar, M., Brown, M.H.: Graphical Fisheye Views. Communications of the ACM 37(12), 73–83 (1994)
12. Johnson, B., Shneiderman, B.: Tree-maps: A Space-filling Approach to the Visualization of Hierarchical Information Structures. In: Proceedings of IEEE Conference on Visualization, pp. 284–291 (1991)
13. newsmap, http://newsmap.jp/
14. Tufte, E.R.: The Visual Display of Quantitative Information, 2nd edn. Graphic Press (2001)

HANASUI: Multi-view Observable
and Movable Fogscreen

Yu Ishikawa[1], Masafumi Muta[1], Junki Tamaru[1], Eisuke Nakata[2],
Akira Uehara[2], and Junichi Hoshino[3]

[1] University of Tsukuba, Graduate School of System and Information, Tsukuba, Japan
{ishikawa.yu,mecab}@entcomp.esys.tsukuba.ac.jp,
tamaru@fz.iit.tsukuba.ac.jp
[2] University of Tsukuba, School of Engineering, Tsukuba, Japan
{s1011195,s1111088}@u.tsukuba.ac.jp
[3] University of Tsukuba, Faculty of Engineering, Information and Systems, Tsukuba, Japan
jhoshino@esys.tsukuba.ac.jp

Abstract. In this paper, we propose the method for creating multi-view mova-
ble fogscreen, and then implement it in our system called "HANASUI".
"HANASUI" displays handheld-like fireworks through a fog screen instead of
sparkles. Our method generates projection data dynamically from a virtual
space and then casts it with multiple projectors, tracking the marker attached to
the device which spouts fog at the fogscreen with infrared cameras and infrared
floodlights. Finally, we conducted a survey to verify the capabilities of
"HANASUI" and its potential for art and entertainment purposes.

Keywords: Fogscreen, Multi-View Observable, Projection Mapping, Entertainment.

1 Introduction

A fogscreen, which uses fog as a projector screen, has proposed as a technological
system for event staging or information presentation [1,2]. A feature of the fogscreen
is that, unlike conventional displays that have used liquid crystal, it doesn't have a
clearly defined edge or the edge is subtle. Another feature is that, because the screen
is made of fog, the projected image can be touched. These points are factors that give
image a great degree of freedom as well as three-dimensionality. Rakkolainen et al.
have constructed an interactive system that applies this characteristic of being able to
directly touch the image, and have identified its potential for use in entertainment and
the arts [1,2]. Furthermore, recent years have seen the commercialization of the fog
screen that can be used in the same way as a touch screen [4], and it is expected that
in future they will become a more familiar sight.

However because a feature of the fogscreen is that light rays are more widely scattered due to the effect of Mie scattering users can only view an image from within a
small range of distance from the fog and on the opposite side to the projector [5].

Y. Pisan et al. (Eds.): ICEC 2014, LNCS 8770, pp. 189–196, 2014.

Because existing systems such as [1,2] have a limited viewable range, the relative positioning of the viewpoint, the fog and the projector are fixed.

Therefore, Yagi et al. have developed a fogscreen that can be viewed from multiple directions by utilizing a cylindrical of screen that allows for Mie scattering and multiple calibrated projectors [5]. Meanwhile, in the Pocket Cosmos developed by Mun et al. [6], the device which generates the fog is fitted with a 3-axis accelerometer, allowing a mobile fogscreen where the fog is directed vertically.

However, although the system developed by Yagi et al. allows freedom in the relative position of the view point and the fog, the relative positions of the fog and the projector remain fixed. And, while the device of Pocket Cosmos [9] has mobility, it doesn't allow for multiple viewpoints, so it is likely that the image on the fog screen can only be viewed by the person holding the device.

As mentioned above, a feature of the fogscreen is its subtle outline, and prior research has suggested its application possibilities in entertainment and the arts, so if a system could be developed which allows for multiple viewpoints and mobility, and also the simultaneous use of multiple devices, it could contribute to the advancement of entertainment and the arts.

Therefore we propose a method to develop a fogscreen that allows multiple viewpoints and mobility, and the simultaneous use of multiple devices. And we carry out an evaluation through the development of "HANASUI", a system based on this method.

HANASUI is system that utilizes a portable, multi-user fogscreen for entertainment. Therefore, we carry out an evaluation through actual user experience to establish whether we have in fact developed a multi-user, portable display, and achieved an eye-catching production.

2   Proposed Method

Here we lay out the development of a portable, multi-user fogscreen using the following method. The process we propose flow we propose is illustrated in figure 1.

1. In order to be observable from multiple viewpoints, several projectors are used simultaneously.

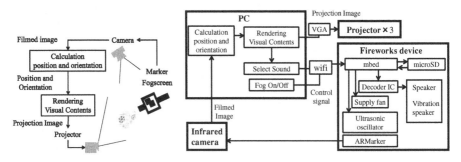

Fig. 1. System Flow   **Fig. 2.** Construction of HANASUI

2. In order that the image is correctly projected when the fog generation point is moved, markers were fitted to the fog generator to read its position and orientation and adjust the projection to match those readings.

How to position the projectors when multiple users are using the system simultaneously, it is necessary for a given user to be able to see the images projected onto the other users' fog screens. In order to achieve this, several projectors are arranged. Here, taking into consideration Mie scattering, we positioned three short focus projectors at approximately 60-degree intervals, at the same level and equidistant from the center of the circle, and with their lamps aimed at the same central point. With this arrangement, we avoid images projected from each projector overlapping due to the directionality of scattered light, and it is possible to construct a fogscreen that can be observed from multiple viewpoints.

2.1 Detecting the Position and Orientation of the Device

In order to detect the position and the orientation of the device, we use markers of known shape and size and a camera with known internal parameters. If these parameters are known, we can know the position and orientation of the markers [10]. Also, in order to avoid interference with marker recognition when the images are projected onto the markers, an infrared camera and infrared floodlight are used and the markers are filmed in the infrared spectrum.

2.2 How to Create the Projector Output Images

In order that each projector can project an image on the fog, it is necessary to create images adjusted according to the projection position of each projector, using the information collected in Subsection 2.2 about the position and orientation of the device. To generate these images, we construct and use a virtual space that is geometrically aligned with the actual space. Geometrical alignment means that the position of the cameras set up to film the markers in the virtual space (virtual marker cameras) and the relative positioning of the projectors (virtual projectors) are aligned with the infrared cameras filming the markers and the projectors in the actual space. By setting up this alignment in advance, the detected marker positions and orientation can be directly reflected in the virtual space.

The acquired the position and the orientation of the device are reflected the device arranged in the virtual space (virtual device) and we arrange the image we want to project on the front of the virtual device. Furthermore, we arrange the virtual cameras in the locations of each of the virtual projectors. We set the field of view of the virtual cameras to be the same as that of the projectors. With this setup, if the virtual cameras film the image at the front of the device, these filmed images are the images are the images that geometrically aligned projectors must project.

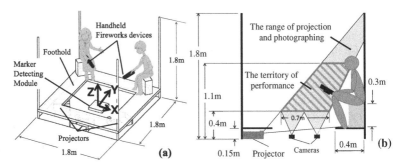

Fig. 3. a) Configuration of HANASUI b) Territory of performance

At the time of this study, the geometrical alignment of   the real and virtual spaces was not automated. A hexagonal prism was arranged in both the real and virtual spaces; the prism was filmed by the virtual cameras; these images were projected; and the projectors were manually moved and adjusted until the projected prism aligned with the actual prism.

3   Implementation of HANASUI

In the section, we cover the implementation of HANASUI, the system through which we developed our purposed multi-user and portable fogscreen. The configuration of the HANASUI system is illustrated in figure 2, and the system as whole is illustrated in figure 3.

HANASUI is made up of a performance stage and a handheld device (the handheld fireworks device figure 4).

The user experiences the HANASUI by holding out the device above the central area of the performance stage.

3.1   Performance Stage

The performance stage is in a darkroom 1.8m high and 1.8m square, and a platform with a 1.1m-square hollow center is located approximately 15cm above the floor. Below the platform three short focus projectors (Casio XJ-ST155 1024x768) are arranged at approximately 60-degree intervals, facing the center of the hollow. On the floor of the hollow space, facing directly upwards, are an infrared floodlight (WTW-F6085) and two infrared cameras (Logicool HD Pro WebCam C910 1920x1080).

In addition, the modularized infrared floodlight and infrared camera is referred to as a marker detection module.

3.2   Marker Detection Module

The marker detection module has the infrared floodlight at the center, and the infrared cameras are placed symmetrically. By using infrared light, it is possible to reliably detect the markers unaffected by light from the projector in the darkroom.

The infrared floodlight and infrared camera are positioned facing vertically upward ceiling means because it is believed that in this way occlusion will not occur when the user peers into the center of the system from above the device. And the use of two cameras is in order to widen the field of recognition.

3.3   AR Markers

With the 1.8m square size of the performance stage and the efficiency of the projectors used on this occasion, 1.3m above the floor was the highest point in the projectors' projection range. Therefore, as a marker that the camera could recognize up to this point, an 80mm-square AR marker was placed in the center of a 95mm-square acrylic plate.

To estimate the marker's position and orientation, an ARToolKit was used, which could estimate position and orientation at 30fps.

3.4   Fireworks Device

The fireworks device (figure 4) plays audio in time with the fog dispersal and image. The fireworks device is fitted with an ultrasonic oscillator, water storage tank, ventilation fan, mbed (microcontroller), speaker, vibration speaker, wireless module, battery, microSD, MP3 decoder IC, and AR marker, and can be controlled wirelessly.

These components are controlled by the internal microcontroller with the signal sent from a computer. The fog is generated using the ultrasonic oscillator, and about 90ml of water is spouted as fog per hour. Furthermore, the form of fog screen from user's view is approximately inverted triangle of which height is 0.15m and base is 0.15m. About 10 users can see the contents on the fog simultaneously. The water tank can hold about 40ml of water so fog can be generated for a maximum of about 20 minutes. Fitting vibration speakers, which emit sounds when it vibrate and are attached to the device, mean that the user experiences vibration simultaneously with audio playback. Ventilation from the fan ensures that the fog doesn't disperse and the projected image is vivid.

3.5   Contents

For the purposes of the test, the experience lasts for three minutes. During that time, six visual contents are shown and switched every 30 seconds. Each time, the visual contents are displayed in the order: flames, cherry blossom petals, sunflower, fireworks, Japanese maple leaf, and snowflake. This sequence was first carried out like a regular fireworks display, and subsequently became a conscious representation of the four seasons.

Each of them is like a performance that is spouted from the front of the handheld fireworks device. Figure 5 shows the view of the fireworks from the user's viewpoint. Also, six varieties of audio were played to match the visual contents. They were played in the following order: the sound of an open fire burning, the song of a Japanese bush warbler and a "shishiodoshi" (a water-filled bamboo tube which clacks

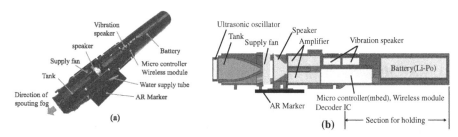

Fig. 4. a) Photograph of fireworks device b) Cross Section of fireworks device

Fig. 5. Virtual contents a) Fire b) Sunflower c) Cherry blossom d) Skyrocket e) Japanese maple f) Snowflake

against a stone when emptied), the chirping of a cicada, the explosion of fireworks, the chirping of a cricket, and the tinkling of a bell.

4   Evaluation Experiment

The evaluation experiment was exhibited on October 24-26, 2013 at the IVRC [8] (International Collegiate Virtual Reality Contest) 2013 Tokyo Finals held at the National Museum of Emerging Science and Innovation.

4.1   Evaluation Experiment

In order to evaluate the system, users were given a questionnaire. 162 questionnaires were collected from visitors aged between 7 and 68 years old.

The questionnaire consisted of six questions to which respondents awarded scores between 1 and 5, and a free description. The questions are shown in table 1, while the scoring scales by Likert scale from 5(yes) to 1(no). The results for question 5 are based on 145 questionnaires, and relate to the experience of two users each holding a fireworks device. For this question, any cases where a user did the experiment alone were marked as a non-respondent.

Table 1. The questions of questionnaire

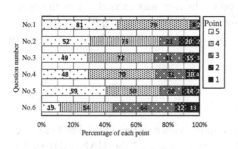

Fig. 6. Results of Questionnaire

	Question items
No.1	Do you think that the performance of HANASUI is beautiful, or not?
No.2	Could you look like the projected contents is emitting from the top of fireworks device, or not?
No.3	Did you think the projected contents on fogscreen was tracking fireworks device, or not?
No.4	Did the sound of fireworks device make NAHASUI more attractive?
No.5	Could you watch the virtual contents projected on fogscreen, or not?
No.6	Did the vibration of fireworks make HANASUI more attractive?

The procedure was that before the experience, the details of the system were explained as, "HANASUI is a performance system that uses fog and projectors in a handheld firework-like device," along with how to hold the device and the fact that the usable range of the fog screen is above the hollow central part of the performance stage. Questionnaire answers were requested after the experience.

4.2 Results

The results of the collected questionnaires are shown in figure 6. It shows the proportional breakdown for each score, with the width of the graph corresponding to 100%.

Free Description. In relation to the evaluation questions, there were opinions related to inadequate sound or vibration, such as, "the sound should be louder," or "I couldn't feel the vibration." But on the other hand, there were comments such as, "the sound was very good," and "the vibration was wonderful."

With regard to users' impressions, in addition to the comment, "it was beautiful," there were many comments saying, "it was magical."

Other than that, many users pointed out issues related to the particular positional setup of the fog screen, such as "when the projector light got in my eyes it was blinding."

Observations. From question 1, more than 90% of users felt the HANASUI performance was beautiful. And with many comments saying it was magical, we can say that it is established as a form of performance.

From question 2, we can say that many users felt that the visual contents seemed to be spouted out from the front of the device.

The results of question 3 tell us that many users felt like the visual contents followed the front of the handheld fireworks device.

From the results of questions 2 and 3, we can say that we have succeeded in developing a mobile fog screen.

Regarding sound and vibration, although the majority of users found that they added to the appeal of the performance, many others did not feel that way. It is likely that the sound volume was inadequate, and so was influenced by sound from the surroundings.

From question 5, we know that many users were able to view the image projected on the other user's fog. On this occasion, no evaluation was carried out of the precision of the projected visual contents, but more than 75% of users gave an evaluation that was "just about make it out" or better. So we can see that we have succeeded in developing a multi-viewpoint fog screen.

5   Conclusion

Here, we have proposed method to develop a multi-viewpoint and portable fog screen using AR markers and virtual space, and we have produced the HANASUI system using that method. And we carried out an evaluation experiment using a questionnaire.

From the results, we have confirmed that many users were able to view the visual-contents projected on another user's fog screen, and that they felt the visual contents were in front of the fog screen-generating device they themselves were holding.

From the above points, we have confirmed that the method proposed here for constructing a multi-viewpoint and portable fog screen is viable. We have also confirmed that many users find the HANASUI system developed using this method "beautiful" and "magical."

HANASUI was awarded the Maywa Denki Presidents Prize at IVRC 2013. Video of the experience and from the user's viewpoint can be seen on YouTube [9].

References

1. Rakkolainen, I., Palovuori, K.: Walk-thru screen. In: Electronic Imaging International Society for Optics and Photonics, pp. 17–22 (2002)
2. Rakkolainen, I.: Tracking users through a projection screen. In: Proceedings of the 14th Annual ACM International Conference on Multimedia, pp. 101–104 (2006)
3. Hayashi, H., Onishi, R., Hirai, S.: Spacial Visual Expression Using Mist in A General Bathroom-Interactibity with Touch Sensor Embedded in A Bathtub. In: EC 2007, pp. 75–76 (2007) (in Japanese)
4. DISPLAIR play with air, http://displair.com/ (accessed December 7, 2013)
5. Yagi, A., Imura, M., Kuroda, Y., Osiro, O.: Multi-Viewpoint Interactive Fog Display. TVRSJ 17(4), 409–417 (2012) (in Japanese)
6. Mun, N., Sone, J., Natsui, N., Hasebe, T., Yoshida, K.: Pocket cosmos-Cosmos in my hand. The Jornal of the Society for Art and Science 3(4), 244–249 (2004) (in Japanese)
7. Kato, H., Billinghurst, M.: Marker tracking and hmd calibration for a video-based augmented reality conferencing system; In Augmented Reality. In: Proceedings of the 2nd IEEE and ACM International Workshop on IEEE, pp. 85–94 (1999)
8. IVRC 2013 official home page, http://ivrc.net/2013/ (accessed July 10, 2014)
9. Hanasui, http://www.youtube.com/watch?v=_kLVEq-qVu4 (accessed December 8, 2013)

Interactive Art, Performance and Novel Interactions

Designing Interactive Public Art Installations:
New Material Therefore New Challenges

Jun Hu, Mathias Funk, Yu Zhang, and Feng Wang

Department of Industrial Design, Eindhoven University of Technology
Den Dolech 2, 5612AZ Eindhoven, The Netherlands
j.hu@tue.nl

Abstract. The new materials in public art installations give the birth to interactivity and participation, which in turn, introduces new challenges, not only in the creative design process, but also in how to involve the participants in this process and in evaluating the targeted experience such as such as social connectedness and inclusion. Six design cases are presented, as examples for interactive and participatory forms of these installations. The design techniques and the user experience evaluation methods overlap in these cases and many of these techniques and methods have been found to be useful in our practice.

1   Introduction

Currently the cities are coming to life in the digital world. How this digital city becomes meaningful to us remains to be seen but the first signs point towards visual solutions that augment the buildings, bridges, statues etc. The augmented layer can be used as decoration, but also as public media where the social interactivity can take pace [1]. One of the ways to approach these challenges is for example interactive public installations. The current development in public art installations involves a significant amount of new material and technology, resulting new dynamic, interactive or participatory forms that require the artists and designers to construct their work from a system view and with a good understanding of human-system interaction. It is no longer about carving stones and casting bronze; it is time to sculpture the interactive experience with the public participation [2, 3].

1.1   Five Generations of Materials

The term "public arts" often reminds people of the traditional art forms such as sculptures, murals and installations in public spaces in cities. Even the bricks in the pavements of a city square or the grass of the lawns in a park can used as the material by the artists for these public arts. For artists, material is of vital importance in expressing their thoughts, motives and emotions [4]. Material is a language of art and it has gone through several generations in the art history. From natural materials to recent smart materials [5], there has been distinctively five generations: the first generation of natural materials such as wood, bamboo, cotton, fur, leather and stones; the second

Y. Pisan et al. (Eds.): ICEC 2014, LNCS 8770, pp. 199–206, 2014.
© IFIP International Federation for Information Processing 2014

generation of man-made materials such as wood-based panels, paper, cement, metal, ceramic and glass; the third generation of synthetic materials such as plastic, rubber and fiber; the fourth generation of composite materials such as fiber-reinforced materials used in aerospace components; the fifth generation of smart materials with one or more properties that can be changed or controlled by external stimuli, such as force, temperature, electricity or magnetic fields. The advances in the material science has pushed the evolution of material technology forward, which has also a great impact on its application in the field of arts [5].

In the traditional public arts, the materials of the first and second generation are most often used. Along with the development of the material technology, the synthetic and composite materials are more and more applied, however the forms of the public arts remain static. The recent development of the smart materials and especially the digital media brings dynamic forms to the public arts that utilize different modalities of the senses. The further development in sensor technology, computer and mobile networks brings interactivity to public arts.

1.2   Four Levels of Interactivity

Based on the work of Edmonds et al [6], Wang, Hu and Rauterberg defined three generations of art and generative technology according to the carrying material, technology and interactivity [7]: 1) Static forms: there is no interaction between the art artifact and the viewer, and the artifact does not respond to its context and environment. 2) Dynamic forms: the art artifact has its internal mechanism to change its forms, depending on time or limited to reacting to the changes in its environment such as temperature, sound or light. The viewer is however a passive observer and has no influence on the behavior of the artifact. 3) Interactive forms: the viewer has an active role in influencing the dynamic form of the art object. The input from the viewer can be gesture, motion, sound as well as other human activity that can be captured by the artifact's sensorial layer. When interactivity is introduced, the "dialog" between the viewer and the perceived dynamic form of the artifact can always vary depending on the difficult-to-predict behavior of the human viewer. Later Hu et al [2] introduced the fourth generation of the public art forms – participatory forms – Interactive art platforms that allow social interactivity and creativity contribute to the physical and digital parts of the artifact. Artists and designers do not create the public media arts as a final result, but create them as platforms for other artists and the public to contribute to the artifact. The creation process, together with the results of this process, forms the dynamic media artifact that grows with the creative input from the social environment and over time.

The new materials in public art installations give the birth to interactivity and participation, and in turn, the interactivity and participation also introduces new challenges, not only in the creative design process, but also in how to involve the participants in this process and in evaluating the targeted experience such as such as social connectedness and inclusion. Next we present several design cases, giving examples to interactive and participatory forms, then sharing our practices and experiences in facing and handling these challenges.

2   Interactive Forms

2.1   Blobulous

Blobulous (Fig. 1) allows participants to interact through projected avatars, blogs of dots, which react to their movement and body signal.The participant's heart rate is mapped to the color of her avatar[8, 9]. Wireless heart rate sensors are used to capture and send heart rate data from users and a ZigBee network to handle communication between sensors and the avatars.

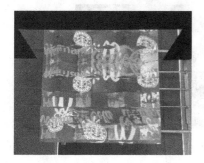

Fig. 1. Blobulous   **Fig. 2.** Yang Sheng

2.2   Yang Sheng

Yang Sheng is an ancient Chinese Philosophy to maintain and improve one's health though daily activities. Tai Chi is one of the common meditation practices which originates in China and is still popular today, but not among the younger generation. To attract the young to this tradition, this installation uses computer vision to track the movements of the Tai Chi players and visualize their movements as well as "chi", the life energy, with a floating sphere controlled by the movements (Fig. 2).

Fig. 3. Replication   **Fig. 4.** Strijp-T-ogether

2.3   Replication

People walk past the wall and find themselves projected on it in a grid of delayed videos; each newly appearing video copying the previous one (Fig. 3). Slowly, the influence and domination of the West is shown with an increasing number of logos which progressively overwhelm and cover the person and the scenery. The drama revolves around the idea that China is replicating the West, to create the awareness of the western culture creating a new patina on top of the Chinese culture.

3   Participatory Forms

3.1   Strijp-T-ogether

Strip T is an old industrial area rebuilt to accommodate and foster creative industries. However there is hardly any social interaction among people from different companies. Strijp-T-ogether is designed to stimulate the social interaction with a mobile application and a projection in the main entrance hall (Fig. 4). The photo of a space is used on the mobile as the background and an addition can be made by drawing or adding other graphical objects. These additions will be projected into the space and will also be shown on the mobile of the others as background. People can then react on each other's drawings and additions to trigger social interaction [10].

3.2   Leave Your Mark

With the installation "Leave your mark", people can "draw" and leave their mark behind on the public space, to express themselves (Fig. 5). The concept involves projection mapping to digitally augment buildings. In some locations the installation will be provided with a camera. The feed of this camera will be projected onto the installation at another location. If a person walks by this second location, she could possibly see someone, a complete stranger, leaving the mark on the first installation. The goal is to increase their feelings of inclusion and connectedness in the city [11].

Fig. 5. Leave your mark

3.3   Moon Rising from Sea

This installation is designed for the city of Taicang, China. The installation is roughly 10 by 10 meters on its base and 8 meters high. On top of the base are constructions that give the impressions of a large sail, and the moon rising from the waves. Images, animations and videos can be projected onto the inner surface of sail in the evenings (Fig. 6), allowing the public to contribute their photos from social media to induce the feeling of social connectedness [8, 11, 12].

Fig. 6. Moon rising from sea

4   Practices in the Design Process

In the design process of above mentioned installations, many design techniques were found to be useful. These techniques including learning from performance art, card-board modelling, acting out and video prototyping, not listing them all.

Dynamic art forms and interactive public installations have much in common: both have a time core to drive the dynamics; both have to manage inside a public space and the space has to be carefully structured for functions and interactions; both have to accommodate active or passive participants with different roles and goals. Traditional dynamic arts have much to offer and it is valuable to explore how the elements and techniques could contribute to interaction design [13-15].

Installations in public spaces are three dimensional, or if we take time into account because of the dynamic nature of interaction, four dimensional. Cardboard modelling, especially when integrated with advanced mechanical and electronic techniques and components, is a powerful tool for tangible or rich interaction [16, 17].

When designing for social interaction in public spaces, the interactive nature of the design requires conceptualizing, visualizing and communicating the dynamics of the interaction. The integration of design processes and software design processes is often necessary [18, 19]. The acting-out design approach [20] utilizes the designers body to simulate the elements and the behavior of the design, providing and communicating the insights at earlier stages of a design process when a prototype is not yet available.

High-fidelity prototyping of installations in a large scale or for a big or busy public space is often costly and challenging, if not impossible. Video prototyping allows the designers to create simulation of the installation and the interaction using simple materials and equipment [21].

A combination of video prototyping and acting out can be also used in context with the help of portable projectors: prepared video prototypes are projected onto artifacts and objects in the real-life context using projection-mapping techniques. This serves as documentation for evaluation, but also as input for further design iterations.

5   User Experience Evaluation

We present some of the methods that were used for evaluation in the projects mentioned earlier and that were found to be handy for designers, instead of extensively reviewing the literature about and reflecting on how user experience shall be evaluated in public spaces.

5.1   Qualitative Methods

Interviews with Experiential Prototypes. Interactive installations for public spaces have to be experienced in the actual space for the users to understand the design and to give valuable input or feedback. This is done for most of the projects mentioned.

Co-Reflection. In the project Strijp-T-ogether, co-reflection was used as a qualitative and constructive approach on evaluating whether the installation triggers social interaction [10]. "Co-reflection sessions can be developed in three parts: exploration on the current situation, ideation through a discovery process and confrontation between users and designers" [22].

Observations in Context. It is important to observe in the context when design for public spaces in order to understand the situations and to get a good grasp of the problems to be solved or the opportunities to be identified. Observing in context has demonstrated its effectives not only to get the input for the ideas and concepts, but also in evaluating whether the design has achieved its goal – but in the latter case, a prototype would be necessary.

5.2   Quantitative Measures

Connectedness. Social Connectedness Scale Revised (SCS_R) questionnaire [23] was chosen to evaluate the level of social connectedness of participants in the projects "leave your mark", Blobulous and Strijp-T-ogether. SCS-R is based on an earlier version of Social Connectedness Scale [24]. SCS-R consists of 20 items (10 positive and 10 negative). The negatively worded items are reverse scored and summed with the positively worded items to create a scale score. A higher score on the SCS-R indicates a stronger feeling of social connectedness.

Social Inclusion. The Inclusion of community in self scale [25] is a simple yet effective pictorial measure consisting of six pairs of circles. Each pair of same-sized circles overlaps slightly more than the preceding pair. Each circle on the left of the pair represents the participant, while the circle on the right represents the community. Connectedness to the community at large is assessed by the participant marking the pair of circles that best describe her relationship with the community. It is found to be useful in projects "Leaving your mark" and "Strijp-T-ogether".

Attractiveness. AttrakDiff [26] is an instrument for measuring the attractiveness of interactive products. With the help of pairs of opposite adjectives, users can indicate their perception of the product. These adjective-pairs make a collation of the evaluation dimensions possible. The following product dimensions are evaluated: Pragmatic Quality, Hedonic Quality - Stimulation, Hedonic Quality - Identity and Attractiveness. Hedonic and pragmatic qualities are independent of one another, and contribute equally to the rating of attractiveness and they are mapped into a visual output. This method has been used to measure the attractiveness of Blobulus [9].

6   Concluding Remarks

The recent development in material and technology creates new opportunities for the artist and designers to creative interactive public art installations, merging physical material with digital content, allowing social engagement and participation. Six design cases are presented in this paper, as examples for interactive and participatory forms of these installations. The targeted spaces and user groups, design concepts and implementing technologies vary, aiming at different social experiences. The design techniques and the user experience evaluation methods overlap and many of these techniques and methods have been found to be useful in our practice. We consider it to be an interesting and promising area in design research on social and cultural computing [27] in public spaces. The practice and experience presented in this paper are first steps of our effort in facing the new challenges in both design and research in this area.

References

1. Hu, J., Frens, J., Funk, M., Wang, F., Zhang, Y.: Design for Social Interaction in Public Spaces. In: Rau, P.L.P. (ed.) CCD/HCII 2014. LNCS, vol. 8528, pp. 287–298. Springer, Heidelberg (2014)
2. Hu, J., et al.: Participatory Public Media Arts for Social Creativity. In: 2013 International Conference on Culture and Computing (Culture Computing). IEEE (2013)
3. Wang, F., Hu, J., Rauterberg, M.: New Carriers, Media and Forms of Public Digital Arts. In: Culture and Computing, pp. 83–93 (2012)
4. Dewey, J.: Art as experience. Perigee (2005)
5. Rauterberg, M., Salem, B., van de Mortel, D.: From Passive to Active Forms. In: Feijs, L., Kyffin, S., Young, B. (eds.) Design and Semantics of Form and Movement (DesForM 2005), pp. 110–117. Koninklijke Philips Electronics N.V., Newcastle-upon-Tyne (2005)
6. Edmonds, E., Turner, G., Candy, L.: Approaches to interactive art systems. In: Proceedings of the 2nd International Conference on Computer Graphics and Interactive Techniques in Australasia and South East Asia, Singapore, pp. 113–117. ACM
7. Wang, F., Hu, J., Rauterberg, M.: New Carriers, Media and Forms of Public Digital Arts. In: Culture and Computing 2012, pp. 83–93. Springer, Heidelberg (2004)
8. Funk, M., Le, D., Hu, J.: Feel Connected with Social Actors in Public Spaces. In: Workshop on Computers As Social Actors, co-located with 13th International Conference on Intelligent Virtual Agents (IVA 2013), Edinburgh, UK (2013)
9. Hu, J., Le, D., Funk, M., Wang, F., Rauterberg, M.: Attractiveness of an Interactive Public Art Installation. In: Streitz, N., Stephanidis, C. (eds.) DAPI/HCII 2013. LNCS, vol. 8028, pp. 430–438. Springer, Heidelberg (2013)

10. Janmaat, J.: How to stimulate soicial interaction within a working area. Department of Industrial Design, Eindhoven University of Technology (2013)
11. Brenny, S., Hu, J.: Social Connectedness and Inclusion by Digital Augmentation in Public Spaces. In: 8th International Conference on Design and Semantics of Form and Movement (DeSForM 2013). Philips, Wuxi (2013)
12. Le, D., Funk, M., Hu, J.: Blobulous: Computers As Social Actors. In: Experiencing Interactivity in Public Spaces (EIPS), CHI 2013, Paris (2013)
13. Zhang, Y., et al.: Learning from Traditional Dynamic Arts: Elements for Interaction Design. In: International Conference on Culture and Computing, Kyoto, Japan (2013)
14. Zhang, Y., et al.: Scripting Interactive Art Installations in Public Spaces. In: 16th International Conference on Human-Computer Interaction, Creta Maris, Heraklion, Crete, Greece (2014)
15. Zhang, Y., Frens, J., Funk, M., Hu, J., Rauterberg, M.: Scripting Interactive Art Installations in Public Spaces. In: Kurosu, M. (ed.) HCI 2014, Part I. LNCS, vol. 8510, pp. 157–166. Springer, Heidelberg (2014)
16. Frens, J.: Cardboard modeling studio: A designerly exploration tool for rich and embodied interaction. In: Proceedings of the Fifth International Conference on Tangible, Embedded, and Embodied Interaction. ACM (2011)
17. Frens, J., Djajadiningrat, J., Overbeeke, C.: Form, interaction and function, an exploratorium for interactive products. In: Proc. of Asian Design Conference (2003)
18. Hu, J., Feijs, L.M.: An Adaptive Architecture for Presenting Interactive Media Onto Distributed Interfaces. In: Applied Informatics (2003)
19. Hu, J.: Design of a distributed architecture for enriching media experience in home theaters (2006)
20. Hu, J., Ross, P., Feijs, L.M.G., Qian, Y.: UML in Action: Integrating Formal Methods in Industrial Design Education. In: Hui, K.-C., Pan, Z., Chung, R.C.-K., Wang, C.C.L., Jin, X., Göbel, S., Li, E.C.-L. (eds.) Edutainment 2007. LNCS, vol. 4469, pp. 489–498. Springer, Heidelberg (2007)
21. Bojic, M., et al.: On the effect of visual refinement upon user feedback in the context of video prototyping. In: Proceedings of the 29th ACM International Conference on Design of Communication. ACM (2011)
22. Tomico, O., Frens, J.W., Overbeeke, C.: Co-reflection: user involvement for highly dynamic design processes. In: CHI 2009 Extended Abstracts on Human Factors in Computing Systems. ACM (2009)
23. Lee, R.M., Draper, M., Lee, S.: Social connectedness, dysfunctional interpersonal behaviors, and psychological distress: Testing a mediator model. Journal of Counseling Psychology 48(3), 310 (2001)
24. Lee, R.M., Robbins, S.B.: Measuring belongingness: The Social Connectedness and the Social Assurance scales. Journal of Counseling Psychology 42(2), 232 (1995)
25. Mashek, D., Cannaday, L.W., Tangney, J.P.: Inclusion of community in self scale: A single-item pictorial measure of community connectedness. Journal of Community Psychology 35(2), 257–275 (2007)
26. User Interface Design GmbH, AttrakDiff Tool to measure the perceived attractiveness of interactive products based on hedonic and pragmatic quality (2012), http://www.attrakdiff.de/en/Home/
27. Bartneck, C., et al.: Applying Virtual and Augmented Reality in Cultural Computing. IJVR 7(2), 11–18 (2008)

Interactive Performance Art Using Musical Instrument Daegeum for Healing

YoungMi Kim*

Singyoung-dong, Jongro-gu, 110-830, Seoul, South Korea
ymkimlab@naver.com

Abstract. The piece called healing bamboo is a drawing concept utilizing daegeum interface as a performance interactive art. The piece has an aim of manifesting spiritual culture of Bamboo healing by drawing fake bamboo on screen while daegeum is being played. Drawing bamboo trees was a representative healing method of the Korean ancestors. Although joys and sorrows of our ancestors differ from those of modern day, the idea of bamboo tree purifying consciousness and making mind upright continued up until now. A performer draws pictures by meditating upon the symbolization of bamboo trees and the old classical scholar' spirits. Accordingly, the daegeum sound that embraces mental values of an oriental culture and the bamboo tree drawing based on such sound offer emotional elements to heal the mind and body of a performer. We reinterpreted the cultivation of mind of bamboo tree healing as a modern tendency walking with the trend without discoloration of its meaning.

Keywords: Healing Art, Interactive Art, Performance, Cultural Technology.

1 Background

With economical advancements, modern people take one step further from just being rich and show high interests in managing healthy lives by healing mind and soul. The healing fever is the reflection of our lives being weary and hard. Because of that, it is necessary to first examine the cause before healing wounds. The emergence of healing appears to be attributable to stress from prolonged recession and demand to cure wounds from interpersonal relationships. Due to such reasons, healing is a new trend culture in the modern world. Art heals wounds in one's mind and soul and by that we can gain stability and pleasure. In most cases healing occurred through drawings and listening to music; however in this paper, we suggest art healing from the perspective of experience. Notably, in the past years, our ancestors recovered and healed wounded self-regard through art and music. In this paper, we focused on the Korean conventional culture forming the base of an oriental culture for consideration.

---

* Please note that the LNCS Editorial assumes that all authors have used the western naming convention, with given names preceding surnames. This determines the structure of the names in the running heads and the author index.

Y. Pisan et al. (Eds.): ICEC 2014, LNCS 8770, pp. 207–213, 2014.

2   Bamboo Trees with Ideology of Healing

Oriental esthetics is mostly embedded with the idea of mental healing. Interestingly, our oriental ancestors said we can disciple one's mind by just looking at an object which has mental values. As historically investigated, the representative plant with mental values is a bamboo tree and classical scholars observed bamboo trees by day and night and developed their mental, by drawing Bamboo trees for healing. This has values of drawing inner side and mind of the painter, not just copying the appearances of the bamboo trees in reality. They assumed the artistic activity of drawing bamboo trees was a way of mind culturing, incorporating philosophy, literary value, moral and cultivation.[1] Bamboo trees were perceived as an emblem of a man of virtue by our ancestors.[2] The symbolization of a bamboo tree as a man of virtue is due to five reasons which embrace powerful virtues.

Fig. 1. The artwork as it is drawn according to a performers play

First is that bamboo tree has firm roots. A benevolent person should emulate bamboo roots and nurture virtues not to be pulled off.

Second is that bamboo tree has straight stem. We should not tilt to one side by straightening our mind.

Third is that bamboo trees are hollow inside. We should learn and cultivate ourselves with open mind, accepting others with open-mindednessor in other words, modestheart.

Fourth is that bamboo tree has straightened joints and has discipline. We should cultivate behaviors through straightness.

Fifth is that bamboo tree never withers, being green for four seasons. It has unvarying mind in any circumstances.

Our forbearers printed the five characteristics of bamboo trees in their minds and drew bamboo trees keeping in their mind spirit. The mind of a bamboo tree is the uprightness, maintaining center and taking a firm stand in the fierce wind (harsh adversity).[3] We can see from bamboo drawings the wisdom of our forbearers that we can learn to stand upright whilewavering in the wind.

3   Development of Bamboo Trees as an Interactive Art

3.1   Art Processing

For <The healing bamboo> piece, we referred to the paintingby Leejung who established pattern tradition of bamboo tree painting in Chinese ink in Chosun dynasty.The Joseon Dynasty of Korea lasted more than 519 years and encompassed the reigns of 27 kings. During this time, which ink-and-wash painting flourished and became highly developed. Leejung's bamboo drawing in chinese ink represents bamboo drawings of Chosun dynasty in chinese ink by taking and developing one's line completely that you can not find earlier styles of bamboo

Fig. 2. Lee jung by bamboo trees (a)bamboo tree painting in chinese ink, Lee jung (b) wind-bamboo drawing, in the first half of 17th century, Lee jung

drawing in chinese ink in his drawings. (see Fig. 2) We created dual version, separating the old paintings of bamboo with thick nodes and wind-bamboo drawing which are Lee Jung's representative pieces. For the first version, we made references to (a)bamboo drawing in chinese ink and for the second version, we designed with references to (b)wind-bamboo drawing.

This drawing portrays the fidelity of classical scholars hardening firm will to live, recovering from hardships by bamboo trees. By the drawing (a) (see Fig. 2) showing bamboo trees which are upright, full of vigor, Leejung cherishes fidelity and integrity that classical scholars should have. (b) In this painting, Leejung focused on expressing condensed spirits of bamboo trees withstanding wind. Although the stem is straightened, the wisdom that we should deal with everything flexibly is passed on to other generations by the portrayal of a stem which is little bit bent. Because of these reasons, <wind-bamboo drawing>is illustrated in the Korean bill. Wind-bamboo drawing by Lee jung is used as a background picture for the current Korean 50, 000 won bill. The attitude of the old classical scholars drawing four gracious plant to cultivate minds and appreciating the drawings to become a man of virtue is much needed in this contemporary world. In the Fig. 3(a) we added modern touch in expressing bamboo with thick nodes in Leejung's Fig. 2(a). With strong drawing line, we added strength in each of the leaves one by one. Heavy breathing is expressed by drawing line of heavy concentration and drawing line of relatively weak breathing is weakened to give a three-dimensional effect by having a feeling of space.

Fig. 3. Healing bamboo (a)"version 1"digital data with a reference to Fig. 2(a) a image (b)"version 2"digital data with a reference to Fig. 2(b) image

In the Fig. 3(b) elasticity of the bamboo is well-illustrated by accurately capturing bamboo stem and leaves fluttering in the wind. The sense of fluttering is well-portrayed as the bamboo stem is thin with thick leaves. This aims to nurture the mind to flexibly deal with an unexpected headwind in the modern life by drawing the bamboo confronting the wind flexibly without shaking in the coming wind. The completed bamboo tree slowly wavers by the wind by 15degrees left and right and maintains dynamic movement until the seal is marked. The Fig. 3(b) adds dynamic interactive elements by improvement of what the Fig. 3(a) lacked which is made one year earlier than the Fig. 3(b).

3.2   Breathing as an Interactive Impersonation Tool

The conventional four gracious plants were drawn by brush and ink. However in this piece, a daegeum as an interface replaces the formative meanings brush and ink took. The daegeum was an musical instrument which healed our ancestors in the past.[4] The daegeum makes very deep and pure sound by resonance and the tone seemed to represent and express feeling of lamentation and pain of a man of virtue that it became the musical instrument of healing cherished by classical scholars.

Fig. 4. The Interface (a)Drawn by brush and ink (b)Daegum: Daegum is one of the representative musical instruments that were played in palaces during Chosun Dynasty

<The healing bamboo> is an art embodied in breathing. For the morning breathing method, which is the representative of an oriental mental cultivation method, we must exhale long and thin breaths through mouth, visualizingthe breath spreads out to every inch of the entire body to remove distracting thoughts. Prior to the exhaling, we need an inhaling procedure, in which we breath in heavily by nose to keep equilibrium. Such breathing procedures manipulate consciousness and removes distracting thoughts from head and maintains a state of equilibrium, leading to mind healing. The bamboo drawing made by calm and consistent breathing through daegeum maintains consistency in light and shade of ink stick. To copy bamboo in heart onto a screen, it is important to find relaxed and untrouble breathing. By this process, modern man can read the heart of the classical scholars which mimics the heart of a man of virtue and can heal mind and soul naturally.

Such breathing procedures manipulate consciousness and removes distracting thoughts from head and maintains a state of equilibrium, leading to mind healing. The bamboo drawing made by calm and consistent breathing through daegeum maintains consistency in light and shade of ink stick. To copy bamboo in heart onto a screen, it is important to find relaxed and untrouble breathing. By this process, modern man can read the heart of the classical scholars which mimics the heart of a man of virtue and can heal mind and soul naturally.

Fig. 5. Interactive Media Art for Healing exhibition, 2009

3.3   Appropriate Technology Design

The user sounds amplitude is the higher, the drawing line is the thicker. The others, the user sounds time is the longer, the drawing line is the longer. Finally, we can display the bamboos steps like black-and-white drawing on the screen using the drawing action quantized by decibel descriptor.[5][6]

Manufactured program, which digitalized analog features, is Adobe Flash program with a huge merit of establishing strong controller, which only the writers could use on. In the Figure 6, we will examine control panel in the upper side from left to right one by one. In the main menu in the left, the sound level of microphone level is at maximum 100. It becomes sensitive as the figure is lowered and will insensitively accept input values as the figure gets higher.

Blow Accumulation is a menu amassing breathing and a special daegeum sound is output when breathing strengths accumulate above a set up value. The accumulated numbers are not shown by figures but are shown by the expression of a gauge bar filled with grey color in graphics. The submenu, Processed Brush Power refers to the concentration when we draw bamboo trees. With a maximum strength of 110, heavier concentration on joints and leaves are portrayed as the figure gets higher. Process Brush Power inputs graphics and are classified by five stages 0-20, 21-40, 41-60, 61-80, 81-110. Sensitivity refers to the drawing speed and bamboo joints are drawn quicker as the figure approaches 50 which is the maximum number.

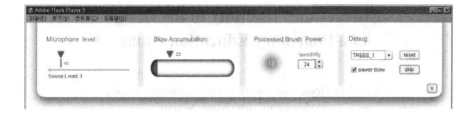

Fig. 6. Display controller

4   Conclusion

Real healing should expand consciousness and purify minds beyond healing body and heart. When we consider that mental crisis of our society is due to the lost meaning of life and the lack of self-control abilities, the necessity of mental cultivation is clearly noted. Our ancestors said a tranquility of mind and a mental healing occurs by just looking at an object of mental values. <The healing bamboo> expresses mental values and ideological meanings possessed by the subject well, through embodiment of gallery. The daegeum sound which mimics clear minds of the classical scholars and the heavy brush touch emotionally approached the mental cultivation of modern men. Consequently, through several exhibition, the approachment of the art as the interactive art seeking healing was positively valued.

References

1. Kim, Y.-M., Choi, J.-S.: Breathe Brush. In: 37th ACMSIGGRAPH 2010, Los Angeles, July 25-29 (2010)
2. Kim, Y.-M., Choi, J.-S.: Bamboo Flute. In: ACE 2009, October 29-30 (2009)
3. Choi, B.-S.: Thought and History of Ink Painting, p. 23. Dongmoonsun, Korea (2008)
4. Kim, Y.-M.: Interactive Ink-and-Wash Drawing. In: Anacleto, J., Fels, S., Graham, N., Kapralos, B., Saif El-Nasr, M., Stanley, K. (eds.) ICEC 2011. LNCS, vol. 6972, pp. 383–386. Springer, Heidelberg (2011)
5. Choi, B.-S.: Thought and History of Ink Painting, pp. 83–88. Dongmoonsun, Korea (2008)
6. Kim, Y.-M., Choi, J.-S.: The Sound Brush Made of Bamboo. In: Butz, A., Fisher, B., Christie, M., Krüger, A., Olivier, P., Therón, R. (eds.) SG 2009. LNCS, vol. 5531, pp. 279–282. Springer, Heidelberg (2009)

Efficacy and Usability in the Design
of a Pharmacy Education Game

Geoffrey Hookham[1], Joyce Cooper[2], Rohan Rasiah[2],
Hayley Croft[2], and Keith Nesbitt[1]

[1] School of Design, Communication and IT, University of Newcastle, Newcastle, Australia
{Geoffrey.Hookham,Keith.Nesbitt}@newcastle.edu.au
[2] School of Biomedical Sciences and Pharmacy, University of Newcastle, Newcastle, Australia
{Joyce.Cooper,Rohan.Rasiah,Hayley.Croft}@newcastle.edu.au

Abstract. This study introduces a puzzle game called the 'Virtual Dispensary' that was developed to assist in teaching dispensing skills to first year pharmacy students. We describe the key game elements and reports on initial findings from a study of the usability and effectiveness of the game.

Keywords: Engagement, Gamification, Pharmacy, Usability, Efficacy.

1 Introduction

Throughout history, games have been used to educate, train, inform and distract [1]. As of 2014 there is a groundswell of enthusiasm surrounding the 'engaging' nature of computer games and the potential to leverage this engagement for more 'effective' education [2]. This motivates a number of research questions around serious games about what is engagement, how to measure effectiveness and the role of usability in ensuring games meet there serious intention.

The game described in this study, the Virtual Dispensary, was developed to assist teaching dispensing skills to first year Pharmacy students. We take an iterative approach to creating the Virtual Dispensary, developing and evaluating game prototypes to ensure we meet the expected educational directions of the serious game and also ensuring that key usability issues that might detract from engagement are identified early in the development process. We report here on some of the key design elements integrated into the game and report on a first usability trial with a representative sample of students. Both the novel domain and the issues uncovered should be of interest to all designers of serious games.

2 The Virtual Dispensary

The online Virtual Dispensary provides pharmacy students with an exploratory space that allows the students to practice typical forensic skills related to prescribing medications. A single play session of the game requires the student to solve a quiz that

Y. Pisan et al. (Eds.): ICEC 2014, LNCS 8770, pp. 214–216, 2014.

requires navigating and interaction with elements in a virtual pharmacy. The structure and gameplay of the Virtual Dispensary prototype places the game within the 'puzzle game' genre, as it consists of conceptual reasoning challenges requiring extrinsic knowledge for successful completion [3].

The game world itself is based on a virtual tour created from sixteen, 360° panoramic photographs of a community pharmacy. The functionality of the community pharmacy tour allows students to navigate about the pharmacy and zoom in to examine products in detail. The tour also provides information about the key locations of the pharmacy by way of auditory descriptions and information pop-ups. Players have the task of identifying and verifying prescriptions, which includes checking medication packaging and labels on interactive 3D models situated at typical locations.

3   Usability Study

The subjects for the study were 10 students currently studying the Masters of Pharmacy program at the University of Newcastle. There were six males, and four females. Four of the subjects were under the age of 23, four were between the ages of 24-34 and two were older than 35. Most subjects (n=9) completed the game in less than 30 minutes while one subject played for slightly longer. After completing the game, subjects completed an anonymous survey, containing eleven Likert-scale questions designed to measure the perceived effectiveness and usability (Table 1) of the Virtual Dispensary. Students could also respond to two open questions to identify the features of the Virtual Dispensary they enjoyed the most and to suggest possible improvements.

In terms of effectiveness, all 10 subjects agreed that the Virtual Dispensary provided an effective way of learning about dispensing. For the two questions related to confidence, 12 of the twenty responses agreed that the game improved their confidence about dispensing while five disagreed. Seven of the subjects formed no opinion about whether or not the application stimulated their interest to learn.

When asked to identify the best thing about the Virtual Dispensary, four noted the scripting examples with checking. Three subjects highlighted the realism of the pharmacy environment and three suggesting the interactive products and packing as key elements. A range of improvements were suggested, these focused on providing more content, in particular three subjects requested increasing the number of products and scripts available. Another four subjects wanted more product information to be integrated into the game. Other subjects suggested integrating even more elements of pharmacy practice, such as patient counselling into the game.

According to the feedback, the application of interactive and game elements was perceived to be a fun and effective learning technique, however this is no indication of the effectiveness in terms of learning outcomes. There were some interesting feedback elements, namely that the majority of respondents indicated that the game functions were well integrated. Further development that provides more product information and interactive components is the next goal of this research followed by better measure of effectiveness using pre and post testing of student knowledge [4].

Table 1. Perceived Effectiveness and Usability Questions and Responses (n=10)

Effectiveness Questions	strongly disagree	disagree	no opinion	agree	strongly agree
Using this type of technology is an effective way of learning about dispensing				5	5
I feel I have gained confidence from learning more about dispensing before my next placement		2	3	4	1
I feel I have gained confidence from learning more about dispensing before my dispensing exam		3		6	1
The Virtual Dispensary Application stimulated my interest to learn		1	7	2	
Usability Questions	**strongly disagree**	**disagree**	**no opinion**	**agree**	**strongly agree**
I thought the application was easy to use		1	2	4	3
I thought the application was fun to use			1	7	2
I thought the application was realistic				7	3
I found the different functions in this application were well integrated	1		4	3	2
I imagine that people would learn to use this application very quickly		2		4	4
I thought there was too much inconsistency in the application	1	4	5		
I need more instructions on how to use the application before I am confident to use it effectively	1	3	3	3	

References

1. Koster, R.: A theory of fun for game design. Paraglyph Press, Scottsdale (2005)
2. Kapp, K.M.: The Gamification of Learning and Instruction: Game-based Methods and Strategies for Training and Education. Pfeiffer, San Francisco (2012)
3. Adams, E.: Fundamentals of Game Design. Pearson Education (2013)
4. Girard, C.,, Ecalle, J., Magnant, A.: Serious Games as new education tools: how effective are they? A meta-analysis of recent studies. Journal of Computer Assisted Learning 29, 207–219 (2013)

Entertainment and Language Learning: Voice Activated Digital Game and Interactive Storytelling Trials in Singapore Schools

Tim Marsh[1], Joo Jin Sim[2], and Dawn Chia[2]

[1] Griffith Film School, Queensland College of Art, Griffith University, Australia
t.marsh@griffith.edu.au
[2] English Language and Literature Branch,
Curriculum Planning and Development Division, Ministry of Education, Singapore
{SIM_Joo_Jin,Dawn_CHIA}@moe.gov.sg

Abstract. We describe the Ministry of Education's (MOE) English Language Oracy Portal project that aims to make learning English engaging and effective through the introduction of game-based learning and interactive storytelling/storybooks incorporating automated speech-assessment-feedback mechanisms in Singapore schools. In particular, we describe pilot studies and trials with 720 students and their teachers from twelve schools, and report the most important findings to inform development to make improvements and recommend strategies for their integration in the curriculum and classroom for the final rollout in primary and secondary schools across Singapore.

Keywords: assessment, studies, trials, serious games, games for learning.

1   Introduction

Game-based learning provides engaging, fun, exciting and entertaining gameplay that motivates students to learn [1, 2, 3]. Research in the field of applied linguistics also suggests that motivation is a key factor in language learning [4] and digital games have been found to possess the potential for motivating the development of speaking skills [5]. Despite English being officially designated in 1965 as the main language of instruction within the Singapore education system, Singapore's English Language Curriculum and Pedagogy Review Committee (ELCPRC) and the Ministry of Education (MOE), identified a wide range of language abilities and language use among Singaporean students and focus groups with employers revealed *"a decline in oral fluency and writing skills"* among Singaporean employees. Therefore, ELCPRC and MOE identified a need *"to ensure that every student is equipped with the English language competency and skills needed for learning, for work and for life in a global economy"*.

This paper describes one effort to address this need by introducing a gaming environment and an interactive storytelling/storybook in primary and secondary schools to motivate Singaporean students to improve their oral English Language (EL) skills. We describe pilot study trials and report on findings before rollout in schools across Singapore.

Y. Pisan et al. (Eds.): ICEC 2014, LNCS 8770, pp. 217–219, 2014.

2   Studies: Pilot and Trials

720 (M, F), 480 primary school students (9-10 years) and 240 secondary school students (12-13 years) from 12 schools across a range of academic abilities took part in studies with the two interactive digital English learning applications: V.A.S.T. (Voice Activated Spy Tech) and Reading Champs, a gaming environment and interactive storybook, respectively (see figure 1). Both applications have rich graphics, animations, audio and interactive features that are comparable in many respects to commercial off-the-shelf interactive games and applications. Both applications incorporate automated speech-assessment-feedback mechanisms in four key areas: accuracy, fluency, word stress, and tone (AFWT), providing personalized guidance to help with students' individual learning needs. The rationale and aims for the EL Oracy Portal applications study trials is to:

- investigate the effectiveness of the applications, in supporting students in the development of their EL oral reading skills
- identify the factors that affect students' ability to make productive use of the feedback provided by the applications
- identify the extent that applications may be incorporated into the formal curriculum and classroom that yields the most teaching and learning value

Three data collection approaches were identified to shed light on the study's rationale and aims: (i) observation of students in classroom sessions (ii) focus group sessions with students and teachers (iii) student and teacher survey/questionnaire.

Fig. 1. Classroom trails in schools (left) with V.A.S.T. and Reading Champs (right)

2.1   Findings

Students enjoyed interacting with V.A.S.T. and Reading Champs judging by observed intonations and excitement when speaking/reading, facial expressions, and laughter. Students moved between in-game and out-of-game/storybook to discuss, collaborate and share with fellow students about in-game features, reading/speaking approaches and strategies for advancing. During this out-of-game/storybook behavior, students appeared to continue to be engaged in game/storybook-related activities. In focus groups, students verified this in-game and out-of-game collaborative behavior, and emphasized that it heightened enjoyment and contributed to learning. Teachers agreed that students enjoyed playing with applications, looked forward to lessons and were positive about collaboration between students outside of the game/storybook. In questionnaires, all students rated applications high (~4, scale 1 to 5) for fun, enjoyable, focused, and for wanting to play/read again. Male students' ratings were slightly higher than female students for mixed classes (M, F). Students' self-report ratings for learning show mid-to-high ratings. Table 1 below shows examples of the issues, concerns and recommendations identified in studies:

(i) **Set-up, Integration & Tutorial:** relating to support, guidance and tutorials	
1	students should be made aware and guided in the use of features through hand-out/tutorial provided by teachers before gameplay
2	minimize technical issues associated with sound-levels and microphone input
3	encourage acceptance/sustained use by student collaboration in-game and off-game in classroom; implement blended learning in-game / off-game
(ii) **Re-Design / Re-development:** generally more critical recommendations:	
4	deter students from continuously skipping through the reading/speaking tasks in V.A.S.T. and encourage more reading/speaking challenges
5	ensure students understand speech assessment feedback to make improvements to their speaking e.g. "awesome", "try again" corresponding to AFWT
6	introduce arrows, breadcrumbs, waypoints to aid navigation
7	incorporate short in-game tutorial on V.A.S.T's complex recording function
8	shift students engaged in wandering around/exploring the gaming environment to engage in missions associated with reading/speaking and learning
9	V.A.S.T.'s in-game analytics should provide clear, accurate and reliable assessments and feedback on students' speech and performance

3   Discussion and Conclusion

Studies show V.A.S.T. and Reading Champs provide appealing automated reading and speaking practice environments that are highly effective for motivating students to improve their oral EL skills in an engaging and entertaining manner. A number of recommendations have been made for their effective implementation and use towards rollout in primary and secondary schools across Singapore.

References

[1] Gee, J.P.: Learning by design: games as learning machines. Interactive Educational Multimedia 8, 15–23 (2004)
[2] Prensky, M.: Fun, play and games: what makes games engaging. In: Digital Game-Based Learning. McGraw-Hill (2001)
[3] Marsh, T., Zhiqang, N.L., Klopfer, E., Chuang, X., Osterweil, S., Haas, J.: Fun and Learning: Blending Design and Development Dimensions in Serious Games Through Narrative and Characters. In: Serious Games and Edutainment Applications. Springer (2011)
[4] Dorneyi, Z., Otto, I.: Motivation in action: a process model of L2 motivation. In: Working Papers in Applied Linguistics, vol. 4, pp. 43–69. Thames University, London (1998)
[5] Johnson, W.L.: Serious Use of a Serious Game for Language Learning. International Journal of Artificial Intelligence in Education 20, 175–195 (2010)

Adaptive Decision Making in Microsimulations of Urban Traffic in Virtual Environments

Fabian Krueger[1], Sven Seele[1], Rainer Herpers[1,2,3],
Peter Becker[1], and Christian Bauckhage[4]

[1] Institute of Visual Computing, Bonn-Rhein-Sieg
University of Applied Sciences, 53757 Sankt Augustin, Germany
sven.seele@h-brs.de
[2] University of New Brunswick, Fredericton, E3B 5A3, Canada
[3] York University, Toronto, M3J 1P3, Canada
[4] University of Bonn, 53115 Bonn, Germany

Abstract. To improve the plausibility of driving and interaction as well as the perceived realism of agents in interactive media, we extend cognitive traffic agents based on personality profiles with emotions. As proof of concept a scenario with a narrowing road was evaluated. To enable agents to handle these scenarios, an existing lane change model was adapted to model the required decision processes and incorporate the driving style defined by static and dynamic aspects of the agents.

Keywords: adaptive agents, serious games.

1 Introduction

The credibility of NPCs in current entertainment software, called agents in the following, often suffers from unrealistic and incomprehensible behavior. Especially in serious games, where individual agents are often closely observed by a player, displayed behavior must be plausible to enhance immersion. By adding personality profiles to agents, observed decisions become more consistent and may increase realism. However, in deterministic systems, the profiles cause identical reactions in identical situations. Such predictable behavior may become implausible if the agent does not adapt to its surroundings or to the player. This contribution will outline how psychological profiles of agents are extended with a model of emotion to dynamically adapt their behavior. The model is applied to a specific road traffic scenario demonstrating the benefits of such an approach.

2 Modeling Adaptive Decisions

Our approach for adaptive decision making is based on two elements: (1) a static foundation, based on the Five Factor Model (FFM) as presented in [1], to achieve consistent behavior patterns for individual agents and (2) a dynamic model to allow

Y. Pisan et al. (Eds.): ICEC 2014, LNCS 8770, pp. 220–222, 2014.

influencing these patterns. A personality profile representing the five personality traits of the FFM is part of each simulated agent. To increase credibility, we proposed a general model for mapping real personality profiles and studies to a consistent form and number range in [2]. This model was used to map findings from a study in [3], which linked personalities to general driving behavior, to our agent profiles. To integrate a mapping into an application, task dependent parameters are derived from the personality to influence the agents' decisions. This will yield consistent individual behavior patterns for each agent.

Although, this recurring consistent behavior is desirable, it becomes implausible if an agent is stuck in a certain situation due to its personality derived behavior. Therefore, it is necessary that agents are able to adapt. Thus, the static personality-based model is extended with a dynamic emotional state.[1] Emotions are integrated into the agent architectures in three parts: experiencing, influencing, and fading. Experiencing has been modeled through predefined incidents. When an agent experiences an incident, the negative and positive emotion of its emotional state are adjusted according to the type of incident. Studies (e.g., [4]) have shown correlations between personality of subjects and their perception of emotions. Thus, the perception depends on the emotional state and personality of an agent. In our case, high neuroticism will intensify negative emotions and high extraversion or conscientiousness will intensify positive emotions [2].The influence of the emotional state is modeled as a temporary modification of personality profiles [2]. In general, the personality of a person is a constant attribute over extended periods of time. However, by modeling the influence of emotions as a change of the personality, it can be added or removed without having to change the existing system. Exponential and linear functions control how the influence of each emotion dimension fades over time. For details see [2].

3   Results

As a proof of concept the presented agent model was applied to a specific traffic scenario in which the lane of an agent is blocked by an obstacle (e.g., a delivery truck). To clear it, the agent needs to change onto an adjacent opposing lane with dense traffic. The agent could pass the obstacle by waiting for an appropriate gap to not influence oncoming traffic (1), by forcing oncoming traffic to slow down or stop (2), or by waiting for an oncoming agent to slow down for it (3). In reality, most drivers would choose case (1). However, with increasing waiting time, drivers will accept increasingly smaller gaps and at some point may choose option (2). To simulate this behavior, the lane change (LC) model MOBIL [5] was added to our agents. It includes a politeness factor to control the aggressiveness of agents in LC decisions, which is derived from an agent's personality in our case. We adapted MOBIL to include changes to opposing lanes by weighting the advantage which agents gain from a LC with their complementary politeness.

The test scenario was simulated with static personality-based drivers (PB) and dynamic emotion-based drivers (EB). In a first step, traffic flows were measured for the

---

[1]   Mood is not considered here, because it persists for prolonged time periods and agents in our application are only observable for a limited time.

free and the blocked lane to measure the emergent traffic behavior. The flow on the blocked lane was low for PB agents since polite drivers would weigh the disadvantage for oncoming agents higher than their own advantage. As a result they get stuck behind the obstacle until a polite agent on the free lane allows the waiting agent to pass. EB agents achieved higher flows on the blocked lane indicating that they will not wait until allowed to pass, but force their way around the obstacle if they have been waiting too long. This effectively models drivers whose patience is limited, just as is the case in real life. The resulting shorter waiting times are more plausible to an observer. Additionally, the model is able to emulate behavior that is frequently observable in real traffic: If a queue had formed behind the waiting agent, several enqueued agents will tailgate the first agent as soon as it starts to pass the obstacle.

4   Conclusions and Future Work

We proposed a model that uses personality profiles to generate consistent behavior patterns for individual agents, improving their credibility. A proof of concept was evaluated in a specific traffic scenario. Static personality-based drivers produced implausible behavior in certain situations (e.g., unrealistic waiting times). Adding an emotion model for adaptive behavior did not only improve plausibility of directly observable agent behavior, but also improved traffic flow, resulting in more plausibility on a macroscopic scale.

In future work it needs to be investigated whether the proposed agent model is able to generate plausible behavior for other (general) scenarios. Additionally, it remains to be evaluated whether players really perceive the proposed agents as more realistic. This could be evaluated by integrating them into an existing application, like the FIVIS project (vc.h-brs.de/fivis), for a detailed user study.

Acknowledgements. The presented work received funding by the DGUV (grant FP307) and the BMBF (grant 17028X11).

References

1. Seele, S., Herpers, R., Becker, P., Bauckhage, C. Cognitive Agents for Microscopic Traffic Simulations in Virtual   Environments. In: Herrlich, M., Malaka, R., Masuch, M. (eds.) Entertainment Computing - ICEC 2012. LNCS, vol. 7522, pp. 318--325. Springer, Heidelberg (2009)
2. Krueger, F., Seele, S., Herpers, R., Becker, P. Dynamic Emotional States based on Personality Profiles for Adaptive Agent Behavior Patterns. Technical Report, Bonn-Rhein-Sieg University of Applied Sciences, Dept. of Computer Science (2013)
3. Herzberg, P. Beyond "accident-proneness": Using Five-Factor Model prototypes to predict driving behavior. Research in Personality. 6 (43), 1096--1100 (2009)
4. Watson, D., Clark, L.A. On traits and temperament: general and specific factors of emotional experience and their relation to the five-factor model. Journal of Personality. 60 (2), 441--476 (1992)
5. Kesting, A., Treiber, M., Helbing, D. General Lane-Changing Model MOBIL for Car-Following Models. Transportation Research Record. 1999 (1), 86--94 (2007)

Autonomous Landing of AR.Drone

Roman Barták, Andrej Hraško, and David Obdržálek

Charles University in Prague, Faculty of Mathematics and Physics, Praha,
Czech Republic
{roman.bartak,david.obdrzalek}@mff.cuni.cz,
andrej@hrasko.eu

Abstract. Inexpensive robotic toys are becoming widely available and though
they are called toys, they provide gradually better sensing features and rising
computational power. Adding new autonomous functions, such as autonomous
landing for flying drones, helps the users with routine maneuvers and so allows
using them with lower risk of breaks caused by loss of control in critical operational phases. In this paper we present software for autonomous landing of an
AR.Drone – an affordable robotic quadricopter. This software uses an easy-to-
customize landing pattern and exploits only the sensors available on the drone.
The whole landing process is simplified to a "push-button" approach for the end
user, allowing for safer overall operation.

1   Introduction

AR.Drone by Parrot Inc. is a high-tech yet affordable flying toy – a quadricopter with
several sensors including two cameras, accelerometer, gyroscope, sonar, and a built-in
controller for basic stabilization. Pre-processed information from sensors can also be
received via Wi-Fi so the computer can serve as a more powerful external brain for
the drone. For controlling the drone from a computer and for visualizing information
from sensors, several software applications exist. We use *Control Tower* [6] as the
basic computer interface to AR.Drone and we extended its functionally with autonomous landing to a user-customizable pattern. The idea is that the user flies the
drone above the pattern and by pushing a button in the software GUI the drone autonomously lands on that pattern. Such functionality is great for beginner users who can
control the drone in free space but are not able to precisely land or are afraid of controlling it low above the ground where mistakes in control or turbulences caused by
airflow could easily cause crashing and then damaging of the drone.

2   Landing Description

For autonomous landing, the drone must reliably detect the landing point. There exist
methods for visual navigation (e.g. using an H-shaped landing pattern [5] or a specific
circular pattern [3]), however they require better visual sensors (cameras) and they
usually do not support horizontal orientation.

Y. Pisan et al. (Eds.): ICEC 2014, LNCS 8770, pp. 223–225, 2014.

We decided for the landing pattern consisting of two colored discs which makes it very easy to be prepared by an inexperienced user. The user can print any two colored discs; it is only important that the colors are different enough from each other and from the typical colors in the landing zone. This makes it much easier to use in real life (instead of being forced to use specially crafted and unalterable unique pattern). In addition to this easy customization of the landing pattern, the other advantage is that such pattern also defines the horizontal orientation.

To preprocess the picture, we straightforwardly use HSV filtering, image erosion, and image dilatation (these basic image pre-processing algorithms are readily available and described in the OpenCV library [7]). Then, to identify each disc in the picture, blob detection algorithm (described in [4]) is used and the center of the disc pair is calculated to set the target landing point.

The drone is controlled using four independent standard *proportional-integral-derivative (PID) controllers* [2] fed by the distance to the target. The input for each PID controller is the coordinate part of the target distance in its specific direction and the output is one control value for the AD.Drone low-level interface functions (the pitch, roll, yaw, and vertical speed). The distance calculation is shown on Figure 1.

More details about the algorithms and their implementation can be found in [1].

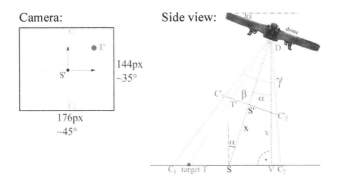

Fig. 1. Distance to the target calculation: dist(T,V) = v * tan(α+β), where β = arctan(tan(γ/2) * pixel_dist(T',S') / pixel_dist(C'$_1$,S'))

The typical process to use autonomous landing is as follows. The user sets the HSV parameters of the two color blobs in the picture and optionally selects the horizontal angle (yaw) of the drone with respect to these two blobs. Any time later the user can invoke the "*land on target*" action to let the drone automatically land or the "*lock on target*" action to hover above the landing point at the current altitude. When the landing pattern disappears from the camera view, the system can optionally attempt to find it by flying in the direction where the pattern was lost ("*estimate target*").

3   Evaluation and Conclusion

During the tests it has proven the AR.Drone is able to land safely even when the environment conditions are too advantageous for manual control (e.g. air flow at ground level). Figure 2 presents the graphs showing the landing time, precision, and reliability of the landing from different original altitudes and orientations with or without the wind generated by two fans close to ground at the landing area.

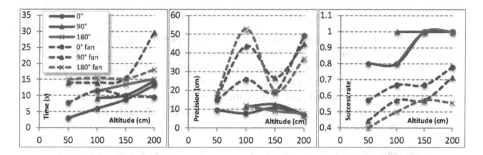

Fig. 2. Dependence of landing time (top left), precision (top right), and reliability (bottom) on the initial altitude (50, 100, 150, 200 cm) and orientation relative to the target (0°, 90°, 180°)

In this work we have shown how standard control software of a low-cost quadricopter AR.Drone can be extended by an automatic landing procedure. That lowers the bad chance to break the drone during landing which belongs to the most dangerous phases of the flight; especially the windy conditions are difficult for manual landing and often cause crashes and damages. This is important for users who exploit the drone as a toy, for playing and entertainment. Our preliminary experimental results show this extension is reliable under normal, non-laboratory conditions.

Acknowledgements. This research was supported by the Czech Science Foundation projects P103/10/1287 and P202/12/G061.

References

1. Barták, R., Hraško, A., Obdržálek, D.: On Autonomous Landing of AR.Drone: Hands-on Experience. In: Proceedings of FLAIRS 28 (2014)
2. King, M.: Process Control: A Practical Approach. John Wiley & Sons Ltd., Chichester (2010)
3. Lange, S., Sünderhauf, N., Protzel, P.: A Vision Based Onboard Approach for Landing and Position Control of an Autonomous Multirotor UAV in GPS-Denied Environments. In: International Conference on Advanced Robotics, pp. 1–6 (2009)
4. Szeliski, R.: Computer Vision: Algorithms and Applications. Springer, Heidelberg (2010)
5. Yang, S., Scherer, S.A., Zell, A.: An Onboard Monocular Vision System for Autonomous Takeoff, Hovering and Landing of a Micro Aerial Vehicle. Journal of Intelligent & Robotic Systems 69(1-4), 499–515 (2013)
6. ControlTower   software,   https://code.google.com/p/javadrone/wiki/ControlTower (accessed May 14, 2014)
7. OpenCV software library, http://opencv.org/ (accessed May 14, 2014)

Generative Methods for Automated Music Video Editing

Julia Stefan

Griffith University, Queensland College of Art
julia.stefan@griffithuni.edu.au

Abstract. In order to enhance viewer experience when watching music videos, a set of methods for generative music video editing has been developed. These algorithms use stochastic selection based on user-defined shot characteristics, as well as temporal constraints to manage narrative structures. The prototype application is introduced and demonstrated by showing two examples of software-generated music videos, and the basic concepts behind the algorithms will be explained.

Keywords: Music videos, generative composition, online videos, non-linear video, adaptability.

1 Introduction

Music videos are a popular format for audio-visual experiments. In recent years, they have been used to explore the possibilities presented by online technologies and interactive applications through the use of moving images. Popular examples include The Wilderness Downtown[1], Like a Rolling Stone[2] and Do Not Touch[3]. In comparison to feature films for instance, the shorter running time of music videos makes them a popular format for experiments. This popularity is further increased due to the genre's aesthetic flexibility and its focus on the creation of rhythm and emotional engagement rather than narrative coherence [1].

By implementing options for user interaction, video sequences may become more personal and therefore more engaging for viewers. Interactive online music videos have been used to explore a number of different concepts for interactivity. These include game-like videos and tree-structured, choose-your-own-adventure type narratives. Interactive online music videos also allow for new possibilities of personalisation by embedding content from social networking websites and search engines. These "hypervideos" [2] generally either depend on viewer participation during playback or preliminary input in order to generate variations. Additionally, many of these videos are based on comparatively rigid structures in order to maintain coherence and to ensure that the director's concepts are still being realised.

---

[1] http://www.thewildernessdowntown.com
[2] http://video.bobdylan.com
[3] http://donottouch.org

Y. Pisan et al. (Eds.): ICEC 2014, LNCS 8770, pp. 226–228, 2014.
© IFIP International Federation for Information Processing 2014

In contrast, the research concerning generative video composition presented in this paper is based on the idea of providing variable music videos, which can be generated in real-time without the requirement of viewer interaction and which therefore depend on processes that are to some extent beyond the director's control [3]. Thus, the methods presented here aim to provide a new creative tool for video directors, as well as an engaging viewing experience for audiences.

2   Music Video Generation

This demonstration presents a prototype application of Dividation, a software for generative music video editing utilising real-time assembling of video sequences from individually prepared pools of video footage using algorithmic decision-making processes based on the creator's clip classifications.

Sequence generation is achieved using stochastic processes based on Markov chains and probabilistic structures to describe the editing dynamics. A database of sufficiently annotated original video footage is used. Assuming the individual shot to be the basic building block of these videos, a sequence is assembled shot by shot according to the video's principal key characteristics as defined by the video director.

Additional structuring methods, such as underlying ordered lists, help to ensure narrative coherence through the specification of forced shots and the definition of temporal windows within which the stochastic selections are constrained.

3   Demonstration

Two music videos are used to demonstrate the video generation method described above: *Majestic* and *Eloise*.

The music video *Majestic* consists of a simple narrative, in which the protagonist is drawn into the televised action of the musicians' performances. Six parameters are used to categorise the video content and are mapped to temporal probabilities. The mapped temporal probabilities describe the amount of visual features that should be seen during particular sections of the song. This music video uses a pool of roughly two hundred clips with a length varying from less than one second up to three minutes. An algorithmic decision-making process is then employed for both the automatic sequencing of the video footage and the cutting of the footage into shots of appropriate lengths.

In comparison, the music video *Eloise* uses a slightly more detailed narrative. Here, the protagonist, Eloise, is seen inside her home, while the musicians are performing the song inside her living room. A secondary protagonist singer urges the woman to leave her house and quit her bad habits, which she finally does. For this video, the editing dynamics are based on the use of three visual parameters and a pre-defined narrative structure. This provides an additional guide to the order of the shots. The video uses approx. 550 pre-cut clips with a length varying from less than one second up to ten seconds. In this example, the algorithmic decision-making process is only applied to the sequencing of the video content. The selected shots are played in their entirety, unless a temporal alteration is required to ensure an accurate synchronisation.

Both videos demonstrate (1) the potential of using generative composition methods for online music video creation, (2) the resulting editing aesthetics, as well as (3) some of the challenges of this process. With the use of randomness as a driving factor for sequence creation, the resulting music videos may not always be coherent to the audience and accurate enough to the editor's intentions. An appropriate management of this problem requires correct and well-balanced definitions of the probabilistic and narrative structures and constitutes a central aspect of this research.

4   Discussion and Future Outlook

Further research will focus on refining the quality of the applied editing algorithms in greater detail and extending the repertoire of specific methods by taking into account the requirements introduced by different progressive and narrative structures. Furthermore, it must deal with the creation of adequate interfaces to involve the editors in the generative composition process. Compared to traditional methods of manual video editing, the creation and editing of music videos by using generative composition methods is a rather abstract creative process because it requires a stronger conceptual involvement in order to properly communicate to the composition software how to edit a specific sequence, rather than manually executing this task oneself. Ongoing research as part of this project will reveal the effectiveness of the editing algorithms in terms of viewer engagement, and its practicality for editors.

References

1. Vernallis, C.: Unruly Media: YouTube, Music Video, and the New Digital Cinema. Oxford University Press, New York (2013)
2. Hammoud, R.I.: Interactive Video: Algorithms and Technologies. Springer, Berlin (2006)
3. Boden, M.A., Edmonds, E.A.: What is generative art? Digital Creativity 20(1-2), 21–46 (2009)

Correlation between Facial Expressions and the Game Experience Questionnaire

Chek Tien Tan, Sander Bakkes, and Yusuf Pisan

Games Studio, University of Technology, Sydney and University of Amsterdam,
Intelligent Systems Laboratory Amsterdam, The Netherlands
{chek,yusuf.pisan}@gamesstudio.org, S.C.J.Bakkes@uva.nl

Abstract. Quantitative methods in the domain of player experience evaluation provide continuous and real-time analyses of player experiences. However, current quantitative methods are mostly either too confined within in-game statistics, or require non-typical laboratory play setups to monitor real-life behavior. This paper presents preliminary results on the feasibility of using facial expressions analysis as a natural quantitative method for evaluating player experiences. Correlations were performed between the facial expressions intensities and self-reported Game Experience Questionnaire (GEQ) dimensions of players in two video games.

Keywords: Facial expressions, video games, player experience.

1   Introduction

A key aspect in game design is the evaluation of player experiences, as the primary goal of most digital games is to provide players with appropriate and often positive overall experiences that are linked to concepts like flow and immersion [1]. Within a game, different instances of gameplay also aim to provide short-term experiences like fear, anger and surprise. It is therefore essential in game design to be able to measure whether (and to which extent) these experiences are achieved. Research into methods to enable efficient and effective player experience analysis is hence a key area in the digital games domain.

This paper contributes to the understanding of using facial expressions analysis for evaluating player experiences by investigating correlations between classifications of facial expressions and self-reported Game Experience Questionnaire (GEQ) dimensions [2].

2   Correlation Study

A repeated-measures design was used to collect the data. Participants had their in-game actions and facial video captured whilst playing two games: (1) Portal 2[1], and (2) Draw My Thing by OMGPOP[2].

---

[1] http://www.thinkwithportals.com/
[2] http://www.omgpop.com/games/drawmything

Y. Pisan et al. (Eds.): ICEC 2014, LNCS 8770, pp. 229–231, 2014.

Table 1. Pearson's correlation coefficient between average facial expression intensities and average scores from each GEQ dimension, for Portal 2 (all $p < 0.001$)

GEQ Dimension	Anger	Joy	Surprise
Competence	0.15	0.41	-0.24
Immersion	0.29	-0.01	-0.07
Flow	-0.22	0.07	0.40
Tension	0.38	0.44	-0.44
Challenge	0.24	0.26	-0.08
Negative affect	0.43	0.13	-0.47
Positive affect	-0.04	0.09	0.16

Participants were recruited via university mailing lists which includes university employees, undergraduates and alumni. 12 participants (4 females) took part in the study aged between 20 and 48 (M = 34, SD = 8). The participants represented a wide mix of player types. with six participants indicated that they have played the Portal series and three have played Drawing games by OMGPOP.

After indicating their informed consent in the study and a background questionnaire, they proceeded to play the two games for 15 minutes each, one after another in an enclosed room by themselves. The opponent in Draw My Thing played against the participant from a separate room over the Internet. At the end of the experiments, the facial videos were then fed through the facial expression recognizer (developed previously [3,4,5]) and graphs were generated for each player. In this study, only anger, joy and surprise expressions were used as they were most reliably detected and are common player responses. These were then used for the below correlation analysis. After each game, participants also filled the full Game Experience Questionnaire (GEQ) [2].

3   Results

Pearson's correlation coefficients (as both facial expression and GEQ data are parametric) between each game experience dimension in the GEQ and each average facial expression intensity were calculated for participants playing Portal 2 and Draw My Thing, as shown in Tables 1 and 2 respectively.

In Portal 2 (Table 1), the facial expressions were significantly correlated to a majority of GEQ dimensions. Anger and joy had primarily positive correlations with the GEQ dimensions except for flow, e.g., anger was significantly positively correlated with moderate to large effect sizes ($0.30 < r < 0.50$, $p < 0.001$) with GEQ dimensions tension and negative affect. The surprise expression had primarily negative correlations except for flow.

In Draw My Thing (Table 2), results were mostly different from those in Portal 2. Focusing on only the larger effect sizes, only challenge showed consistent significant correlations in the same directions. Challenge were both positively correlated with anger and joy, and negatively correlated with surprise. Other than the challenge dimension, the other correlations for Draw My Thing were either in the opposite direction or had vastly different effect sizes, when compared to Portal 2.

Table 2. Pearson's correlation coefficient between average facial expression intensities and average scores from each GEQ dimension, for Draw My Thing (all $p < 0.001$)

GEQ Dimension	Anger	Joy	Surprise
Competence	-0.37	-0.18	0.53
Immersion	-0.10	0.07	0.08
Flow	0.18	0.25	-0.07
Tension	0.14	-0.14	-0.25
Challenge	0.35	0.38	-0.30
Negative affect	-0.35	-0.42	0.22
Positive affect	-0.12	0.12	0.15

4 Preliminary Conclusions and Future Work

One key finding is that significant correlations were exhibited between the facial expressions and the GEQ dimensions. In this study, only challenge showed consistency of a large effect size and direction across both games played. This correlation implies that challenge intensities can potentially be automatically inferred from facial expressions across different game genres. There were also large correlations exhibited in the rest of the GEQ dimensions but they did not align in both games, which means that different games might induce different bindings of facial expressions with gameplay experiences.

The next major step will be to analyse these results in combination with our prior results that involve further qualitative and quantitative measures [4,5]. For future experiments, we also hope to evaluate the correlations of the facial expressions with other physiological signals like EDA and EMG, in order to perform a finer-grained analysis.

Acknowledgements. This research was supported by the Games Studio and the Centre for Human Centred Technology Design at the University of Technology, Sydney.

References

1. Bernhaupt, R.: Evaluating User Experience in Games: Concepts and Methods. Springer (2010)
2. Nacke, L.E.: Affective Ludology: Scientific Measurement of User Experience in Interactive Entertainment. PhD thesis, Blekinge Institute of Technology (2009)
3. Tan, C., Johnston, A.: Towards a Nondisruptive, Practical, and Objective Automated Playtesting Process. In: Workshops at the Seventh Artificial Intelligence and Interactive Digital Entertainment Conference, pp. 25–28 (2011)
4. Tan, C.T., Pisan, Y.: Towards Automated Player Experience Detection With Computer Vision Techniques. In: CHI Workshop on Game User Experience (2012)
5. Tan, C.T., Rosser, D., Bakkes, S., Pisan, Y.: A feasibility study in using facial expressions analysis to evaluate player experiences. In: Proceedings of the 8th Australasian Conference on Interactive Entertainment Playing the System - IE 2012, pp. 1–10. ACM Press, New York (2012)

Implementing Virtual Clients in Quake III Arena

Stig Magnus Halvorsen[1,2,3] and Kjetil Raaen[1,2,3]

[1]The Norwegian School of IT (NITH), Oslo, Norway
{halsti,raakje}@westerdals.no
[2]Simula Research Laboratory, Bærum, Norway
[3]University of Oslo, Oslo, Norway

Abstract. Performing server and network experiments on video games can be cumbersome because it usually requires a large number of players to generate sufficient server and network load. A solution is automated artificial intelligence-controlled virtual clients that behave as real players. This paper describes an implementation of virtual clients in the open source video game *Quake III Arena*, which converts the game into an open source tool for generating server load with realistic network traffic for investigating game system scalability.

Keywords: Virtual Client, Quake III Arena, Quake 3, Load Generation.

1 Introduction

Network and server load can be generated through the use of live sessions with real people as test candidates, as it was done in [2]. Alternatively, automated artificial intelligence (AI)-controlled virtual clients, or simply "virtual clients", can be used as demonstrated in [3]. The latter is beneficial as it allows experiments to be done by a single scientist requiring little time and hardware. We want to follow the second approach in our research and in [1], we proposed several open source games as potential tools for scientific work. None are ideal for server and network experiments because no tools are provided for server load and network traffic generation. This paper documents the addition of *virtual clients* to *Quake III Arena* (Q3A) to solve this lack of tools. Q3A is an open source game already discussed in [1]. The modified game can be used as a load-generating tool that scientists may use or alter to test and evaluate their concepts.

2 Implementing Virtual Clients

We were inspired by Q3A's implementation of the single player game mode. The design solves a similar problem to ours because it requires some server-side logic within the client to function properly. Single-player mode is started by first launching a local and "hidden" server with a specified map, followed by launching the client logic that connects to the local server.

Our solution is designed to launch from a console, using the engine's built-in *console variable* (cvar) system. A virtual client can hence be enabled by setting the proper cvars through program arguments, followed by connecting to a server.

Y. Pisan et al. (Eds.): ICEC 2014, LNCS 8770, pp. 232–234, 2014.

The virtual client retrieves a message containing the configuration of the server on connection. This is used to create a local shadow copy of the game server, with the same loaded map, entities and configuration. The entire procedure utilizes a modified version of the local server initialization process from the original single player mode.

Once the shadow server is initialized, it sleeps approximately a second to synchronize the shadow server with the game server. The received data from the game server contains the initial position and view angles of the client, which is used to add a bot to the shadow server at the exact same position. The bot library enables the interaction of bot entities with the map. The bot's commands are transmitted to the shadow server in the same way as connected regular clients. All commands are processed in a server function that takes a given command as a parameter. The function is modified to enqueue the received command in the client's command queue. The engine notices the new command in the client queue and immediately transmits it to the game server. Updates from the game server are forwarded to the shadow server by copying the player and entity states from each received update into the bot and entity structures of the shadow server.

3   Results

To evaluate how the virtual clients affect the server, we ran an experiment with 0-48 virtual clients connected to a single, unmodified Q3A server. Figure 1 shows the server's network load. The server's *Data in* graph shows that bandwidth increases proportionally with the number of clients. *Data out* increases quadratically because each client needs updates from all the other clients within its *view area* [4]. Figure 2 illustrates server CPU and memory utilization. CPU utilization increases until it reaches approximately 71% with 21 connected virtual clients. The server starts to struggle since the operating system needs to share its processing capabilities with other processes. Memory usage remains constant as the

Server with 0-48 Connected Virtual Clients

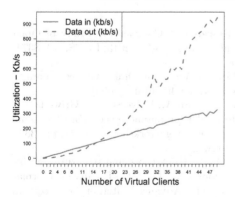
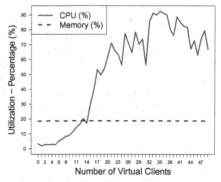

Fig. 1. Network Load   **Fig. 2.** CPU & Memory Utilized

game engine always pre-allocates enough memory for the maximum number of supported clients.

Our implementation is capable of running in graphical and console mode. Table 1 shows an average of the various client types' resource usage. The data is the average of ten readings from a host with a quad core 2.6Ghz CPU (max 400%) and 4GB memory. The console version utilizes one thread, while the two others use six. The console client requires significantly less processing power and memory than the others, while network differences are minimal. The console version allows up to 57 instances on this specific host, multiple host machines should be used for large scale testing.

Table 1. Various Client Types and their System Load

Type	CPU	Memory	Bandwidth in	Bandwidth out
Regular player	252.42%	79 MB	1.64 Kb/s	5.80 Kb/s
VC Graphical	234.26%	94 MB	2.00 Kb/s	5.14 Kb/s
VC Console	6.94%	29 MB	1.41 Kb/s	6.00 Kb/s

4   Evaluation and Conclusion

Q3A has been modified into a load-generating tool for investigating game system scalability, by implementing virtual clients that produce server load with authentic network traffic. Researchers can implement their concepts into the game and analyze performance differences by utilizing the virtual client support. This can be used to improve the credibility of [3] and similar research.

Q3A is old and may not be advanced enough for some researchers, but is likely a better test platform than small prototypes such as the one utilized in [3]. Virtual clients may be considered complex in comparison to client packet capture and playback. However, packet traces cannot support evaluation of server processing load. The current implementation supports only one virtual client per instance of the software, wasting resources when launching multiple.

References

1. Halvorsen, S.M., Raaen, K.: Games for Research: A Comparative Study of Open Source Game Projects. In: an Mey, D., et al. (eds.) Euro-Par 2013. LNCS, vol. 8374, pp. 353–362. Springer, Heidelberg (2014)
2. Claypool, M., Claypool, K.: Latency and Player Actions in Online Games. Communications of the ACM - Entertainment Networking 49, 40–45 (2006)
3. Raaen, K., Espeland, H., Stensland, H.K., Petlund, A., Halvorsen, P., Griwodz, C.: Lears: A lockless, relaxed-atomicity state model for parallel execution of a game server partition. In: ICPPW 2012: Parallel Processing Workshops, vol. 41, pp. 382–389. IEEE Computer Society, Washington (2012)
4. Stefyn, D., Cricenti, A.L., Branch, P.A.: Quake III Arena game structures. Swinburne University of Technology. Technical reports No. 110209A, Faculty of Information and Communication Technologies. Centre for Advanced Internet Architectures (February 2011)

TwitterFM: An Experimental Application in Entertainment and Social Broadcasting

Theodoros Kalaitzidis and Nikitas M. Sgouros

Department of Digital Systems, University of Piraeus
18534, Piraeus, Greece
sgouros@unipi.gr

Abstract. We describe TwitterFM a web application that explores ways by which social broadcasting via Twitter can be enriched with entertainment features. The system views Twitter as a dynamic set of 'radio stations', each one transmitting under a keyword (hashtag). The user can 'tune in' to the radio stations he wants. Once this happens all messages transmitted by this station are rendered into speech via TTS accompanied with music selected by the user and/or the system. TwitterFM analyzes the affective content of each rendered message and colors accordingly the sub-window in which it is displayed.

Keywords: Entertainment Applications, Microblogging, Social Broadcasting.

1   System Description

Entertainment is inherently a social process as it provides an experiential setting for the elicitation of affective reactions and behaviors. Social broadcasting, on the other hand, has greatly enabled access to information by providing decentralized models for the dissemination of news and opinions and by allowing information diffusion through social processes such as content sharing and retransmission. Combining entertainment and social broadcasting can create novel media forms that facilitate access and consumption of information and provide media-enriched, socially influenced and customized solutions for content presentation. We describe TwitterFM [1] a web application that explores ways by which entertainment processes can enrich social broadcasting and support microblogging environments such as Twitter. Twitter supports a light and informal style of communication that we believe is suitable for casual interaction with the user similar to what is the case with entertainment radio.

TwitterFM views Twitter as a dynamic set of 'radio stations', each one transmitting under a keyword (hashtag). The user can select the hashtags she is interested in and organize them in various radio bands. She can then 'tune in' to the radio station she wants. Consequently all messages transmitted by this station are turned into speech via TTS and rendered accompanied with music selected by the user and/or the system. Furthermore, the system analyzes the affective content of each rendered message and colors accordingly the sub-window in which it is displayed. TwitterFM employs a mashup architecture combining five web APIs: Twitter, Alchemy, TinySong, LastFM and YouTube. The Twitter API provides the text messages that are used as input to

Y. Pisan et al. (Eds.): ICEC 2014, LNCS 8770, pp. 235–237, 2014.

the system. In particular, it provides the keywords that generate significant amount of interest at the current point in time and the original text of the messages that correspond to the keywords selected by the user. The Alchemy API is used for affective analysis of the content of each Twitter message used by the system. TinySong offers a simple interface for collecting links to the music tracks that match with the keywords selected by the user. It is used for identifying the tracks that the user wants to enter in his playlist and to collect additional info on these tracks that will be used for retrieving them from YouTube. LastFM API is used for retrieving similar music and artists to the ones selected by the user in her playlist while YouTube is used to reproduce the tracks selected by the user. In addition, TwitterFM uses its own rudimentary API for coordinating the use of the five APIs described above thereby allowing the user to view/change Twitter trends and/or look for and suggest appropriate music. The system offers appropriate endpoints for other applications to use the results of TwitterFM in these areas. Finally the system uses the FreeTTS API for converting the text of Twitter messages to speech. TwitterFM seeks to recreate the radio experience when listening to Twitter messages. To this effect it uses a radio metaphor for structuring user interaction. In particular, the system uses an analog radio description of the keywords that are trending in Twitter and the ones selected by the user (see Fig. 1). The messages received by the system are organized in 'bands' similar to the way radio stations are organized in radio bands (FM. MW etc). One of these bands called 'Trends" is generated automatically by the system based on the top trending keywords in Twitter at each point in time. The rest of the bands are determined by the user. In particular, the user selects the keywords that will be included in each of these bands and these keywords appear on the radio screen as 'frequencies'. If the user selects any one of these keywords in the band then the system moves the needle on top of the selection and the system starts collecting Twitter messages containing this hashtag. These messages are then converted into speech with FreeTTS and their affective content is analyzed using Alchemy. A tweet is labeled as 'positive' or 'negative' and the label is accompanied by a numerical value indicating the confidence of Alchemy for the label. Depending on the label and its confidence TwitterFM colors each text either red for negative or green for positive along with all the intermediate shades depending on the level confidence. For example in Fig. 1 the middle tweet has been labeled as positive with confidence 0.8 (bright green) compared to the left one which was labeled as positive with confidence 0.2 (light green). The user can create a list of music tracks that wants to be played along with the tweets. The systems plays sequentially the tracks in this list and also allows the user to search for tracks and edit its playlist. TwitterFM constantly monitors the number of remaining tracks in its play list and if this number is less than a threshold it tries to append to the list tracks and artists similar to the ones in the playlist using the LastFM API.

Users found the system original and interesting. The major problem they had involved the actual content of Twitter messages which very often contains web-specific information such as links to web sites that when spoken can be distracting. A solution could involve screening the textual content of each message and removing these links from the spoken part. In addition, due to the limitations of the TTS system, TwitterFM ignores all punctuation marks in the message content. This results in a spoken interpretation of the message that is flat and monotonous. Both problems expose a more general issue with microblogging systems that convert between different types of media. These systems should allow content creators to prescribe the ways with which their messages will be rendered in different modalities. This could possibly create conflicts with the consumers of these messages. Another issue concerned the placement of spoken messages in the audio stream. Currently, all messages are rendered as soon as they are received and message speech is often mixed with the current audio track. Users suggested rendering the spoken messages between audio tracks similar to what happens to commercials in entertainment radio. In terms of related work there exist a number of apps that read aloud content from social network sites (e.g. iHear, Flipboard or SpokenLayer). However these apps do not enrich the content in some meaningful fashion the way TwitterFM does. TwitterFM is one of a number of web applications that perform post processing on Twitter messages in order to enrich or customize their content. Similar applications with TwitterFM in this category include SocialAudio and SocialRadio. TwitterFM differs from both systems as it provides a radio-band analogy for organizing the hashtags selected by the user and in that it provides a synchronous textual presentation of tweet content enriched with affective analysis. There has been significant interest in the automatic generation of music playlists (e.g. [2]) and, very recently, for original music synthesis in social broadcasting ([3]).

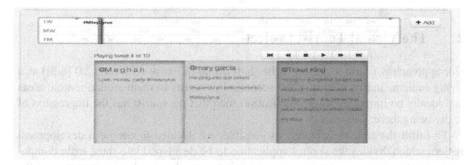

Fig. 1. TwitterFM user interface

Acknowledgements. Presentation of this paper was partially supported by the University of Piraeus Research Center.

References

1. Kalaitzidis, T.: Development of a social TTS application, M.Sc. Thesis, Dept. of Digital Systems, University of Piraeus (December 2013)
2. Coelho, F., Devezas, J., Ribeiro, C.: Large-scale Crossmedia Retrieval for Playlist Generation and Song Discovery. In: Proceedings of the 10th Conference on Open Research Areas in Information Retrieval, Portugal (2013)
3. Moreale, F., de Angeli, A., Miniukovich, A.: TwitterRadio: Translating Tweets into Music. In: CHI 2014, Canada (2014)

Using Drones for Virtual Tourism

David Mirk and Helmut Hlavacs

University of Vienna, Research Group Entertainment Computing, Vienna, Austria
{david@mirk,helmut.hlavacs}@univie.ac.at

1 Introduction

Virtual reality offers tourism many useful possibilities to create or extend virtual experiences that tourists may accept and use as partial alternatives for real visitation [4,5]. Especially in some areas of tourism, e.g. marketing, entertainment or education virtual reality will become more and more valuable. The vision of this work is to allow users of a client software application to receive real-time video images of different places of the world and watch them locally. As a special feature, and unlike to fixed stationary webcams, the user should be as free as possible to define where the "Virtual Eye" resides and what it is looking at.

2 The Virtual Tourist Project

Our approach is to use a cheap off-the-shelf drone (a Parrot ARDrone 2.0 [6,8]) as a flying camera, and be used in a live scenario by tourists to roam around remote areas and ideally be immersed in the application such that the tourist has the impression of really being there.

To fulfill the task as complete as possible, we decided to choose a development pattern which divides the control application to be developed into three main components. Firstly, the server application, which is responsible for the direct control of the ARDrone, transmitting the calculated navigation vectors to the ARDrone. The second main component defines the graphical user client (client application), which processes and transmits the direct input to the ground station via TCP. Finally, the existing SDK for this purpose must be modified and extended in order to allow the user to use a wide a range of different control devices (e.g. "Oculus Rift").

The ARDrone 2.0 is very susceptible to outer influences. Moderate wind gusts deviate the drones very quickly from their original course which leads to a behavior where the electronics of the quadrocopter try to counteract this divergence with abrupt control maneuvers. This makes it difficult to provide a stable (vibration-free) video sequence to the user [1,2,3]. Furthermore, the rigid mounting of the video cameras leads to an undesirable side effect: basics quadrocopters control their flight direction by changing the speeds of their propellers and thus changes their attitude. At an acceleration to the front the drone tilts with the front camera toward the ground, on a flight back into sequence then turned toward the sky. To avoid this effect a modification with a steerable front camera on a ball joint would be necessary.

Y. Pisan et al. (Eds.): ICEC 2014, LNCS 8770, pp. 238–240, 2014.
© IFIP International Federation for Information Processing 2014

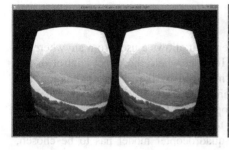 

Fig. 1. View through Oculus Rift (Carin-   **Fig. 2.** Outdoor
thia/Austria)

A practical test arrangement showed that it is not possible to give the user complete freedom of the control over his permit virtual eyes. For this reason, a virtual route in the form of GPS waypoints must be predefined, on which the ARDrone travels within certain tolerances. As a result the user directly controls only the flight speed of the virtual tour, not the drone navigation directions. However, this allows a completely free focus and control of the front camera orientation.

2.1   Navigation

Due to the small narrow field of view of 91 degree and the rigidly mounted front camera a user-controlled direct navigation of the ARDrone would only be possible after several exercise passages. The specification of a flight course, which on the one hand is free of any obstacles (thus the risk of collisions decreases), and on the other hand provides optimized designed sightseeing courses (i.e., they lie within the flight range of the ARDrone and show the most important sights), allows the user to enjoy a satisfactory experience without the need of having knowledge of the actual flight behavior and functional ways of the quadrocopter.

2.2   Virtual Reality

The ARDrone 2.0 and the provided SDK already provides numerous possibilities for real-time symbol or character recognition to developers. Necessary calculations are made directly on the ARDrone hardware/firmware and the results are processed in a client application. The Oculus Rift is a virtual reality headset, originally designed for immersive gaming. To create a strong sense of immersion it is designed to almost fill the wearer's entire field of view and to completely block out the real world. The pin-cushioned image for each eye (640×800 resolution) is corrected by lenses in the head-set. The used combination of 3-axis gyros, accelerometers, and magnetometers make it capable of absolute (relative to earth) head orientation tracking without drift [8,9,10].

3   Conclusion and Future Work

The aim of this project was to develop a system that allows a user from anywhere on the world to control a ARDrone 2.0 via the Internet where the direct control of the direction of the quadrocopter is exclusively managed by the server application and only the alignment of the front camera is assumed by the user. However, the difficulties and problems that occurred while developing and testing this solution with the consumer grade Parrot ARDrone 2.0, led us to the conclusion that for a practicable use of the Virtual Tourist in tourism, new quadrocopter model has to be chosen, which fulfills more of the given requirements.

References

1. Balas, C.: Modelling and linear control of a quadrotor. School of Engineering, Craneld University (2007)
2. Brooks, A.C.: Real-time digital image stabilization (2003), http://www.dailyburrito.com/projects/DigitalImageStabilization.pdf
3. Czyba, R.: Attitude stabilization of an indoor quadrotor (2009), http://www.emav09.org/EMAV-nal-papers/paper64.pdf (April 2013)
4. Guttentag, D.A.: Virtual reality: Applications and implications for tourism. Department of Geography and Environmental Management, MES Candidate in Tourism Policy and Planning, University of Waterloo, Waterloo, ON, Canada N2L 3G1 (2014)
5. Letellier, R.: Virtual reality - a new tool for sustainable tourism and cultural heritage sites management. AIT, Bangkok, Thailand, Phimai (February 1999)
6. Parrot. Ar.drone open api platform (2014), https://projects.ardrone.org/
7. Sarumi, O.A., Balogun, V.F., Thompson, A.F.: A 3d geo spatial virtual reality system for virtual reality
8. Mondragon, I.F., Olivares-Mendez, M.A., Campoy, P., Martinez, C., Mejias, L.: Unmanned aerial vehicles uavs attitude, height, motion estimation and control using visual systems. Auton. Robot. (2010)
9. Tico, M.: Digital image stabilization. Nokia Research Center, Palo Alto (2013), http://cdn.intechopen.com/pdfs/9242/InTech-Digital_image_stabilization.pdf (September 04, 2013)
10. Silven, O., Niskanen, M., Tico, M.: Video stabilization performance assessment (2013), http://www.ee.oulu/nisu/projects/publications/videostabilizationperformance.pdf (May 04, 2013)

Informative Sound and Performance
in a Team Based Computer Game

Patrick Ng, Keith Nesbitt, and Karen Blackmore

School of Design, Communication and Information Technology
University Of Newcastle, NSW, Australia
{Patrick.H.Ng,Keith.Nesbitt,Karen.Blackmore}@newcastle.edu.au

Abstract. This study focuses on the role of sound in the popular multiplayer online battle arena game, Dota 2. Our initial results indicate that team performance improves with the use of sound. By contrast, some individuals performed better with sound and some without.

Keywords: Dota 2, Auditory Display, Auditory Icons, Earcons.

1   Introduction

For game developers, integrating informative sound has the potential to provide additional feedback to the player. In this paper we explore the relationship between sound and performance by evaluating the role of sound in player performance in the multiplayer online battle arena game, Dota 2.

Prior works within the field of auditory display have identified two key ways that sound can be used to improve the functionality and efficiency of user feedback Gaver described the design of 'Auditory Icons' in the interface, an approach that builds on the everyday listening skills of users [1]. Blattner suggested an alternative means of creating auditory messages called 'Earcons', that rely upon musical conventions such as pitch, timbre and dynamics to communicate abstract information [2].

Research conducted on video game audio and performance has shown mixed results in regards to whether sound has a positive or negative impact on performance. Tafalla reported that participants playing the game DOOM with the soundtrack scored almost twice as many points to those playing without the sound [3]. In contrast, Yamada et al found that the presence of music had a negative effect on performance [4]. Further studies into the effects of sound on performance levels have found that players perform the weakest when playing without sound while the highest scores were obtained when playing with music unrelated to the game [5]. Each of these findings suggest that sound could play a factor on players performance levels in games.

As information gathering plays an important task for players in most games, further research is required to better understand the role sound plays in performance. To this end, this preliminary study was conducted to examine the effects of informative sound in a team based game. The main question we consider in this research is: "Can sound be used to improve player performance in computer games?"

Y. Pisan et al. (Eds.): ICEC 2014, LNCS 8770, pp. 241–243, 2014.

2   Evaluating Performance

A total of 20 participants (19 males, 1 female) took part in this experiment. Of these participants, 18 were undergraduate students aged between 18-25 years while 2 participants were postgraduate students aged between 26-40 years. In the *sound on* condition, players were required to have the in game background music and sounds from the game turned on. This included voice chat. Participants in the *sound off* condition were not allowed to have any sounds from the game on and played in complete silence. Other sounds, such as personal music, were not allowed in either of the two conditions. In both conditions players were allowed to communicate using text based chat to each. The server selected to host all matches was US west. This server provided the best possible latency levels for all players based on their Internet connection speeds. The game mode selected was *all pick* which allows players access to all heroes in the game.

We recorded a total of 140 comparative measures (7 performance measures x 5 players x 4 teams) for analyzing individual performance. Of these 82 showed improvements in performance when sound is included, 10 showed no difference and 48 displayed a reduction in performance. We collated the individual performance data further, calculating the average individual results across the 7 measures. Out of these 7 measures, 1 showed a reduction in performance, 6 showed improvements when sound was present (see table 1). The difference for the measure of 'Hero levels' was found to be significant.

Table 1. Average Individual Performance with Sound On and Sound Off

Individual Measure	Sound Off	Sound On
Hero Levels*	17.2	18.6
Hero Kills	6.8	7.1
Hero Deaths	10.8	11.5
Kill Assists	7.1	7.4
Total Gold Earned	12555	13170
Gold per Minute	312.8	314.8
Experience Points per Minute	427.9	453.8

In addition to recording individual performances, we also recorded 16 team measures in total (4 teams x 4 performance) for measuring team performance. Out of these, nine showed an increase in performance with sound on while seven showed a decrease in performance. We analysed the team performance data further, calculating the average team results for the three expert teams (see table 2). Out of the 4 measures, 3 showed improvements in performance when sound is present while only 1 measure recorded a reduction in performance with sound.

Table 2. Average team performance (3 expert teams)

Team Measure	Sound Off	Sound On
Total Gold Earned	62383.3	64331.7
Total Experience Points Earned	85693.3	94206.7
Hero Kills	35.7	37.8
Hero Deaths	7.1	7.4

3   Discussion

In this study we have undertaken a preliminary examination of the role of information and sound in video games. Specifically, we looked at whether sound could offer improved performance levels in the multiplayer online battle arena game, Dota 2. In our preliminary experiment, we attempted to measure the difference in performance levels by adding and removing sound from the gameplay. We tested both individual and team performance levels in two different sound conditions (on and off) using seven individual and four team measures. Our analysis of the initial results has shown mixed results in terms of whether players and teams performance actually improved when there is sound. While over half of the total individual comparative measures have shown improved performance with sound, 58 displayed either no difference or a reduction in performance. We also found a similar pattern in team performance where 9 of the comparative measures displayed an increase with sound while 7 showed a reduction in performance. A post survey conducted after the experiment revealed that 18 of the 20 players felt that removing sound affected their performance negatively.

The next stage of our work will address some of the issues encountered with the design of this preliminary study. We will focus on two expert teams who play an extended number of games against each other so that the additional data gathered might highlight further significant differences in performance.

References

1. Gaver, W.: Auditory Icons: Using Sound in Computer Interfaces. Human-Computer Interaction 2(2), 167–177 (1986)
2. Blattner, M.M., Sumikawa, D., Greenberg, R.: Earcons and icons: their structure and common design principles. Human-Computer Interaction 4(1), 11–44 (1989)
3. Tafalla, R.J.: Gender differences in cardiovascular reactivity and game performance related to sensory modality in violent video game play. Journal of Applied Social Psychology 37(9), 2008–2023, doi:10.1111/j.1559-1816.2007.00248.x
4. Yamada, M., Fujisawa, N., Komori, S.: The effects of music on the performance and impression in a racing game. Journal of Music Perception and Cognition 7(2), 65–76 (2001)
5. Tan, S., Baxa, J., Spackman, M.P.: Effects of Built-in Audio versus Unrelated Background Music on Performance in an Adventure Role-Playing Game. International Journal of Gaming and Computer-Mediated Simulations 2(3), 1–23 (2010),
    doi:10.4018/jgcms.2010070101

A Need for Interactive Music Videos

Metic Cakmak and Helmut Hlavacs

University of Vienna, Research Group Entertainment Computing, Vienna, Austria
metincakmak@gmail.com, helmut.hlavacs@univie.ac.at

1   Introduction

Music videos [9] have been companions to modern pop and rock songs for decades now. However, all music videos share one common property: they are static. Once having been filmed, they remain as they are, never again change, though in the past more and more examples of interactive selection of content and perspectives have appeared [1,2,3,4,5,6,7,8]. New computing technologies on the other hand nowadays make possible real-time rendering of complex scenes with stunning, photo realistic quality. These features have mainly been used in modern high-quality computer games. In our work we transfer this technology to the realm of music videos. This makes it possible to produce dynamically produced music videos, having the capability to change, to adapt, to be created newly again and again, each time they are watched. Consumers can even interact with them just like they can interact with computer games.

2   Automated and Interactive Music Videos

The practical work of this study was the creation of a video clip for a rap song using the engine Unity 3D. At first we have analyzed hundreds of video clips of rap songs, and categorized their content. Then we analyzed the rap song at hand and planned the scenes according to the song text. The scenes have been realized directly in a 3D environment which we created in Unity 3D.

The rapper "Massimo Schena" is a young Austrian musician. He writes usually about actual and major issues facing teenagers in the community. The main topics are drug abuse, unemployment of teenagers, the lack of chances offered to teenagers, the lack of education and other teenager related issues.

At first we created a 3D character of Massimo using the Blender 3D character creation tool. Then the animations of moves which he likes to do during a performance were created with the same tool. We have created the animations according to a video clip capturing the moves. The rapper mostly prefers dance styles like break dancing, freestyle, dougie, hip hop and jerk and the hand gestures included mainly def wave, the slim shady chop, and the ninja star .

After the creation of the character and the animations, we selected an appropriate song from the repertoire of Massimo called "Mehr Perspektiven"[1], a song demanding more chances and options for teenagers to live a fruitful life.

---

[1] https://www.youtube.com/watch?v=veyDvOcGUBM

Y. Pisan et al. (Eds.): ICEC 2014, LNCS 8770, pp. 244–246, 2014.

Fig. 1. Suicide   **Fig. 2.** Drunk

Based on the scenes, we created three different versions of a video. The static version never changes, while the automatic version can change camera angles, type and number of characters seen, and the sequence of the scenes, which are dynamically adapted on the fly. Finally, the interactive version makes it possible to actually change scenes. For instance, in scene 5, the viewer can prevent the teenager form committing suicide by clicking the mouse.

3   Experimental Evaluation

We asked a test audience to evaluate, whether our enhancements concerning interactivity and automation indeed lead to more entertaining videos. In particular we started with two hypotheses:

1. Automation and interactivity make video clips more interesting / attractive.

2. Automated and interactive video clips are preferred to be seen in the future.

We chose a within-subjects design with 20 subjects, watching the static, the automated, and the interactive videos 8 times each. In order to check for memory effects we chose ten subjects to watch the videos sequentially, while the other ten subjects watched them in random order (in the end there were no differences between the groups). We chose individuals as much as possible from different age, gender or social groups. However, the most reachable audience for us were young students and therefore the majority of our audience is rather young. After watching the videos we asked the participants to fill out a questionnaire containing 20 questions. While 80% of respondents think that the third video clip is more preferable for the near future, 15% think the second video clip and only 5% of them think that the first video clip will be more preferred.

Also, we have implemented a paired t-tests to pair questions for testing our hypotheses. As a conclusion we can say that both automation and dynamical change, as well as interaction will be important features to add to future music videos. Above all, interaction is key to create music videos which keep the audience interested. As music videos try to bring a visual stimulus to the audience, it is important to keep this stimulus fresh and surprising throughout many subsequent presentations, and people want to be able to influence the outcome at least to some degree. This is similar to normal stories, which become boring after a while, since we think that surprise, change and new stimuli are key to keep an audience interested over some time.

4   Conclusion and Future Work

Our hypotheses are confirmed by our experiments, which show significant differences between the presented videos. However, more research is definitely necessary to include more viewers from different age groups, test for differences between gender groups and social background, or come up with videos with different content, and higher quality.

References

1. Red Hot Chilli Peppers, Look Around, http://redhotchilipeppers.com/news/301-look-around-interactive-video
2. Death Grips, I've Seen Footage, http://pitchfork.com/news/47844-death-grips-ive-seen-footage-becomes-interactive-choose-your-own-adventure-party-website/
3. Bob Dylan, Like a Rolling Stone, http://video.bobdylan.com/credits.html
4. Night Bus, When the night time comes, http://www.mtv.com/artists/nightbus/
5. Music Video Interactive, http://www.mvimusic.com/
6. OK Focus, http://okfoc.us/
7. OK Go, Pilobolus, All is not lost, http://www.allisnotlo.st
8. The Creators Project, http://thecreatorsproject.vice.com/blog/meet-okfocus-and-check-out-their-new-interactive-music-video-for-tanlines-not-the-same
9. Vernallis, C.: Experiencing Music Video: Aesthetics and Cultural Context. Columbia University Press (2004) ISBN 0-231-11798-1
10. Escher, E.: Rapper's handbook: A guide to freestyling, writing rhymes, and battling. Flocabulary LLC, New York (2006)

Author Index